Following God

Life Principles from
The Women of Acts

Following God

Life Principles from
The Women of Acts

A BIBLE STUDY BY
XAVIA ARNDT SHEFFIELD

AMG Publishers
Chattanooga, TN 37422

Following God

LIFE PRINCIPLES FROM THE WOMEN OF ACTS

Copyright © 2009 by Xavia Arndt Sheffield
First Printing, November 2009

Published by AMG Publishers.

ISBN 13: 978-0-89957-344-1
ISBN 10: 0-89957-344-4

Cover design Michael Largent at Indoor Graphics, Chattanooga, TN
Text editing and page layout by Rick Steele and Jennifer Ross

Printed in the United States of America
17 16 15 14 13 12 –W– 8 7 6 5 4 3 2

To the Glory of God

To Patricia Batis, Margaret Negelspach
and Peggy Edman

who first listened to me teach Women of the Bible
and who encouraged and stayed
with me throughout the journey

To all women who long to know
God's plan and place for them

Acknowledgments

To AMG Publishers and Dan Penwell, for the opportunity to write this Bible study

To my editor, Rick Steele, for all of his expert advice and help

To my pastor-husband, The Rev. Dr. Richard L. Sheffield, my in-house seminary-trained resource for answering many questions, for his proof-reading of the final galleys, and his helping me with the computer!

To my children, Jennifer and Andrew, who cheered me on

To Margaret D. McGee, author of *Stumbling Toward God, A Prodigal's Return* and *Sacred Attention, A Spiritual Practice for Finding God in the Moment* for her input on some of the questions

To a faithful family while growing up in South Dakota, who planted seeds in my heart that have bloomed

To all the women I have known in the church who have taught me much about God's goodness

 XAVIA ARNDT SHEFFIELD

About the Author

Xavia Arndt Sheffield grew up a Methodist in South Dakota. She holds a BA degree in Music and an MA degree in Speech/Theater from South Dakota State University. While in college, she was involved in a Lutheran traveling evangelism ministry. And, she has been married to a Presbyterian minister for thirty-five years! They have served congregations in Sudbury, MA; Lima, OH; Washington, D.C., and Columbia, MD.

With an interest in church history combined with women's issues in the church, she has taught Women of the Bible, Great Women in Church History, Women in the Early Church, and Women in the Medieval Church.

Xavia has written meditations for the *Upper Room* daily devotional guide, and is currently writing a series of "shirtpocket" gift books for Treble Heart Books.

She enjoys all aspects of being in the church and has taught children's and adult Sunday School; directed Vacation Bible Schools, Christmas pageants and church musicals; created special Advent programs, Sunday School kick-offs and education fairs; directed and composed children's music, played the handbells, and sung in the choir!

Xavia and her husband have two grown children, a daughter, Jennifer and a son, Andrew.

About the Following God Series

Three authors and fellow ministers, Wayne Barber, Eddie Rasnake, and Rick Shepherd, teamed up in 1998 to write a character-based Bible study for AMG Publishers. Their collaboration developed into the title, *Life Principles from the Old Testament*. Since 1998 these same authors and AMG Publishers have produced five more character-based studies—each consisting of twelve lessons geared around a five-day study of a particular Bible personality. More studies of this type are in the works. The release of Xavia Arndt Sheffield's *Life Principles from the Women of Acts* is the eighth release in the Following God Character Series. Although the larger Following God Bible Study series is approaching 30 titles, the interactive study format that readers have come to love remains constant. As new titles are being planned, our focus remains the same: to provide excellent Bible study materials that point people to God's Word in ways that allow them to apply truths to their own lives. More information on this groundbreaking series can be found on the following web pages:

www.FollowingGod.com

www.amgpublishers.com

Preface

The primary focus when teaching from the book of Acts always seems to be on the apostles, and particularly on Paul. The name of the Book is, after all, "The Acts of the Apostles." But, these men of God neither started nor sustained the Christian church by themselves. They needed the women of God as partners in order to make it work. And when you really study this book of the Bible, you not only discover how many of them participated in founding the church, but you also see that the "acts" of these women reveal a courage, a commitment, and a faith that is as impressive and important as that of the apostles. In fact, they were essential to the very survival of the early Christian movement. Their stories are about relationship and partnership and shared leadership for the sake of the gospel.

There are three reasons, I believe, why women were so readily accepted as leaders in the early church. First, and most importantly, was the way Jesus Christ treated them with respect and compassion. He was the greatest liberator of women who ever lived. Jesus himself bestowed upon women a new status apart from their cultures. In Christ, women were no longer second-class citizens, even in a patriarchal society. They were full and equal members of the family of God. Throughout Judea, He befriended, saved, healed, and afirmed all kinds of women.

■ At the temple in Jerusalem, He removed the shame of a woman who had been condemned as an adulteress.

■ Through the great faith of a Syrophoenecian woman, He first brought the gospel to a Gentile and then healed her daughter.

■ To a Samaritan woman, He first revealed his role as Messiah, and she, in turn, became the first evangelist to her people. And, after His resurrection, it was to women that He first appeared and instructed to go and tell the eleven.

Jesus Christ overturned stereotypes and opened the door to new roles for women. And the early church got it right when it followed His teachings regarding a woman's place in His church.

Second, the Holy Spirit equally empowered women on the day of Pentecost when He made no distinction between women and men. Every member of the early church, female and male, was given valid and important gifts that could be used in service to the community of believers. And since it was baptism of all, with water and by the Spirit, that initiated people into Christ, every Christian shared the same rights and duties.

And third, the apostles valued women's gifts and women became active partners with them in the spread of the faith. There is clear evidence that they were included as full members of the early Christian communities and that leadership roles were shared among them. The broad and usual belief of those early Christians was stated by the apostle Paul in Galatians 3:28: *"There is no longer Jew or Greek, there is no longer slave or free, there is no longer male and female; for all of you are one in Christ Jesus."* (See also Romans 10:12, Colossians 3:11.)

This verse does not say that gender is abolished in Christ, but that a patriarchal understanding of social roles was inappropriate within the Christian movement.

The stories of these women show that the early Christians were more concerned about spreading the gospel than in worrying about who was right, wrong, or more important. Their stories will at times shock you, bring you to tears, or fill you with joy. These are the women who lived solely for Christ and who are our examples of what it means to be fully alive in Him.

These are the women who helped start the Christian church. Their stories need to be told.

XAVIA ARNDT SHEFFIELD

Table of Contents

1

Acts and Women: An Overview

The Book of Acts is a story of great drama. It has all the elements of a best-selling novel or a blockbuster movie—shaking buildings and "special effects," kings and queens, angels and demons, dreams and visions, conversions and persecutions, greed and benevolence, miracles and martyrdom, and death and resurrection. It is the story of the founding of the Christian church.

It is best known for its story of the apostle Paul and his trials, tribulations, and drama on the high seas. But there are many other men—and women—involved in the story of the church. We know the names of some of the men: Peter, Stephen, Barnabas, Silas, and Timothy. But what about Sapphira, Tabitha, Rhoda, Lydia, Priscilla, and Bernice? There are all kinds of *women* involved in the founding of the church: mothers and daughters, good and evil queens, business-women and slaves, prophetesses and persecutors, liars and complainers, leaders and evangelists, widows and wives, and Jews, Gentiles, Greeks, and Romans. There are women mentioned in seventeen of the twenty-eight chapters of Acts—no less than thirty named and unnamed individual women or groups of women. And they are between the lines and behind the scenes in *every* chapter.

As I read the Book of Acts, I see women everywhere—in the crowds, among the believers, included in the giving of the Spirit (several times), running house churches and other important

The Book of Acts is a story of great drama. . . . It is the story of the founding of the Christian church.

There are women mentioned in seventeen of the twenty-eight chapters of Acts—no less than thirty named and unnamed individual women or groups of women. And they are between the lines and behind the scenes in every chapter.

ministries, as teachers and prophets, and as the primary benefactors of the Christian movement. They, too, proclaim the gospel message wherever they go, help build up the churches that are started, and work right alongside the men in their *common* purpose of being witnesses to the resurrection of Jesus Christ. Women clearly "acted" both behind and in front of the scenes to help evangelize their world. And if you have never been introduced to them, now is the time.

Just for fun, take this matching quiz to find out how many of the women in Acts you know.
(Place the description number next to the correct name.)

1. A well-known Bible woman of the Gospels who was present at Pentecost
2. She lied to Peter and the early church and was struck dead
3. She made coats and other garments for widows and the poor and was raised from the dead by Peter
4. A businesswoman of Philippi who was the first Christian convert in Europe (Macedonia)
5. She opened her large home to the Jerusalem church
6. She and her husband were leaders in the church at Rome, Corinth and Ephesus, were a missionary team and traveling companions of Paul
7. She was the mother of Timothy (named in 2 Tim. 1:5)
8. Four unmarried women who prophesied
9. The maid who answered Peter's knocking at the door after his release from prison
10. One of two Herodian sisters who heard Paul at Caesarea
11. A woman of Athens who believed the message of Jesus
12. The Queen of Ethiopia whose eunuch was converted and baptized by Philip

_____Bernice

_____Eunice

_____Sapphira

_____Mary (Mother of Jesus)

_____Philip's daughters

_____Dorcas/Tabitha

_____The Candace

_____Damaris

_____Lydia

_____Priscilla

_____Rhoda

_____Mary (Mother of John Mark)

Acts and Women

OUTLINE AND TIMELINE OF ACTS WITH WOMEN MENTIONED

The Book of Acts can broadly be divided into two main sections: Chapters 1 through 12 are concerned with the beginnings of the Christian church in Jerusalem and its spread into greater Palestine. Chapters 1–7 record the witness of the apostles and Stephen in Jerusalem; chapters 8–12 record the further witness of the apostles and Philip in Judea and Samaria.

Chapters 13 through 28 are dominated by the ministry of Paul and include the spread of Christianity from Antioch (in Syria) all the way to Rome. The four great centers of the early Christian church were Jerusalem, Syrian Antioch, Alexandria, and Rome.

Chapter 1: The promise of the Holy Spirit; the ascension of Jesus into heaven; the election of Matthias to replace Judas

Women Mentioned: Certain Women   Acts 1:14
      Mary, the mother of Jesus   Acts 1:14

Chapter 2 (AD 30): The giving of the Holy Spirit; Peter's message to the Jews; the fulfillment of Scripture; the first converts; the activities of the Church

Women Mentioned: All of them (at Pentecost)   Acts 2:4
      Prophesying daughters and   Acts 2:17–18
      female slaves

Chapter 3: Peter's healing of a lame beggar; Peter preaches at the Temple

Women Mentioned: None by name, but probably with believers at the Temple (3:11)

Chapter 4: Peter and John arrested and brought before the council; many more new converts; the believers pray for boldness in their witness; the Church shares its possessions

Women Mentioned: None by name, but probably among 5,000 new converts (4:4)

Chapter 5: The deceit of Ananias and Sapphira; the apostles perform signs and wonders; great numbers join the Church; the apostles arrested and put into prison and released by an angel; they resume teaching

Women Mentioned: Sapphira   Acts 5:1–2, 7–10
      Jerusalem disciples,   Acts 5:14
      women and men

Chapter 6: Seven are set apart for service to widows and the poor; more new disciples; Stephen performs signs and wonders; Stephen arrested

Women Mentioned: Hellenistic (Grecian, Greek) widows   Acts 6:1
      Hebrew widows   Acts 6:1

Chapter 7: Stephen's speech before the council, recounting the history of the Jews; Stephen is stoned while Saul of Tarsus looks on

Women Mentioned: Daughter of Pharaoh   (Exodus 2:5–10)
      Acts 7:21

From the first 7 chapters (the witness in Jerusalem), list the stories and women that you were already familiar with as well as the stories and women you did not know were in Acts.

_____

_____

_____

_____

"For the promise is for you, for your children, and for all who are far away, everyone whom the Lord our God calls to him."

Acts 2:39

Chapter 8: Persecution of the Church begins; the disciples are scattered; Philip preaches in Samaria, where many are baptized, including Simon the Sorcerer; an angel directs Philip to an Ethiopian eunuch
Women Mentioned: Persecuted disciples,   Acts 8:3; 9:2
women and men
Samaritans   Acts 8:12
The Candace   Acts 8:27

Chapter 9 (AD 35): Persecution continues; the conversion of Saul; Saul preaches in Damascus and Jerusalem; Peter's ministry in Lydda and Joppa
Women Mentioned: Dorcas or Tabitha   Acts 9:36–43
Widows of Joppa   Acts 9:39–41

Chapter 10: The conversion of Cornelius; Peter's vision about the Gentiles; the Gentiles receive the Holy Spirit
Women Mentioned: None by name, but probably with Gentiles receiving Spirit (10:45)

Chapter 11 (AD 44): Peter's report to Jerusalem about the Gentiles; the first Gentile church in Syrian Antioch; Saul and Barnabas teach in Antioch for a year, gaining many new converts, who are now called "Christians"
Women Mentioned: None by name, but probably with new converts in Antioch (11:21)

Chapter 12: Herod has James killed; Peter is arrested and imprisoned; an angel frees him; Herod dies
Women Mentioned: Mary, the mother of John Mark   Acts 12:12
Rhoda, Mary's maid   Acts 12:13–15

From chapters 8 through 12 (the witness in Judea and Samaria), what have you learned about the early witness of the church? How have women been involved?

_____

_____

_____

_____

Chapter 13 (AD 48): Paul and Barnabas are set apart by the Spirit; Paul begins his first missionary journey; Paul and Barnabas preach in Antioch of Pisidia
Women Mentioned: High-standing women in Antioch of Pisidia   Acts 13:50

Chapter 14: Paul and Barnabus in Iconium, Lystra, Derbe and then back to Antioch in Syria
Women Mentioned: None by name, but with great numbers of Jews & Greeks (14:1)

Chapter 15 (AD 50-52): The Jerusalem Council; the council's letter to the Gentiles; Paul begins second missionary journey with Silas
Women Mentioned: None by name, but probably with all the believers (15:3)

"Meanwhile the church throughout Judea, Galilee, and Samaria had peace and was built up. Living in the fear of the Lord and in the comfort of the Holy Spirit, it increased in numbers."

Acts 9:31

Chapter 16: Timothy joins Paul and Silas; Paul's vision to go to Macedonia; the conversion of Lydia; Paul and Silas arrested; an earthquake frees them from prison; Paul orders a spirit from a slave girl

Women Mentioned: Timothy's mother   Acts 16:1
                            Lydia   Acts 16:12–15, 40
                            The Philippian women   Acts 16:13
                            Slave girl of   Acts 16:16–19
                            Philippi or Pythoness slave

Chapter 17: Paul and Silas in Thessalonica, Berea, where many believe, but others help the Jews expel them; Paul in Athens, where he speaks on Mars Hill

Women Mentioned: Leading Thessalonian women   Acts 17:4
                            Greek women of Berea   Acts 17:12
                            Damaris of Athens   Acts 17:34

Chapter 18 (AD 53–57): Paul begins third missionary journey; he arrives in Corinth, where he meets Priscilla and Aquila, who become missionaries with him and teach the great Apollos; Paul strengthens all the churches

Women Mentioned: Priscilla   Acts 18:2, 18, 26

Chapter 19: Paul in Ephesus; Paul heals and converts many people who practiced magic; the revolt of the silversmiths over the goddess, Artemis

Women Mentioned: None by name, but probably with believers in Ephesus (19:1, 18)

Chapter 20: Paul goes to Macedonia and Greece; Paul brings a young boy back to life; Paul's visit to Troas and Miletus; Paul addresses the elders of Ephesus

Women Mentioned: None by name, but probably with believers in Macedonia (20:2)

Chapter 21 (AD 57–59): Paul greets the disciples at Tyre, Ptolemais and stops in Caesarea to greet Philip the evangelist; a prophet, Agabus, tells Paul not to go to Jerusalem; Paul's arrest in Jerusalem

Women Mentioned: Tyrian disciples and their wives   Acts 21:5–6
                            Philip's daughters   Acts 21:8–9

From chapters 13 through 21 (Paul's three missionary journeys), how has Paul interacted with different women? Who is mentioned?

_____

_____

_____

_____

Chapter 22: Paul speaks to the people, recounting his conversion and mission to the Gentiles; Paul is brought before the Jewish Council

Women Mentioned: None by name, but women with persecuted disciples (22:4)

> **"I have set you to be a light for the Gentiles, so that you may bring salvation to the ends of the earth."**
>
> **Acts 13:47**

Chapter 23: Paul addresses the Council; Paul's nephew thwarts a plot to kill him; Paul's vision of the Lord, telling him to go to Rome.
Women Mentioned: Paul's sister   Acts 23:16

Chapter 24: Paul is accused of provoking the Jews throughout the world; he appears before Felix the Governor and is imprisoned for two years
Women Mentioned: Drusilla   Acts 24:24

Chapter 25: Paul appears before Festus and appeals to the emperor; he is brought before King Agrippa II
Women Mentioned: Bernice   Acts 25:13, 23

Chapter 26: Paul appears before Agrippa, tells him of his conversion and witness to the Gentiles; Festus calls him crazy; Agrippa sees no guilt in him
Women Mentioned: Bernice   Acts 26:30

Chapter 27: Paul sails for Rome; stormy seas and shipwreck
Women Mentioned: None named, but with disciples (friends) at Sidon (27:3); and perhaps among the 276 passengers aboard ship (27:37)

Chapter 28: Paul's ship is run aground on Malta, where he heals many; he sails for Rome and greets many disciples along the way; great numbers of people are converted in Rome, where he lives for two years
Women Mentioned: None by name, but probably with great numbers at Rome (28:23)

From chapters 13 through 28, list the women who were associated with the apostle Paul in his travels.

_____

_____

_____

Acts and Women

FACTS ABOUT ACTS

The Gospel writer Luke, the physician, and the only Gentile author in the New Testament (perhaps born a Greek), *probably* wrote the Book of Acts between 80 and 85 AD (or as late as 135 AD). Luke is best known for the "Christmas" narrative in his Gospel, which includes the visit of Gabriel to Mary, the beautiful song of Mary called the Magnificat, the birth of John the Baptist, the story of his parents, Zechariah and Elizabeth, and of course, the birth of Jesus. His is the only Gospel to record the angels and the shepherds.

Luke was from Syrian Antioch and may have been included in the group of Hellenists there to become the earliest Gentile converts (Acts 11:19-21). Luke may have been a brother of Titus and is believed to be present in the Book of Acts, having met Paul in Troas, where he began traveling with him and, as a result, was a witness to many of its stories. The "we" sections of Acts begin in Acts 16:10 and may refer to Luke's participation in Paul's travels all the way to Rome. Paul refers to Luke by name in Colossians 4:14; 2 Timothy 4:11; and Philemon 24.

What can we tell about Paul and Luke's relationship and working partnership from these verses?

_____

_____

_____

Did You Know?
BELOVED PHYSICIAN

In Colossians 4:14, Paul refers to Luke as *"the beloved physician."* As a doctor, Luke would have been a member of a highly skilled profession of his time. In both his Gospel and in his Book of Acts, his compassion for the sick and the downtrodden, including women, comes through in his many stories of healing. In addition, Luke uses words in the description of some diseases that were confined to medical writers and also mentions different types of diseases.

Luke addresses both his Gospel and the Book of Acts to a man named Theophilus. This Greek name means "dear to God" or "friend of God." It is thought by some scholars that Theophilus was a Roman official, possibly a procurator, since the phrase in the Gospel, "most excellent" is used to address him. The Roman procurator of Judea, Felix, was addressed as "Your Excellency." The *Eerdman's Bible Dictionary* further defines him: "Theophilus was most likely a Gentile 'God-fearer' in need of an 'orderly account' of the gospel, about which he may have had some knowledge."[1] God-fearers were Gentiles who worshipped the God of Israel, but were not full converts to Judaism and did not know the gospel of Jesus Christ. A recurring pattern in Acts is the teaching of the full message of Christ to those called God-fearers or God-worshipers. See his name in Luke 1:3 and Acts 1:1.

Luke's main purpose for writing Acts was to record the establishment and expansion of the faith and to show how Christianity was intended for the whole world. Acts is the fulfillment of Jesus' words to His apostles before His ascension: *"But you will receive power when the Holy Spirit has come upon you; and you will be my witnesses in Jerusalem, in all Judea and Samaria, and to the ends of the earth"* (Acts 1:8). Acts is a witness to the power of the resurrection.

 Acts is also witness to the *unity* of the body of Christ and to the *equality* of all its members in its earliest days, quite unlike the disunity of that same body today with its many denominations and divisions. How do you think these divisions affect the church's witness today?

_____

_____

_____

_____

Acts is a witness to the power of the resurrection.

Acts is an important book because it gives us a history of the early Christian church that we would not otherwise possess. It shows how Christianity began with the Jews at Pentecost and spread throughout the Roman Empire, beginning in Palestine (Israel) on the eastern edge of the Mediterranean Sea and extending across the northern Mediterranean regions all the way to Rome. Its time frame is the three decades immediately following the death and resurrection of Jesus.

It is interesting to note the structure of the Book of Acts. The activities of the apostles in Acts are parallel to those of Jesus in Luke's Gospel. The Gospel of Luke can be summed up with the theme: "Jesus in action"; the

You could say that the whole message of Acts is that the life of Jesus goes on in the life of the early church.

Acts of the Apostles, in the words of J. B. Phillips, is thematically labeled *"The Young Church in Action."*[2] In both writings, there is an emphasis on the leading of the Holy Spirit, on prayer, concern for the poor, the proper use of money, the fulfillment of Scripture, and the witness to God's power. You could say that the whole message of Acts is that the life of Jesus goes on in the life of the early church.

Luke probably did not call his book "The Acts of the Apostles." It was given this name by the early church toward the end of the second century. In addition, the "acts" or "ministries" of only three of the apostles (Peter, James, and John) are mentioned in the Book of Acts.

📖 Look in Acts 1:13 and write down the names of the remaining eleven disciples (called apostles in Acts) of Jesus.

_____

_____

_____

_____

Tradition states that Thomas preached in Parthia; Andrew in Scythia; and John in Asia.[3] Peter may also have preached to the Jews in Pontus, Galatia, Bithynia, Cappadocia, and Asia.

It has been suggested that a more accurate name for this book would be "The Acts of the Holy Spirit Through the Apostles" or "The Gospel of the Holy Spirit," because the Spirit is clearly the guiding force throughout. The Spirit is really the "main character" in the whole story of the early Church. The Holy Spirit falls upon a group of 120 believers gathered in an upstairs room in Jerusalem during the Jewish festival of Pentecost, and from that point on the Spirit guides and strengthens them for the task of not only proclaiming the resurrection of Jesus, but for performing all the other activities of the early church, from baptizing to healing the sick. The Holy Spirit is mentioned at least sixty-five times in the Book of Acts. Another suggested name for Acts is "The Gospel of the Resurrection" because the witness of the apostles and Paul (and other women and men) is to the resurrection of Jesus.

The Holy Spirit is mentioned at least sixty-five times in the Book of Acts.

Acts and Women

LUKE'S MENTION AND TREATMENT OF WOMEN

The fact that some scholars view Luke as having a high regard for women is significant for this study. He mentions female characters often in his text. In his Gospel, Luke records ways in which Jesus began the transformation of women by lifting them to a new significance in society. In Acts, Luke emphasizes this transformed role and portrays women in ministry roles that were previously denied them in Judiasm and secular cultures.

Jesus was the initiator and model for the way women were treated in the early church. Listed below are some of the ways in which he made clear that women were important to the purposes of God.

Jesus…

- broke all the rules and regulations set down for women in the patriarchal society
- saw a significance in women that was denied them in their society
- did not limit the activities of women in their homes or communities—their world was to be as wide as the world which men saw as their own
- challenged contemporary views of women and talked to them in public
- called for a transformation of men's attitudes toward women
- treated women as persons instead of objects
- lifted women to an equality with men unknown in first-century Palestine
- initiated a startling redemptive and transformational process for women designed to lift and restore them to the position they enjoyed at creation as *full* partners with men
- taught that the needs of both women and men were important
- made it possible for the early church to accept active women members and powerful women leaders

APPLY How do you relate to these attitudes of Jesus toward women in your own life?

_____

_____

_____

_____

_____

In contrast, we can see by the list below that first-century Judaism held views of women that were contrary to the ideas of Jesus.

- The dominant model of a virtuous woman was one who remained at home and obeyed her husband
- When ready for marriage, a woman's father and her prospective husband bartered an agreement for her, rarely with her consent
- Men could make demands on women, but women could not make demands on men
- A man could divorce his wife, but there was no way a woman could divorce her husband
- Many rabbis regarded women as socially and religiously inferior to men, and some even expressed contempt for them
- A woman was legally defined as chattel (any property not related to real estate, such as livestock), and many questioned whether or not she even possessed a soul
- Men were cautioned against speaking to women, especially in public
- Women were legally barred from giving testimony or appearing in a court of law
- Women were not counted in a quorum necessary for the formation of a synagogue
- In the Temple, women were restricted to an outer court (Court of the Women)

In his Gospel, Luke records ways in which Jesus began the transformation of women by lifting them to a new significance in society. In Acts, Luke emphasizes this transformed role and portrays women in ministry roles that were previously denied them in Judiasm and secular cultures.

- Women were rarely tutored or taught the *Torah,* but they were obliged to obey its commands
- Women were generally seen as evil, ignorant, and immoral

APPLY Do any of these kinds of restrictions apply to your life? How do you deal with them?

_____

_____

_____

_____

_____

_____

Other scholars, however, suggest that Luke downplays the importance of roles given to women in the new church, offering that women are only receivers and benefactors. This is due primarily to three things: the place of women in the Roman Empire—that of second-class citizens, the patriarchal society, and the fact that he does not want to offend his audience. They also suggest that Luke highlights men's positions and authority while downplaying the *major* roles of women.

Still others point out the inclusion of women's stories right along with the men's stories. Luke continues the parallelism between his Gospel and Acts in the *pairing* of women and men. In some stories, he features both a woman and a man, such as in the story of Ananias and Sapphira in Acts 5 and Priscilla and Aquila in Acts 18. In others, he uses a parallel story either before or after another one. Examples of this include the healings of Aeneas and Tabitha in Acts 9 and the baptism of the jailer and his household along with the baptism of Lydia and her household in Acts 16. See parallel stories in Luke 1:5–23; 1:26–38; 2:25–38; and 15:4–10.

Luke also puts the names of individual men and women together, such as Dionysius and Damaris in Acts 17:34; and in the many references to women *and* men (Acts 5:14; 8:3; 9:2; 13:50; 17:12; 21:5; and 22:4).

📖 Read some of these passages in both Luke and Acts and write down some of the parallels you see in the stories.

_____

_____

_____

_____

_____

_____

It is significant that Luke mentions as many women as he does and that he places many of them in *major* roles in the early church. He indeed does show us that without women, the Christian church may not have survived. The ingrained cultural prejudices of Luke's day were overcome by the Holy Spirit, and the narrative of Acts shows us how the Spirit also led women to participate in every important ministry of the early church.

Did You Know?
WOMEN IN ISRAEL

In contrast to the cultural and religious restrictions placed on women in first-century Judaism, women in Israel had a status and a freedom equal to men before the Babylonian exile in 587/586 BC. Even in that patriarchal society, women were still considered equal in the eyes of God. They had important roles, were never excluded from worship, and were honored as models of wisdom. Wives and mothers were protected by the law and ranked equally with that of fathers, and daughters were not considered property to be bartered.

How does the Holy Spirit guide the church today?

_____

_____

_____

THE ROMAN EMPIRE, CHRISTIANITY, AND WOMEN

Superbly engineered roads and bridges, as well as good communications in the Roman Empire, enabled Paul, the apostles, and all the disciples to travel easily from place to place, facilitating the spread of Christianity to the entire region. For its first thirty years Christianity, like Judaism, enjoyed protection under Roman law. Paul had the protection of the Roman government until the final years of his life because he was a Roman citizen and he emphasized the benefits of good government.

There were four Roman emperors who ruled during the early spread of Christianity. The first was Tiberius (AD 14–37). The Emperor Tiberius did not persecute the Christians.

The next emperor, Gaius Caligula (AD 37–41), was insane, proclaimed himself a God, hated the Jews fiercely, and committed many atrocities against them. During the reign of Caligula, the great famine, which is foretold by Agabus the prophet in Acts 11:28, occurs.

Beginning his reign only four years later, the Emperor Claudius (AD 41–54) expelled all the Jews from Rome, including Priscilla and Aquila (See lesson 10). It was Claudius who also appointed Agrippa II as king of the Jews and selected Felix as procurator. Claudius had a successful reign, during which many roads, aqueducts, bridges, and baths were built across the Empire. Eusebius, in *The Church History*, tells how Claudius died: "Claudius's poor luck with women, however, culminated when his niece, Agrippina, his fourth wife, poisoned him with a bowl of tainted mushrooms so that her son might succeed."[4]

Agrippina's son was Nero (by a previous marriage), who ruled the empire from AD 54–68. It was Nero who sent Festus as Felix's successor. After the great fire of Rome, for which he blamed the Christians, Emperor Nero began to commit atrocities against them and their leaders, the apostles—and even his own family. During Nero's reign, Paul and Peter were martyred.

Once Judiasm and Christianity began to diverge, Christians lost the special privileges given to the Jews. Jews were specially exempted from taking part in the cult of emperor-worship. Christians also sought this exemption, since they recognized only one God and served only one Lord, Jesus Christ. But when the church became largely composed of Gentiles, it was no longer possible to shelter it under the wing of Judaism. Christians refused to offer a pinch of incense on an altar to the divine Emperor, and the Roman government interpreted this act of insubordination as unpatriotic. Because of this, the official Roman attitude towards Christianity became less and less favorable.

APPLY What is the attitude toward Christianity in various parts of our world today? How and where are Christians persecuted?

_____

_____

_____

_____

_____

The position of women in the Empire varied. Most in the ancient world were considered second-class citizens, and their lives were tied to those of men. But in the eastern provinces and in Rome, women were able to own property, acquire an education, and even participate with men in public, commercial, and religious life. Most often, however, these positions were tied to wealth and therefore, it was wealthy women who had the advantage. In reality, men still controlled most aspects of society in spite of some gains that women might have made.

As for religion, the Romans and Greeks were very "religious" in their own devotion to their many gods and goddesses. Each of the major cities had its own deity. In Athens, it was Pallas Athene; in Rome it was Jupiter Optimus Maximus; and in Ephesus, it was Artemis. In Athens, Paul *". . . was deeply distressed to see that the city was full of idols"* (Acts 17:16). In Ephesus, we read the story which is commonly known as the "revolt of the silversmiths," because Paul speaks against the great goddess, Artemis, and states bluntly that *"gods made with hands are not gods"* (Acts 19:26). In this passage of Acts, we read that Paul interferes with the Ephesian trade of making silver shrines of Artemis.

Ordinary people prayed to these gods and goddesses for all kinds of help in life. Stuart G. Hall, in *Doctrine and Practice in the Early Church,* says, "Many people in the Empire were in fact genuinely religious, believing that they could improve their prospects in this world by behaving well towards the gods, and hoping for some kind of agreeable after-life." It was amidst this religious backdrop that Paul introduces the people of the Roman Empire to the one, true God of Israel.

How difficult do you think this was for Paul and his associates, both female and male?

_____

_____

_____

_____

_____

The position of women in the Roman Empire varied. Most in the ancient world were considered second-class citizens, and their lives were tied to those of men.

FOR ME TO FOLLOW GOD

Life Principle For Lesson One: God's Place for Women

The good news is that God thinks very highly of women. He created women to compliment men, and the role of women is equally important to God's purposes for men. Women are a necessary part of the complete image of God. In Genesis 1:27, it says: *"So God created humankind in his image, in the image of God he created them; male and female he created them."* I think it's interesting to note that often we don't hear the whole verse in Genesis 2, which refers to Eve being a *partner* to Adam. The whole verse says: *"Then the Lord God said, 'It is not good that the man should be alone; I will make him a helper as his partner"* (Genesis 2:18). Various other translations use only *partner* (NEB), or a *suitable companion* to help him (TEV).

 What is your interpretation of this Genesis passage?

_____

_____

_____

We often hear that women are simply "helpmeets," inferring that this is a lesser position. But helper, in this case, is not a demeaning position. Its fuller meaning is of one who aids someone who needs assistance, and who works *beside* rather than *beneath*. It is in Genesis 3 that we read about the beginning of the subordination of women as a result of *human* sin. But Jesus Christ died to forgive that sin and began the restoration of women to their original place in creation. Furthermore, the coming of the Holy Spirit both confirmed and empowered women to become all they were intended to be in the eyes of God. It was the Holy Spirit who led the early church in everything it did. Jesus made us into new creations; the Holy Spirit came to help us live like those new creations. When we allow the Holy Spirit to define women, we find a deep well of blessing for the whole of creation.

 How do you bless the church today with what God has given you?

_____

_____

_____

We read in Acts how thousands of women and men receive the power of the Holy Spirit and *with* the apostles, spread the message of the gospel to the ends of the known world in the short span of thirty years. It is clear from the stories in Acts that something has changed. Women, through Jesus Christ and in the giving of the Holy Spirit, *have* been restored to their original position in creation—as equal *partners* with men. It is clear all the way through Acts that the Spirit of God is the moving, decisive, and final word on where women belong in God's creation and in His church. And that is wherever *God* wants them—not where their cultures want them, not where their husbands want them, not even where their church wants them. J. Lee Grady in his book, *10 Lies the Church Tells Women, How the Bible Has Been Misused to Keep Women in Spiritual Bondage,* says: "God does not want His church to be controlled by men or women. He wants it to be controlled by the Holy Spirit."[6] The Spirit

> **The good news is that God thinks very highly of women. He created women to compliment men, and the role of women is equally important to God's purposes for men.**

gifts everyone with the power to proclaim the gospel, whether it is through teaching, prophesying, leading, serving or evangelizing.

 How do you feel about this statement?

_____

_____

_____

I remember with great joy when the Spirit of God touched my life. I was in graduate school, and my life was a little off-track. I longed to be free of some of the situations in which I found myself. So I took that necessary first step and asked God for his forgiveness and healing. He answered me in a very profound way. I became involved in a Spirit-filled campus ministry that built me up instead of tore me down, encouraged me instead of used me, and freed me instead of bound me to a set of expectations. But the most exciting thing it did for me was that it gave me an opportunity to become a *witness* to God's love. Along with three other young Christian women, I became part of a travelling evangelism team and took two tours of the central and western parts of our country, proclaiming the gospel. It remains one of the highlights of my life.

Like everyone in Acts, women and men alike, we are called to be witnesses to the resurrection in our own unique ways. Not all will be evangelists; some will be teachers, some prophets, some healers. *"To each is given the manifestation of the Spirit for the common good"* (1 Corinthians 12:7). Are you using your gift of the Spirit to build up, encourage, and free others? I guarantee that if you are, God's grace will come back to you in ways you cannot even imagine.

I am continually amazed at what those early Christians accomplished in such a short period of time. But I also remember that it was the Spirit who was empowering *everyone*—giving women and men alike gifts and a place to use them. Just think if we could allow the power of the Holy Spirit to lead our hearts and direct our activities so completely that we could continue to spread the gospel with the same zeal and commitment of those early Christians and with the same respect and acknowledgement that God has a place for everyone. God has a place for you, women and men. Ask the Holy Spirit to guide you in becoming a bold messenger for Christ in this broken world, because your witness is the continuing story of the Christian church. The times and places have changed, but the message is still one of hope and salvation for all.

 What place do you think God has given you?

_____

_____

_____

 Lord of all women and men, guide our lives with your Holy Spirit as you guided those first Christians and all who have followed you throughout the ages. Reveal your gifts to us, that we might use them to bless your church. Help us reflect your image to all those we meet, and give us the power to become bold witnesses to the gospel in our own times and places. In Jesus' name we pray, Amen.

> **Ask the Holy Spirit to guide you in becoming a bold messenger for Christ in this broken world, because your witness is the continuing story of the Christian church.**

Works Cited

1. Allen C. Myers, Revision Editor, *The Eerdman's Bible Dictionary* (Grand Rapids, MI: William B. Eerdman's Publishing Company, 1987), 998.

2. J. B. Phillips, *The New Testament in Modern English* (New York, NY: The Macmillan Company, 1964), 239.

3. Paul L. Maier and Eusebius, *Eusebius, The Church History* (Grand Rapids, MI: Kregel Academic, 2007), 93.

4. Ibid., 91. Used by permission of the publisher. All rights reserved.

5. Stuart G. Hall, *Doctrine and Practice in the Early Church* (Grand Rapids, MI: William B. Eerdman's Publishing Company, 1991), 4.

6. J. Lee Grady, *10 Lies the Church Tells Women: How the Bible Has Been Misused to Keep Women in Spiritual Bondage* (Lake Mary, FL: Charisma House, 2000), 200. Used by permission of the publisher.

Notes

2

"One in the Spirit": Pentecost and Propheysing Women

Waiting may be one of the hardest things we do, and waiting for God's timing is even harder, but always worth it. This lesson is not only about waiting, but it also details one of the most incredible results of waiting in the entire Bible—the giving of the Holy Spirit to both women and men.

As Acts opens, Jesus is meeting with His disciples, now called the apostles, on the Mount of Olives. He instructs them to remain in Jerusalem and wait for the promise of the Father, the baptism of the Holy Spirit (Acts 1:5). Jesus ascends into heaven, as two men in white robes tell the disciples that He will return someday—just as He left.

They return to Jerusalem to the house where they are staying. Others waiting and praying with the apostles are **certain women,** including **Mary the mother of Jesus** and Jesus' brothers (Acts 1:14). In all, there are 120 women and men, from whom the Christian church began. Included in this number, there are probably other women (Acts 1:15). Just as Jesus affirmed women and invited them into His inner circle, they are also now a part of the group that will be instrumental in founding His church.

While waiting, the remaining apostles hold a meeting to decide who will replace Judas Iscariot. The death of Judas is recorded, and Peter quotes Psalms 69:25 and 109:8, which predict Judas' death and replacement. The conditions for election are that the

This lesson is not only about waiting, but it also details one of the most incredible results of waiting in the entire Bible—the giving of the Holy Spirit to both women and men.

new apostle had to have been with Jesus from the beginning of His ministry (from His baptism by John) until His ascension. The apostles seek God's will in prayer and elect Matthias by casting lots between two men.

Acts 2 describes the day of Pentecost, when **all of them** *"were together in one place"* and were filled with the Holy Spirit (Acts 2:4) *"Divided tongues as of fire"* appear and settle on the heads of the believers, and they all begin to speak in other languages. All the Jews, women and men, who have come from all over the Roman Empire for the Feast of Pentecost, as well as those living in Jerusalem, are amazed to hear their own language.

Peter stands and addresses the crowd and tells them how the prophet Joel had foretold this event, now enabling sons and **daughters** and both men and **women slaves** to prophesy (Acts 2:17–18). He goes on to tell them the story of Jesus—how David had predicted the coming of the Messiah and how God had raised Christ from the dead. He tells them they must repent of their sins and be baptized, and ends with: *"For the promise* [of the Spirit] *is for you, for your children, and for all who are far away, everyone whom the Lord our God calls to him"* (Acts 2:39). The message stirs the crowd, and **three thousand people** believe and are baptized.

The new believers devote themselves to the apostles' teaching, prayer, fellowship, and the breaking of bread. They share all they have with each other, meet together daily in the Temple, and praise God with glad and generous hearts. The apostles perform many signs and wonders and the church continues to grow.

Note the verses about the Holy Spirit in the first two chapters of Acts and see how the Spirit is the guide for all that is happening in the community of believers (see Acts 1:2, 5, 8, 16; 2:4, 17, 18, 33, 38).

WHO WAS WAITING?

The Verse in Which the Women Appear:

Acts 1:14: *"All these were constantly devoting themselves to prayer, together with* **certain women***, including* **Mary the mother of Jesus***, as well as his brothers."*

Certain Women

The reality is that we do not know the exact identities of these women. Luke does not give their names or say how many were there. However, scholars have made suggestions about who they *might* have been, based on the Gospel stories of the women who followed Jesus. And the J. B. Phillips translation does identify them as *"the women who had followed Jesus."* In addition, there are references in all of the Gospels to the many women who followed Jesus from Galilee all the way to the cross and beyond.

Luke says:

> *"The twelve were with him, as well as* **some women** *who had been cured of evil spirits and infirmities:* **Mary,** *called Magdalene, from whom seven demons had gone out, and* **Joanna,** *the wife of Herod's steward Chuza, and*

Pentecost and Prophesying Women

DAY ONE

"All of these were constantly devoting themselves to prayer, together with certain women, including Mary the mother of Jesus, as well as his brothers."

Acts 1:14

Susanna, *and* **many others**, *who provided for them out of their resources*" (Luke 8:1–3). He goes on to mention them several times in the narrative of Jesus' death, burial and resurrection (Luke 23:49, 55–56; 24:2–5) and again, names some of them: *"Now it was* **Mary Magdalene, Joanna, Mary the mother of James,** *and* **the other women** *with them who told this to the apostles"* (Luke 24:10).

Matthew's Gospel tells us:

*"***Many women** *were also there, looking on from a distance; they had followed Jesus from Galilee and had provided for him. Among them were* **Mary Magdalene,** *and* **Mary the mother of James and Joseph,** *and the* **mother of the sons of Zebedee***"* (Matthew 27:55–56; also 27:61).

In Mark's Gospel we read:

"There were also **women** *looking on from a distance; among them were* **Mary Magdalene,** *and* **Mary the mother of James the younger and of Joses,** *and* **Salome.** *They used to follow him and provided for him when he was in Galilee; and there were* **many other women** *who had come up with him to Jerusalem"* (Mark 15:40–41, 47; 16:1). Some scholars believe that Salome is the mother of James and John, the sons of Zebedee and two of Jesus' disciples. She is also sometimes identified as the sister of Mary the mother of Jesus.

And finally, in John's Gospel:

"Meanwhile, standing near the cross of Jesus were his **mother,** *and his* **mother's sister, Mary the wife of Clopas,** *and* **Mary Magdalene***"* (John 19:25). Mary the wife of Clopas could be the same as Mary, the mother of James the younger and of Joses (or Joseph). Or, as some suggest, Mary the mother of Jesus could even be the mother of James and Joses, since these are names given to two of Jesus' brothers in Matthew 13:55 and Mark. 6:3. Another Mary, one of seven in the New Testament, could have been identified as being the sister of Mary the mother of Jesus.

If most of these women were with Jesus and the disciples, then it could be concluded that at least some of them *may* have been present with the apostles. Why wouldn't they have been there? These women were the ones who stayed with Jesus to the end, while the men disappeared. Twice, Luke refers to the disciples being with others (Luke 24:22, 33), and verse 22 says that they were *women*. Some even suggest that the two on the road with Jesus after His resurrection were two of the other women who had been at the tomb. (Mark 16:12)

This verse also says, *"but they did not believe them"* which is the same response that Mary Magdalene had just gotten from the disciples in Mark 16:11. They would have believed the men. If all or most of these women are in that room, what do you think the relationship between the apostles and the women is at this point?

_____

_____

_____

There are still other possibilities as to who these women might be. In Paul's letter to the Corinthians, he asks, *"Do we not have the right to be accompanied*

> *If most of these women were with Jesus and the disciples, then it could be concluded that at least some of them may have been present with the apostles. Why wouldn't they have been there?*

by a believing wife, as do the other apostles and the brothers of the Lord and Cephas [Peter]? (1 Corinthians 9:5). We know that Peter had a wife, and this passage seems to suggest that at least some of the other apostles and the brothers of Jesus had wives who traveled with them.

Finally, Paul L. Maier, in *First Christians,* seems to concur with all of these conclusions, as well as adding to the list:

> "Who were the 120 first Christians? The disciples; . . . the Galilean followers of Jesus, including the Seventy (Luke 10:1); his mother Mary and his half-brothers (or relatives) who had now converted to the faith; Mary, Martha, Lazarus, and the Bethany contingent; plus miscellaneous Judean followers, such as the Emmaus disciples, John Mark, and his mother."[1]

📖 Look up some of these references. Why do you think these women would be there?

_____

_____

_____

The importance of various women in Jesus' own ministry makes it clear that women were included in God's plan for His church from its inception.

It is impossible to know how many women there were, since they are often mentioned as a group and their anonymity may suggest that those who joined the movement were often too many to list by name, so they were simply referred to as "the women."

However, even with all of these speculations about who these women **might** have been, we cannot be sure. Ross S. Kraemer, in *Women in Scripture,* concludes:

> "It is difficult to draw historical conclusions from the absence of these women in Acts. . . . Their absence more likely reflects the author's intention. While emphasizing the gender-inclusiveness of the movement, he [Luke] may minimize the presence of women whose claims to authoritative leadership could conceivably have been on a par with those men presented as Apostles. Such an interpretation is strengthened by the prominence and authority of Mary Magdalene in many non-canonical gospels and traditions."[2]

James Carroll, in his book, *Practicing Catholic,* comments further: "...one of the most important Christian texts to be found outside the New Testament canon is the so-called Gospel of Mary, a telling of the Jesus-movement story that featured Mary Magdalene (decidedly not the woman of the alabaster jar) as one of the Church's most powerful leaders."[3] And further, in an article in *Smithsonian Magazine*, June 2006, he states: "Just as the 'canonical' Gospels emerged from communities that associated themselves with the 'evangelists,' who may not actually have 'written' the texts, this one is named for Mary, not because she 'wrote' it, but because it emerged from a community that recognized her authority."[4]

Luke, by reporting the presence of women with the apostles, reiterates Jesus' own rejection of male dominance. Later attempts by the church "fathers," beginning in the second century, however, began to encourage old patterns of patriarchy again. The importance of various women in Jesus' own ministry makes it clear that women were included in God's plan for His church from its inception.

APPLY How do you feel included in God's plan for His church?

_____

_____

_____

Mary, the Mother of Jesus

The one woman who is named in Acts 1:14 is Mary, the mother of Jesus. When we look at her whole life as presented in the Gospels, we see that Mary has a very special calling from God. And now, she is a woman who is about to experience a *new* coming of His Spirit. In this last glimpse of her in the Bible, her special mission is over, and her new life is in the **redefined family** of God, not just as mother, but also as "sister" (Matthew 12:50).

📖 See also John 19:26–27, where Jesus re-defines the relationship between Mary and John, the beloved disciple. How do you think the apostles are relating to Mary now?

_____

_____

_____

The message of Mary in Acts is that she *remains* God's humble servant as she was at the beginning, and she is there to witness to his saving power in her own unique way. Her faith in God has never wavered, and now she is continuing her life-long devotion and service to her Lord in a different time and place. She has essentially showed us, from beginning to end, what it means to be a true follower of Jesus Christ. The editors of *Mary in the New Testament*, put it this way: "He [Luke] is content in his last mention of Mary to show her with one accord with those who would constitute the nascent church at Pentecost. . . . The real import of Acts 1:14 is to remind the reader that she has not changed her mind."[5] Mary's "new call" is to remain with Christ's disciples and become part of His new creation, the church. Mary, who gave birth to the Son of God, has the privilege of also being present at the birth of His church.

APPLY Do you think Mary had a "higher" role than the others in that room? Why or why not?

_____

_____

_____

Others in the Room

Others in the room include the brothers of Jesus. This is surprising because they were among His opponents during His earthly ministry (John 7:5). James thought Jesus was out of His mind when he went off and began to preach. Jesus appeared alone to James after His resurrection and it is thought that James brought the others to faith in Him. James is also mentioned in Galatians 1:19 as *"James the Lord's brother."*

Every Gospel mentions brothers *and* sisters of Jesus. There are different interpretations of "his brothers." First, there are those who do not believe

> *Mary, who gave birth to the Son of God, also has the privilege of being present at the birth of His church.*

that Jesus had blood brothers, based on the belief in the perpetual virginity of Mary. Second, there are those who believe that Jesus did indeed have brothers *and* sisters by his father Joseph and his mother Mary. They are named in Matthew 13:55 as James, Joseph, Simon and Judas, and in Mark 6:3 as James, Joses, Judas and Simon. Other references to brothers *and* sisters include: Matthew 12:46–47; 13:55–56; Mark 3:31–32; Luke 8:19–20; and John 2:12. A third interpretation is that Joseph was married before and they were his children. And finally, there are those who believe that they were Jesus' cousins by Mary's sister. But, the important thing here is that they were *all together* in that room, indicating the positive effect Jesus had on a diverse group of people, from his own family to "many women."

A listing of the *possible* women present with the apostles:

Specifically named as being followers of Jesus and/or being with Him at the crucifixion, burial and/or resurrection:	Mary Magdalene, from whom seven demons went out Joanna, the wife of Herod Antipas' steward, Chuza Susanna Mary, the mother of James and Joses (Joseph)- wife of Clopas? Mother of the Sons of Zebedee, James and John- Salome? She left her home to follow Jesus. Mary, the mother of Jesus. The sister of Mary, the mother of Jesus.
Wives:	Peter's wife Other apostles' wives? Jesus' brothers' wives?
Women of Means: (Financial Support)	Mary, the mother of John Mark—*possibly* the owner of the house where they were staying and in which the Last Supper, resurrection appearances of Jesus and the coming of the Holy Spirit took place Other wealthy widows who provided resources
Women "cured of evil spirits and infirmities," forgiven of sin, or otherwise touched by Jesus (The Gospel Stories):*	The woman with an issue of blood The adulteress The anointing woman The Samaritan woman The Cananite/Syrophenician woman and her daughter The bent-over woman Jairus' daughter Peter's mother-in-law Mary and Martha of Bethany
Jesus' Relatives	His sister(s)

*Even though most of these women were not mentioned as "following Jesus," some of them could *possibly* have been present in the group at the crucifixion. There are men who were healed by Jesus whom we are specifically told "followed him."

How Are They Waiting?

Acts 1:14: *"All these were constantly devoting themselves to prayer. . . ."*

Luke often refers to all of the believers being together, underscoring the unity of the comm*unity*. Other translations of the Bible help with a fuller understanding of the unity of this group. For example, the Revised Standard Version (RSV) and the King James Version (KJV) state that they were *"with one accord"*; the New English Bible (NEB) adds the word *"together"*; the Today's English Version (TEV) renders it *"as a group, and together"*; J. B. Phillips says, *"by common consent all these men, together with the women. . . ."*; while the Contemporary English Version (CEV) has it: *"with a single purpose in mind."* They were already one in spirit, even before they were one *in the Holy Spirit*.

This unity is further expressed in the act of prayer. It is significant that Luke mentions that they are all at prayer at the very beginning, because he is alluding to the fact that prayer was to become one of the primary activities of the apostles in the early church. Throughout Acts, Luke tells us that prayer was a common and frequent act of the early church. Prayer precedes every major event in Acts and is mentioned over thirty times in the Book.

This small group of Jesus' followers did what He did. Jesus devoted himself to calling on his Father for help, strength and direction. He prayed before he did anything. And he taught us how to pray.

📖 Look up the Lord's Prayer in Matthew 6:9–13 and Luke 11:1–4 and say those verses together as a group. Now write down your individual prayers for yourself and others.

_____

_____

_____

_____

_____

It is particularly noteworthy that prayer precedes the giving of the Holy Spirit in other instances, as in this one. In Acts 4:31, at the second infilling of the Spirit, it was *"When they had prayed, . . ."* Similarly, after the Samaritans had become believers, *"The two* [Peter and John] *went down and prayed for them that they might receive the Holy Spirit"* (8:15). And, at Jesus' own baptism, he was praying before the Spirit descended upon him (Luke 3:21).

In the same way, the early church prayed as a group, as the **unified** body of Christ, whenever the apostles or any of their number were in prison or in danger: *"While Peter was kept in prison, the church prayed fervently to God for him"* (Acts 12:5). The Bible tells us to pray at all times like those first disciples. For example:

1 Thessalonians 5:16–18: *"Rejoice always, pray without ceasing, give thanks in all circumstances; for this is the will of God in Christ Jesus for you."*

> Luke often refers to all of the believers being together, underscoring the unity of community. This unity is further expressed in the act of prayer.

Philippians 4:6:*"Do not worry about anything, but in everything by prayer and supplication with thanksgiving let your requests be made known to God."*
Ephesians 6:18:*"Pray in the Spirit at all times in every prayer and supplication."*

 APPLY Does your church have a prayer group or prayer chain that regularly prays for people who are ill or in danger in some way? Does your corporate worship pray for the in-filling of the Spirit?

_____

_____

_____

These women are
beginning to rise
above their cultures
and circumstances
in order to meet the
larger vision of who
they are in Christ.

Another sign of the unity of the group is that the women are participating in prayer *with* the men. It is significant that women are mentioned at all at such a gathering of men because when Jews of that time gathered for study or prayer, it was a meeting of *only* men. In fact, it took ten men, called a *minyan*, to convene for worship or form a synagogue, and women literally did not count. Yet, here we have the followers of Jesus, women and men, praying *together*. This scene indicates that the gender equality practiced by Jesus was beginning to be experienced by women. The transition from the limitations placed on them in Jewish and pagan cultures to the freedom promised in Christianity was taking hold.

This whole scene is an affirmation that Jesus taught His disciples well about the importance and place of women. These women are beginning to rise above their cultures and circumstances in order to meet the larger vision of who they are in Christ.

 APPLY What vision do you have of your life in Jesus Christ? Is it being fulfilled in your life right now?

_____

_____

_____

_____

*Pentecost and
Prophesying Women*

DAY THREE

THE RESULT OF WAITING—THE HOLY SPIRIT

The Verse in Which the Women Appear: Acts 2:4
"All of them *were filled with the Holy Spirit and began to speak in other languages, as the Spirit gave them ability."*

The Story of Pentecost: Acts 2:1–4 *"When the day of Pentecost had come,"*

At that time, Pentecost was grandly celebrated with religious ceremonies, eating, drinking and music. Good sailing weather enabled Jews from every nation in the known world to assemble in the Holy City for this great feast day. This explains the list of countries given in the chapter and the international crowd that was present (Acts 2:9–11). Most every known language was represented. God had chosen to pour out His Spirit *during* this Jewish festival.

Did you know that Pentecost was a Jewish festival then? Is it still called Pentecost by Jews?

_____

_____

"they were all together in one place." (Acts 2:1)

The same group of 120 believers was presumably still in the same house in Jerusalem when the Spirit arrived. The promise came to those who were gathered **together** in prayer. Some scholars suggest that the house where they were staying belonged to Mary, the mother of John Mark, where tradition says the Last Supper and some post-resurrection appearances of Jesus took place. It was located on the western hill of Mt. Zion, the hill on which Jerusalem stood. (Locate this on the map of Jerusalem on the following page).

"and suddenly from heaven there came a sound like the rush of a violent wind, and it filled the entire house where they were sitting." (Acts 2:2)

The coming of the Holy Spirit was a noisy affair with a myriad of "special effects." It was a fulfillment of prophecy and an answer to the community's expectant prayers. It was a clear sign of God's faithfulness to his people. God had promised the giving of His Spirit and He kept that promise. (See Luke 24:49; John 14:26; and Acts 1:4–5, 8.)

📖 Look up these references and read about the promises of God. Write down similarities.

_____

_____

_____

_____

But, this was not the debut of the Holy Spirit. The Spirit of God was present from the beginning of creation: *". . . and the Spirit of God was moving over the face of the waters"* (Gen. 1:2, RSV). The New Revised Standard Version says, *"while a wind from God swept over the face of the waters."* The Hebrew word translated as "wind," *ruach,* can also be translated "breath" and "spirit." Wind/Spirit is one symbol used to represent God's power and presence throughout both the Old and New Testaments (Psalms 104:4).

Other references to the Spirit include Jesus' baptism (Matthew 3:16) and Jesus being led into the wilderness (Matthew 4:1). This same Spirit of God took hold of that first community of women and men and led them from that moment on as they were empowered to become God's witnesses.

> *"All of them were filled with the Holy Spirit and began to speak in other languages, as the Spirit gave them ability."*
>
> ## Acts 2:4

✏️ Did You Know?
❓ PENTECOST

The Jewish Festival of Pentecost was one of the three times per year when the entire household of Israel made a pilgrimage to Jerusalem. Pentecost, literally meaning "fiftieth," derives its name from the fifty days that separate it from Passover. Also called "The Feast of Weeks" (literally, a week of weeks), it traces its origin to Leviticus 23:15–21 and Deuteronomy 16:9 and was a celebration of the wheat harvest. The Jews brought the first fruits of their harvest in thanksgiving to God. Jews later celebrated Pentecost as the time when they were given the Law of Moses. Today, Pentecost in the Christian church is celebrated fifty days after Easter and commemorates the birth of the church and the coming of the Spirit.

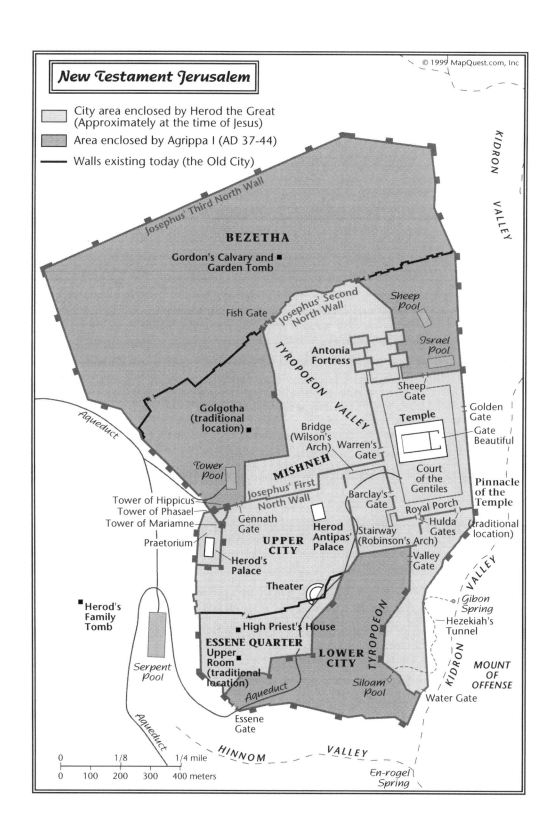

© 1999 MapQuest.com, Inc

New Testament Jerusalem

City area enclosed by Herod the Great
(Approximately at the time of Jesus)

Area enclosed by Agrippa I (AD 37-44)

Walls existing today (the Old City)

KIDRON VALLEY

Josephus' Third North Wall

BEZETHA

Gordon's Calvary and ■
Garden Tomb

Josephus' Second North Wall

Fish Gate

Sheep Pool

Israel Pool

TYROPOEON VALLEY

Antonia Fortress

Sheep Gate

Golgotha (traditional location) ■

Temple

Golden Gate

Gate Beautiful

Bridge (Wilson's Arch)

Warren's Gate

Aqueduct

Tower Pool

MISHNEH

Josephus' First North Wall

Barclay's Gate

Court of the Gentiles

Pinnacle of the Temple

Royal Porch

Tower of Hippicus
Tower of Phasael
Tower of Mariamne

Gennath Gate

UPPER CITY

Herod Antipas' Palace

Stairway (Robinson's Arch)

Hulda Gates

(traditional location)

Praetorium

Herod's Palace

Theater

High Priest's House ■

Valley Gate

TYROPOEON

VALLEY

Gibon Spring

Hezekiah's Tunnel

■ Herod's Family Tomb

ESSENE QUARTER
Upper Room (traditional location)

LOWER CITY

KIDRON

MOUNT OF OFFENSE

Serpent Pool

Aqueduct

Siloam Pool

Water Gate

Essene Gate

Aqueduct

HINNOM VALLEY

0   1/8   1/4 mile
0   100 200 300   400 meters

En-rogel Spring

📖 Look up Matthew 3:16 and compare it with Acts 2:1–4.

Note the differences in the appearance of the Holy Spirit at these two events.

_____

_____

_____

"Divided tongues, as of fire, appeared among them, and a tongue rested on each of them." (Acts 2:3)

The tongues, *as of fire*, are significant in that they also represent God's presence. Fire accompanies the divine presence elsewhere in Scripture (Exodus 3:2; 13:21–22; 19:18; Isaiah 66:15–16) as well as divine judgment (2 Thessalonians 1:8). When John the Baptist spoke of Jesus, he said, *"He will baptize you with the Holy Spirit and fire"* (Matthew 3:11). The Spirit appeared among them as a community as well as individually. A tongue rested on **each** of the women and men present that day as a distinguishing mark of a people belonging to God. It is clear from this story that the arrival of the Holy Spirit was anything but private and hidden from view. It is also clear that women as well as men received the Spirit—and in the same way.

"All of them were filled with the Holy Spirit and began to speak in other languages as the Spirit gave them ability." (Acts 2:4)

The phrase *"All of them"* implies the full presence of the same 120 people mentioned in 1:14–15. And, as this verse clearly states, no one was left out of the outpouring of God's Spirit. In neither the filling of the Spirit nor in the gift itself was any distinction made between women and men. It doesn't say that only a select few were filled with the Spirit. It also does not say that only the apostles were filled with the Spirit. Women and men alike were given the gift of the Spirit because **all** were recognized as important to the community of believers. From that moment on, the Holy Spirit became **the** dominant reality in the life of the early church. The Spirit was the source of all courage, power, joy, and guidance and gave *each* of them the ability to carry on the message of salvation. We have seen how prayerful, faithful, and patient they have been and their waiting has been rewarded.

APPLY Think of a time when God has rewarded you for waiting a long time for something.

_____

_____

_____

_____

They were all not only filled with the Holy Spirit, but they all began to speak in other languages. Mark 16:17 says that these signs will accompany those who believe: *"they will speak in new tongues."* There are different interpretations of "other languages" or "tongues." William Barclay offers one interpretation. He says that the crowd of Jews from all over the region spoke, at most, two languages. Almost all Jews spoke Aramaic and almost everyone in the world spoke Greek at that time. He states that, "Luke, a

Gentile, had confused speaking with tongues with speaking in foreign languages."[6] But Maier, in *First Christians,* counters, ". . . but this does violence to Luke's text, which plainly reports the foreigner's reaction: 'We hear them telling in our own tongues the mighty works of God' (2:11)."[7] Another interpretation of the tongues is that each apostle was able to speak in the language of the place they were to witness. And still another says that the power of the Spirit enabled *"all of them"* to proclaim the Gospel of Jesus Christ to others in ways that they could understand (Acts 2:6–8). "Spirit language," as opposed to "speaking in tongues," which requires an interpreter, is *understandable* to everyone who hears it. It is God's language and it speaks to the hearts of all people.

 How do you think Jewish men from around the region reacted to hearing *women* speaking in "Spirit language?" How do you think the Spirit-filled women felt?

_____

_____

_____

The book of Acts is full of occasions when the Holy Spirit appears among God's faithful people and, on each occasion, gives them all the gift of proclamation. And in the proclaiming, God's people are understood by all who come into contact with them.

"In the last days it will be, God declares, that I will pour out my Spirit upon all flesh, and your sons and your daughters shall prophesy, and your young men shall see visions, and your old men shall dream dreams. Even upon my slaves, both men and women, in those days I will pour out my Spirit; and they shall prophesy."

Acts 2:17–18

THE FULFILLMENT OF PROPHECY

The Verses in Which the Women Appear (Acts 2:17–18; cf. Joel 2:28–29)

"In the last days it will be, God declares, that I will pour out my Spirit upon all flesh, and your sons and your **daughters** *shall prophesy, and your young men shall see visions and your old men shall dream dreams. Even upon my slaves, both men and* **women***, in those days I will pour out my Spirit; and* **they** *shall prophesy."* (Acts 2:17–18)

"Then afterward I will pour out my spirit on all flesh; your sons and your **daughters** *shall prophesy, your old men shall dream dreams, and your young men shall see visions. Even on the male and* **female slaves***, in those days, I will pour out my spirit."* (Joel 2:28-29)

Prophesying Daughters and Female Slaves

Jesus was revolutionary in his treatment of everyone, especially women. And Joel's prophecy is revolutionary. Joel foretells of a time when the gift of the Holy Spirit will be made available to everyone, regardless of age, gender or social status. The women and men of the early church recorded in Acts are among the first to fulfill Joel's prophetic words. Women are now equally called to God's service and prophetic work. Even slaves, who often have been at the bottom of social hierarchy, now have equal status with prophets. Even today, those filled with God's Spirit are completely transformed and liberated to become proclaimers, some through prophecy, of the gospel message.

Prophecy is something that we usually think of in terms of the Old Testament, even though there are prophets and prophetesses mentioned in the Gospels. On the day of Pentecost, the gift of prophecy entered the Christian church by the Holy Spirit. There were both female and male prophets in the early church, and according to Paul, prophecy was a gift given to particular individuals for the upbuilding of the church (Romans 12:6; 1 Corinthians 12:10, 28–29; Ephesians 4:11; 1 Thessalonians 5:20). He considered it basic to the structure and operation of the church. Women would now share in one of the most significant of spiritual gifts.

📖 Look up the verses in Paul's letters about prophecy in Paul's first letter to the Corinthians (1 Corinthians 14:1–5). What do they say about it?

_____

_____

_____

_____

"In the last days it will be, God declares, that I will pour out my Spirit upon all flesh. . . ." (Acts 2:17).

Following the giving of the Holy Spirit, some in the crowd accuse the believers of being drunk. But Peter says that is impossible, since it is only nine o'clock in the morning. Peter's response is to quote the prophecy of Joel to prove that the outpouring of the Spirit is the inaugural event of Israel's "last days" during which *"everyone who calls upon the name of the Lord will be saved"* (Acts 2:21). Some have called this speech the first sermon of the new church. Peter points to the first half of Joel's prophecy as the fulfillment of the promise, claiming that the events of Pentecost fulfill prophecy—a time when God will pour out His Spirit on all people, regardless of race, age, or gender.

APPLY How does the fulfillment of Joel's prophecy speak to women in today's world?

_____

_____

_____

Joel prophesies a time when differential treatment based on gender disappears in that daughters, as well as sons, will prophesy. Differences based on age will also be inconsequential, since both young men and old will have visionary experiences. And finally, distinction based on class will also be of little account, since even slaves (both female and male) will be endowed with the divine spirit. Joel's prophecy is a promise of God to bless all people.

📖 The same promise is described by the prophet Isaiah in Isaiah 44:3 and the prophet Ezekiel in Ezekiel 39:29. Compare the language in each to Joel 2:28–29. What phrase is almost identical?

_____

_____

_____

_____

> The "Acts of the Women" will be different now—they shall prophesy and be free from human and cultural restrictions, labels, and other conditions. "It's a girl!" will now be just as important in human history as "It's a boy!"

Pentecost and Prophesying Women

Peter "rewrites" Joel's prophecy a bit. He substitutes "in the last days" for "after these things" and adds "God declares" at the beginning and "they shall prophesy" at the end. The gift of prophecy, then becomes a distinguishing mark of the Christian movement. That is, a movement of empowered and illumined proclamation by everyone in the church. Pentecost initiates Israel into a new epoch—"the last days" of God's salvation history—when things said and done by Jesus' successors take on the added urgency of a mission to restore God's kingdom to Israel.

> ". . . and your sons and your daughters shall prophesy, and your young men shall see visions, and your old men shall dream dreams. Even upon my slaves, both men and women in those days I will pour out my Spirit; and they shall prophesy." (Acts 2:17–18)

Joel's prophecy shapes the church's mission in Acts. These are no longer days of waiting but days set apart for mission—the mission of giving witness to the risen Jesus. Following the passage from Joel, the shape of this witness includes two primary tasks: signs and wonders and the proclamation of God's word. Acts' constant repetition of the prophecy's catchphrases (*signs and wonders*) and concepts (*Spirit, baptism, filling, inspired prophets, conversion*) expands the full significance of the Spirit's outpouring at Pentecost.

And what does this do for women? Jesus has already lifted women to their "proper" place in creation—that of full partnership with men—and He had no reservations at all about women taking part in the ministry of proclamation. Now God's Spirit is telling us that women are equally as prized as men. The "Acts of the Women" will be different now—they shall prophesy and be free from human and cultural restrictions, labels and other conditions. "It's a girl!" will now be just as important in human history as "It's a boy!"

FOR ME TO FOLLOW GOD

Life Principle for Lesson Two: Waiting on God

"But you promised!" Perhaps we hear those words most often from children when they express disappointment at our failure to keep a promise we made to them. We may fail, but God *never* fails to keep his promises. In Acts, Jesus tells his disciples before His Ascension that the "promise of the Father" will come in the form of the Holy Spirit. They prayerfully wait with the others and *believe* that God will keep that promise—and He does in ways that they could not even have imagined. The Holy Spirit literally turns their lives completely upside-down.

Not only are they baptized by the Spirit, but an Old-Testament prophecy or promise is also fulfilled. The fulfillment of this prophecy also turns their lives completely upside down, especially the lives of the kinds of people to whom Jesus ministered—women, the sick and elderly, and those shunned by society. Joel's prophecy makes it clear that *everyone* is included in God's promise.

The truth of the gospel is that what those early disciples experienced on the day of Pentecost so long ago can still be experienced by us today. When we believe and prayerfully wait for the promises of God, they will be revealed to us, and our lives will also be turned completely upside down in ways that we cannot even imagine. *"For in Him* [Jesus Christ] *every one of God's promises is a 'Yes'"* (2 Corinthians 1:20).

APPLY What promises of God have been revealed to you in your life?

_____

_____

_____

_____

However, we must wait for God's timing. God knows better than anyone not just **what** we need, but **when** we need it. Waiting takes **faith** and **patience** and **trust** and **letting go of our own wills**, like those early Christians did. First it takes faith. We can learn a lot about faith in the eleventh chapter of the book of Hebrews, often called "the faith chapter" of the Bible. It begins by saying, *"Now faith is the assurance of things hoped for, the conviction of things not seen. Indeed, by faith our ancestors received approval"* (Hebrews 11:1).

📖 Read this chapter of Hebrews and write down your observations about faith.

_____

_____

_____

_____

Next, it takes patience. A lot of us are impatient. We want what we want, and we want it now. And in this world of instant gratification, we often get it. Again, in Hebrews 6:12, it says: *"so that you may not become sluggish, but imitators of those who through faith and patience inherit the promises."* Through faith and patience, those early Christians inherited the promise of the father, the Holy Spirit.

APPLY What have you waited for with both faith and patience and ultimately received from God?

_____

_____

_____

_____

_____

Next, it takes trust—trust that God will reveal his promises to us. Proverbs 3:5 tells us that if we trust God, he will guide us. *"Trust in the Lord with all thine heart; and lean not unto thine own understanding. In all thy ways, acknowledge him, and he shall direct thy paths"* (KJV). Those first Christians trusted God to guide them in everything they did, everywhere they went, and everything they needed.

> *Waiting takes faith and patience and trust and letting go of our own wills, like those first Christians did.*

APPLY How do you trust God for your life?

_____

_____

_____

_____

And finally, and probably the hardest thing to do, is to let go of our own wills. The greatest prayer that any of us can ever pray is *"thy will be done."* *Thy* will, not my will. Because when we pray that prayer, we get the best that God has to offer us and not anything that our finite minds can even fathom.

APPLY Write down a time in your life when you let go completely and said, "Thy will be done."

_____

_____

_____

_____

The gift of the Holy Spirit is still available to us now as it was in the first century. The fulfillment of prophecy tells us that the Spirit of God is for all of us, slave or free, male or female, Jew or Greek, rich or poor, white or black, old or young, town or country, plain or fancy, married or single, etc., etc., etc. Let us be mindful that *everyone* we meet is meant for the kingdom of God and for the Spirit.

Isaiah 40:31 tells us: *"But those who wait for the Lord shall renew their strength, they shall mount up with wings as eagles, they shall run and not be weary, they shall walk and not faint."* The Spirit not only changed lives on the day of Pentecost, but it took control of that early community, and we are told in Acts 2:42–47 what a truly "Spirit-filled" church looked like:

> *"They devoted themselves to the apostles' teaching and fellowship, to the breaking of bread and the prayers. Awe came upon everyone, because many wonders and signs were being done by the apostles. All who believed were together and had all things in common; they would sell their possessions and goods and distribute the proceeds to all, as any had need. Day by day, as they spent much time together in the temple, they broke bread at home and ate their food with glad and generous hearts, praising God and having the good-will of all the people. And day by day the Lord added to their number those who were being saved."*

APPLY Which of these characteristics does your church have?

_____

_____

_____

_____

Let the Spirit of the living God renew your life and your church today. And *"Wait for the Lord; be strong, and let your heart take courage; wait for the Lord!"* (Psalms 27:14).

Let us be mindful that everyone we meet is meant for the kingdom of God and for the Spirit.

Lord of all women and men, unite us in Your Spirit and make us one in the body of Christ. Help us value every person and see each one as Your child. Help us use each gift of Your Spirit for the building up of Your church. Be our guide in everything we do that we might find Your way and Your will. In the name of Jesus Christ, we pray, Amen.

Works Cited

1. Paul L. Maier, *First Christians, Pentecost and the Spread of Christianity* (New York, NY: Harper & Row Publishers, 1976), 16.

2. Ross S. Kraemer, Associate Editor, *Women in Scripture* (Grand Rapids, MI: William B. Eerdman's Publishing Company, 2000), 457.

3. James Carroll, *Practicing Catholic,* (Boston, New York: Houghton Mifflin Harcourt Publishing Company, 2009) 156. Used by permission of the author.

4. James Carroll, *Who Was Mary Magdalene?* (*Smithsonian Magazine*, June 2006) 115. Used by permission of the author.

5. Raymond E. Brown and John Reumann, *Mary in the New Testament* (Philadelphia, PA: Fortress Press, 1978), 177.

6. William Barclay, *The Daily Study Bible, The Acts of the Apostles* (Louisville, KY: Westminster John Knox Press, 1975, 2003), 24

7. Maier, *First Christians,* 19.

Notes

3

Sapphira and Other Female Disciples

The Spirit-filled church almost immediately begins to suffer persecution from jealous Jews who have trouble with the doctrine of the resurrection and with Jesus as their Messiah. Peter and John are arrested for the first time. But perhaps the more serious threat comes from within its own ranks, when jealously and greed combine to put the church to its first tests of faith and unity.

Transition—Chapters 3 and 4

The Spirit-filled ministry of Peter and John continues in chapter 3. On their way to Solomon's Portico at the Temple for prayer, Peter and John encounter a man, lame from birth, begging at its gates. They tell this man about Jesus Christ and he is immediately healed. He follows them into the Temple, and the people are filled with wonder and amazement at witnessing the former cripple walking and leaping and praising God. Peter speaks boldly to the Jews about Christ and tells them that it was by His power that the man was healed. The apostle reminds the Jews of the prophecies predicting the coming of the Messiah, who was raised up for their salvation, and that they rejected and killed him. Peter asks them to repent and turn back to God, that they too, may be forgiven. He ends by telling them, *"When God raised up his servant, he sent him first to you, to bless you by turning each of you from your wicked ways"* (Acts 3:26).

> **But perhaps the more serious threat is from within its own ranks, when jealousy and greed combine to put the church to its first tests of faith and unity.**

Chapter 4 opens with the religious leaders becoming annoyed at Peter and John for teaching on the resurrection of the dead. As a result, Peter and John are arrested for the first time. But in spite of this, five thousand people become believers. After the apostles reveal to the Jewish authorities by what power the cripple was healed, they are released with a warning not to speak any more about Jesus. Peter and John tell them that they *"cannot keep from speaking about what we have seen and heard"* (Acts 4:20). They return to their friends and the people pray for boldness for their continuing witness. They are filled with the Holy Spirit, who gives them the courage they need. The new church continues to be of one heart and soul and the people share everything they have with each other.

Chapter 5 opens with the story of **Sapphira** and **Ananias,** two members of the early church, whose story reveals the deception and greed of the human heart and how it affects the unity of the church. When they lie to Peter and the Holy Spirit about what they have given, they are struck dead. But in spite of God's judgment on Sapphira and her husband, the Spirit continues to strengthen the new church, and the apostles perform many signs and wonders. Still more people become believers, **great numbers of both men and women.** Many, even from the towns around Jerusalem, bring their sick and tormented to Peter for healing.

Persecution of the apostles continues by the Sadducees, *"those who say there is no resurrection."* (Luke 20:27). They are arrested again and thrown into prison. But an angel of the Lord releases them and they are told to continue their witness. When the high priest and elders send for them, they find them teaching in the temple. Peter and the apostles are brought before the Sanhedrin and warned again to stop their teaching. Peter tells them that they must obey God and proceeds to tell them once again about Jesus, which enrages them. Some want to kill them, but a respected lawyer named Gamaliel convinces them that the apostles are not a threat and that this will soon pass. His advice is accepted; they are flogged and released.

📖 Look up the verses in these chapters about the Holy Spirit and note how it is leading both the apostles and the church. (Acts 4:8, 25, 31; 5:3, 9, 32)

_____

_____

_____

Sapphira and Others

DAY ONE

ONENESS OF HEART: AT FIRST

To fully understand the story of Sapphira and Ananias, it is important to describe the climate of the early church in Jerusalem in regard to its attitude about the sale of property for the good of all. This is the second description of the early church in Acts, describing the unity and generosity of its earliest members.

> *Now the whole group of those who believed were of one heart and soul, and no one claimed private ownership of any possessions, but everything they owned was held in common. With great power the apostles gave their testimony to the resurrection of the Lord Jesus, and great grace was upon them all. There was*

not a needy person among them, for as many as owned lands or houses sold them and brought the proceeds of what was sold. They laid it at the apostles' feet, and it was distributed to each as any had need. (Acts 4:32–35)

Luke begins this summary in Acts 4 with the community's practice of sharing goods, which is a commentary on how we are to use our money and possessions. The early church members had an innate sense of responsibility toward each other and a real desire to share all they had with those in need. Their "oneness of heart" takes on visible expression in the pooling of their possessions.

The *Abingdon Bible Commentary* says: "The emphasis here (vv. 32–37) is upon the unanimity, the unselfishness, the brotherly love of its members, and upon the public ministry carried on (verse 33), marked as it was by power and grace."[1]

Through the power of the Holy Spirit, these first Christians were able to share in a way that took care of everyone. The transforming power of God's love is what makes us generous, not any power within ourselves. It is love that makes the poor rich and the rich thankful and generous; love that shares itself freely with no thought of reward or personal gain, and love that is valuable and gives value to all other things. The needs of others become more important to the first Christians than the need for possessions.

APPLY Describe what your possessions mean to you. How do you share what you have with others?

_____

_____

_____

_____

Jesus had a lot to say about possessions. The statements He made serve as powerful symbols of what our own values are in relation to the groups we belong to, whether family, social or religious. Probably the most familiar story in the Gospels about possessions is of the rich, young man who was told by Jesus, *"If you wish to be perfect, go, sell your possessions, and give the money to the poor, and you will have treasure in heaven; then come, follow me. When the young man heard this word, he went away grieving, for he had many possessions"* (Matthew 19:21–22).

And Luke, in his Gospel, quotes Jesus as saying, *"So therefore, none of you can become my disciple if you do not give up all your possessions"* (Luke 14:33). If our possessions are *more* important to us than Jesus Christ, we cannot be called his disciples. And if we are not generous with what God has given to us, we need God's grace to enable us to develop a spiritual maturity to replace our spiritual poverty.

APPLY How does the generosity of others in your community or church affect you?

_____

_____

_____

> The early church members had an innate sense of responsibility toward each other and a real desire to share all they had with those in need. Their "oneness of heart" takes on visible expression in the pooling of their possessions.

> The transforming power of God's love is what makes us generous, not any power within ourselves.

The word *diaspora* is a Greek word meaning "dispersion." Throughout the Old Testament, beginning with the Assyrian conquest, the Israelites were dispersed and became a people of exile. Dispersion of Jewish exiles became a way of life and continued into the Greco-Roman period, when Jews were scattered over much of the ancient world. The letter of James begins by saying, *"To the twelve tribes of the Dispersion."* (James 1:1) Peter, similarly, says in his first letter, *"To the exiles of the Dispersion in Pontus, Galatia, Cappadocia, Asia and Bithynia. . ."* (1 Peter 1:1).

Sapphira and Others

DAY TWO

Before Sapphira and Ananias are introduced, we hear about Barnabas, who is also a wealthy landowner and a *diaspora* Jew from Cyprus who has joined the Christian community. He also joins Paul in his missionary travels later in Acts. He is a positive example of the generosity of the believers in sharing the proceeds of the land that he sold.

"There was a Levite, a native of Cyprus, Joseph, to whom the apostles gave the name Barnabas (which means 'son of encouragement'). He sold a field that belonged to him, then brought the money, and laid it at the apostles' feet." (Acts 4:36–37)

Perhaps Sapphira and Ananias are watching closely, and see that the community is singling him out for special mention because of what he has done. I think it is human nature to want recognition for what we do and what we give. It is also human nature to want to recognize those who give to the church. One of my pet peeves is all of the seemingly endless brass plaques you find in some churches that make sure everyone knows who gave what and when and for what. I have seen plaques on windowsills, in elevators, even in bathrooms, and I think, is the need for recognition so great that we have to make sure we are given credit, even in God's house? I think the reward is in the giving, rather than in the recognition. What can we give anyway other than what God has given to us?

Jesus told us not to sound trumpets before ourselves so that everyone might praise us for our deeds *or* for our almsgiving. He said, *"But when you give alms, do not let your left hand know what your right hand is doing, so that your alms may be done in secret; and your Father who sees in secret will reward you"* (Matthew 6:2–4).

If we can be content to know that God will reward us for what we *really* give, then our giving can take on a holy purpose and be used for his glory rather than for our own egos. When was the last time you gave something anonymously? How did that feel?

_____

_____

_____

HATCHING THE PLAN TOGETHER

Verses in which Ananias and Sapphira appear: Acts 5:1–2

*"But a man named Ananias, with the consent of his wife, **Sapphira,** sold a piece of property; with his wife's knowledge, he kept back some of the proceeds, and brought only a part and laid it at the apostles' feet."*

In this period of the great outpouring of the Spirit, the new church is undergoing a test in all of its responsibilities. The story of Sapphira and Ananias is an example of Luke's pairing of female and male characters and is a negative example in the community of goods—one of self-service rather than other-service. The actions of Ananias and Sapphira break that "oneness of heart" that has, thus far, characterized the Spirit's leading of the new church.

It is a story about our human nature. It deals with money and the pitfalls of wealth as well as the desire to be noticed and well-liked. It shows how dishonesty, deception, greed and divided loyalties disrupt the unity of the believers.

 What other kinds of things can disrupt unity in a church or other institution or family?

_____

_____

_____

The story is about the harsh reality of the consequences of sin. It is one of the stories that shocks us for its refusal to offer forgiveness and restoration. It is the first story in Acts in which an individual woman stands out, and it is also the story of two early Christians who are struck dead for their sin.

The story of Ananias and Sapphira is hardly the first story in the Bible where God's people faced judgment for keeping items that weren't rightfully theirs. In fact this story in Acts parallels the Old Testament stories of Achan (Joshua 7:1–26) and Saul and the Amalekites (1 Samuel 15). In both Old Testament stories, the central character knowingly disobeys God by keeping back some of the war booty. The deception leads to immediate death for Achan, as he is killed at God's command, and God renounces Saul as king. An unrepentant Saul eventually dies a premature death as God's blessing upon him had been removed. In Ananias and Sapphira's case, God did not judge them for keeping some of the money from the sale of their possessions; He judged them for misleading others into believing that they had given the entire proceeds to the church.

 How do you react to a God who strikes his servants dead for disobedience?

_____

_____

_____

We meet Ananias first in relationship and partnership with his wife in planning their deception. The narrative presumes that spouses could act as joint owners and make mutual decisions, since Sapphira is identified as being complicit in the deception. In their marriage, Ananias consults with his wife about the sale and disposition of property. This shows Sapphira as having an equal voice in the economic management of her household. In fact, says Richard I. Pervo in *Women in Scripture,* she *"may be the most fully 'equal' woman in the New Testament."* She was also equal in another more serious way—she was punished in the same way for lying.

The text clearly says that they conspired their act of deception and lies against the church *together*. It may first suggest that the property belonged to Sapphira, since Ananias had to get her consent. Then, the plot is hatched to keep back some of the proceeds. The Contemporary English Version (CEV) suggests an even more sinister plan; it says *"they agreed to cheat"* (Acts 5:2).

> **"But a man named Ananias, with the consent of his wife Sapphira, sold a piece of property; with his wife's knowledge, he kept back some of the proceeds, and brought only a part and laid it at the apostles' feet"**
>
> **Acts 5:1–2**

The text clearly says that they conspired their act of deception and lies against the church together.

So, at its inception, this act by *both* was a deliberate attempt to look better than they were and to purposefully deceive the church by lying about it. We aren't told why Sapphira chose to become her husband's accomplice in the deed. Whether she actively approved the sale and distribution of the assets or simply silently failed to resist him, we don't really know for sure. But Luke's intent is clear: he is stressing the complicity of *both* partners in the deception.

APPLY How do you feel about Sapphira's actions? What would you do?

_____

_____

_____

_____

It is important to remember that they were not obligated to give any of the money to the church. It was entirely up to them how much they gave. Their sin consisted of surrendering a part *as if* it had been the whole, giving the *impression* that they were being completely sacrificial in their giving, like Barnabas. But, in the process of wanting the praise of others, and perhaps a higher position in the church, they got the wrath of the Holy Spirit instead.

Their sin consisted of surrendering a part as if it had been the whole, and keeping back the other part for themselves, giving the impression that they were being completely sacrificial in their giving, like Barnabas.

APPLY What kind of impression do you like to give to those around you, especially at church?

_____

_____

_____

Let us look at Ananias first in Acts 5:3–6:

> 'Ananias,' Peter asked, 'why has Satan filled your heart to lie to the Holy Spirit and to keep back part of the proceeds of the land? While it remained unsold, did it not remain your own? And after it was sold, were not the proceeds at your disposal? How is it that you have contrived this deed in your heart? You did not lie to us but to God!' Now when Ananias heard these words, he fell down and died. And great fear seized all who heard of it. The young men came and wrapped up his body, then carried him out and buried him.

How did Peter know about the lie? Why do you think he was so quick to condemn him?

_____

_____

_____

What was the reaction of the people present? How do you react?

_____

_____

_____

_____

DON'T ALWAYS AGREE WITH YOUR HUSBAND

Sapphira: Pronounced (suh fai' ruh) from the Aramaic, "sappira" meaning "good" or "beautiful"

Ironically, her name means "good" or "beautiful" and the name Sapphira was restricted to wealthy Jerusalem women. She appeared to have everything going for her—wealth, beauty and prominence in the church and community. But her character reveals a dishonest and insecure nature and a need for recognition. We are given no information about hers or Ananias' backgrounds, but they were probably Jews who had become Christians and joined the church in Jerusalem. They were faithful disciples of this first community of believers. They appear to be among its most wealthy and prominent members. Sapphira, Ananias, and Barnabas appear to be of the same social class of landowners, who sell property and present the proceeds to the apostles for the good of the community.

Verses in Which the Woman Appears: Acts 5:7–10
"After an interval of about three hours his **wife** *came in, not knowing what had happened."*

Now it is Sapphira's turn. The important thing here is that she *alone* responds the way she does based on their agreement. Sapphira has the opportunity to tell the truth about the land that she and Ananias have sold, but she too, chooses to lie. Since they are not brought in together, she has the chance to change her mind about the whole thing. She is even the one who is given the opportunity to answer Peter about the price, when Ananias is not.

 Why do you think Sapphira went along with her husband? Have you ever done that, even though you disagreed with him? What caused you to do that? How did it turn out?

_____

_____

_____

Peter said to her, 'Tell me whether you and your husband sold the land for such and such a price.' And she said, 'Yes, that was the price.' Then Peter said to her, 'How is it that you have agreed together to put the Spirit of the Lord to the test?' (Acts 5:8–9)

First, note the differences in the couple's conversations with Peter. Peter asks different questions of each of them and asks only two of Sapphira. She seals her *own* fate when she is asked about the price. She lies with her *own* lips, rather than being accused by Peter. In her answer, she makes it known that she is a *full partner* in the deception. She reveals *herself* to be someone who thinks it better to hide what she and her husband have done rather than telling the truth to the church and to God.

'Look, the feet of those who have buried your husband are at the door, and they will carry you out.' Immediately she fell down at his feet and died. When the young men came in they found her dead, so they carried her out and buried her beside her husband. (Acts 5:9–10)

> **Sapphira appeared to have everything going for her— wealth, beauty and prominence in the church and the community. But her character reveals a dishonest and insecure nature and a need for recognition.**

She suffers the same fate as Ananias. If they had not been struck dead, how do you think others would have treated them, knowing that they had lied to the church?

_____

_____

_____

Conclusions

First of all, this story is an example of the way Luke liked to pair male and female characters in his narratives. However, even though Ananias and Sapphira are paired at the beginning of the story as co-conspirators in their action of lying to God and God's people, they each act individually when Peter questions them separately about it. He intends for both women and men to learn the lesson. We are ultimately responsible to God for ourselves.

Second, it illustrates the sacredness of our stewardship. This couple seems to be motivated by financial concerns and the need to be noticed for what they do. Their giving to the church is done to impress others and to build themselves up rather than to help others. If they had not been exposed, the people would probably have continued to think well of them.

Third, this story warns us of the dangers of lying to the Holy Spirit. Peter shouts to Ananias, *"You did not lie to us, but to God!"* In both Matthew and Luke, Jesus says to Satan, *"Do not put the Lord your God to the test"* (Matthew 4:7; Luke 4:12). And Luke, in the case of Ananias, puts the responsibility on Satan for causing him to lie, *"why has Satan filled your heart to lie to the Holy Spirit. . . ?"* (Acts 5:3). And to Sapphira, he says, *"How is it that you have agreed together to put the Spirit of the Lord to the test?"* (Acts 5:9). It is Satan who has already infiltrated this new community of believers in an attempt to undermine it from within. The lesson is to keep from yielding to the temptation of the father of all lies (John 8:44).

And finally, this story tells us that even from its earliest and greatest days, the church was made up of all kinds of people—those with both pure and ulterior motives. In Proverbs 6:16–19, it clearly states the things that God hates, and lying is one of them. What are some of the others?

_____

_____

_____

_____

There are many who are disturbed by this story and its swift and negative judgment instead of forgiveness. The *Abingdon Bible Commentary* helps:

> "The teaching of Jesus emphasized high ethical principles and the apostles took up the strain. The deed of Ananias and his wife was destructive. The brotherhood of this early community could not be spoiled from without, as the book of Acts shows. The life of the church was more seriously endangered by hypocrisy or treachery within."[3]

The forces that would destroy the church from within had to be weeded out. Here, God has moved with great discipline to ensure its purity and survival in its earliest days.

Their giving to the church is done to impress others and build themselves up, rather than to help others.

The forces that would destroy the church from within had to be weeded out.

"And great fear seized the whole church and all who heard of these things." (Acts 5:11)

As the story unfolds, it has a profound effect on the believers—it gives them a great sense of awe and dread. The reaction, in both cases, is the same. It teaches a lesson and serves to keep the new church on the right course.

It is interesting to note that in these passages about this couple, the word "church" appears for the first time as the name for the Christian community (5:11).

OTHER WOMEN WHO BELIEVED

Verse in Which the Women Appear: Acts 5:14

"Yet more than ever believers were added to the Lord, great numbers of both men and **women.***"*

Ordinary Jews living in and around Jerusalem heard and believed the message of the resurrection and were baptized into the fellowship of the early church. They were people looking for better lives—for hope and healing, for meaning, and for a purpose beyond themselves. The women in Acts 5:14 were responding to the message of Jesus for them—a message of re–creation, redemption and renewal—and for a message that told them they were important and equal to the task of proclaiming the gospel. The Spirit of the living God was calling women and men alike to Himself.

This verse serves as a general reminder that *both* women and men joined the church. The early church had no trouble with its evangelism program and church growth goals! In the first two chapters of Acts alone, we see the explosive growth of the Christian community go from 120 faithful disciples to three thousand members after just one Spirit-filled sermon by Peter (Acts 2:41). And by the time Peter and John are arrested for the first time for preaching the gospel and warned not to do it anymore, *"many of those who heard the word believed, and they numbered about five thousand"* (Acts 4:4). Then, as a result of many signs and wonders, we have even more being added to the membership. Other Bible translations indicate in 5:14 that *"multitudes"* (KJV) or *"crowd"* (TEV) were added to the church.

APPLY What motivates you to join a particular church?

_____

_____

_____

What are some of the ministries of your church that cause people to join?

_____

_____

_____

_____

> **"Yet more than ever believers were added to the Lord, great numbers of both men and women"**
>
> **Acts 5:14**

> **The early church had no trouble with its evangelism program and church growth goals!**

In order to grasp the full impact of the growth of the church during this time, we need to look at the full context of this verse, contained in verses twelve through sixteen. This is the third summary describing the unity of the church in Jerusalem and highlights the powerful acts of the apostles.

> *Now many signs and wonders were done among the people through the apostles. And they were all together in Solomon's Portico. None of the rest dared to join them, but the people held them in high esteem. Yet more than ever believers were added to the Lord, great numbers of both men and women, so that they even carried out the sick into the streets, and laid them on cots and mats, in order that Peter's shadow might fall on some of them as he came by. A great number of people would also gather from the towns around Jerusalem, bringing their sick and those tormented by unclean spirits, and they were all cured.* (Acts 5:12–16)

The scene is so reminiscent of Jesus. People brought their sick and demon-possessed into the streets to be touched and cured by Peter just as they had thronged to Jesus for healing and wholeness (Luke 4:37, 5:15; 6:17–19).

📖 Look up these verses and note the similarities.

_____

_____

_____

_____

Empowered by the Holy Spirit, and following in Jesus' footsteps and by His example, the apostles are busy carrying out His instructions to them. These dramatic signs and wonders produced awe and respect in those who witnessed them, resulting in many new converts.

 What are the signs and wonders of today's church?

_____

_____

_____

It is significant that Peter preached to the people out in the open on Solomon's Portico (or porch). Neither he nor the thousands of new converts were keeping such a transforming message to themselves. It was too important. And the people, it says, *"held them in high esteem"*—perhaps admired them for their courage and extra-ordinary faith in what they believed. The power of the Holy Spirit is moving in the midst of the people to create and continue the work of Jesus Christ in the world—as His church.

Did You Know?

SOLOMON'S PORCH

Solomon's Portico, which was a covered colonnade on the eastern side of the Temple, became the regular meeting place of the early church. It was a place where the rabbis met with the people to teach them. It is mentioned twice in the book of Acts (3:11 and 5:12) and was the site of Jesus' teaching on one occasion (John 10:23).

Sapphira and Others

DAY FIVE

FOR ME TO FOLLOW GOD

Life Principle for Lesson Three: Judgment and faith

The pictures of families posing with their possessions in a 1994 book, *Material World,* by Peter Menzel, continue to stare back at me to this day, many years after I first looked at them. I remember the powerful emotions I had when I first looked through the book. The contrasts are stark and truly remarkable. There are families surrounded by piles of stuff as well as other families surrounded by only a few jars and jugs. I also noticed that some families, usually the ones with fewer possessions, included religious objects, such as a Bible or a statue of Mary or the Koran, among their things.

In the introduction to Menzel's book, Paul Kennedy states that these religious items remind us that "even in our material world, most human beings feel a deep need for the transcendent and the intangible."[4] Something comes through in the pictures where these kinds of items are included. There are smiles and joy on the faces of those who are displaying an item representing their faith, even in the midst of what appears to be the most desperate of circumstances. Are they the ones, like those early Christians, who shared everything they had in an attempt to meet the needs of others instead of just themselves? Are they the ones who don't count their things as their most valuable possessions?

 If you posed with all of your possessions, what would be the most important thing among them?

_____

_____

_____

The sharing of possessions and proceeds from the sale of those possessions are at the heart of the story of Sapphira and Ananias. Their possessions *seem* to be more important to them than being as honest and generous as they can be. They *seem* to be even more important to them than those in the church who are in need. Their story reveals the deception and greed of the human heart, even in the church. And the consequences of their actions are God's reaction to the *condition* of their hearts. When they lie to Peter and the Holy Spirit about what they have given, they are struck dead. Their tragic, untimely deaths teach us that God has no patience with *deliberate* sin.

The sin that provoked the lie they told was greed. Jesus addressed the problem of greed in Luke 12:15: *"And he said to them, 'Take care! Be on your guard against all kinds of greed; for one's life does not consist in the abundance of possessions.'"* He tied it *directly* to our possessions. And he has no patience with it. He also has no patience with lying. Lying seems to be especially prevalent in our society today. And yes, it still happens in the church, and when it does, it disrupts the unity of the body of Christ now just as it did in the first century. But while others can be fooled, God knows our hearts and judges us accordingly. The Psalms have a lot to say about how God deals with lies and deception.

"You destroy those who speak lies. . . . " (Psalms 5:6)

"No one who practices deceit shall remain in my house; no one who utters lies shall continue in my presence." (Psalms 101:7)

Psalms 10:3, 7 combines greed with deception: *"those greedy for gain curse and renounce the Lord. . . . Their mouths are filled with cursing and deceit and oppression."*

 Sapphira had the opportunity to tell the truth about the land she and Ananias had sold, but she chose to lie instead. When we have the opportunity to tell the truth about something, do we? We also have a choice—to deceive or live by faith; to be led by our human nature or by the Spirit of God. When have you given in to your human nature over listening to God? What was the result?

Lying seems to be especially prevalent in our society today. And yes, it still happens in the church. And when it does, it disrupts the unity of the body of Christ just as it did in the first century.

_____

_____

_____

_____

APPLY According to Peter's words to Ananias, it was Satan who filled his heart and caused him to lie. It is always Satan who causes us to sin. Jesus called him the father of lies. And Peter's words to Sapphira ask why she *agreed* to the lie. Even in the best days of the church, God had to deal with Satan. How do you think God is dealing with those who lie in His church today?

_____

_____

_____

The reaction of the entire church was one of great fear. God got everyone's attention. But He got on with empowering the apostles to bring even more people into His church. They continued to perform many signs and wonders, so that people would continue to join the church *in spite of* the unfortunate incident that had just taken place.

Our churches today are full of those who have joined them for all kinds of reasons—a charismatic preacher, a friendly congregation, good programs for children, Bible study or fellowship. But the most important reason is not any of these. It is the promise of eternal life through Jesus Christ who said, *"I am the way, and the truth, and the life. No one comes to the Father except through me"* (John 14:6). We find our purpose and our life in the one who came to save us.

> ## "I am the way, and the truth, and the life. No one comes to the Father except through me"
> ## John 14:6

All of our hearts can be freed from the sins of Sapphira and Ananias if we will only depend on God for our lives. God is still working to bring even more women and men to His church, in spite of the sins of greed, deception and lies and self-serving that permeate our society and even our churches.

 Lord of all truth, keep our minds and hearts free from lies and deception, that You might be glorified. Purge us of any untruth within us and help us overcome it with the guidance of Your Holy Spirit. And teach us the truth about You, that we might be set free. In Your precious name we pray, Amen.

Works Cited

1. Eiselen, Frederick Carl; Lewis, Edwin; and Downey, David G., Editors, *The Abingdon Bible Commentary* (New York, NY, Nashville, TN: Abingdon Press, 1929), 1100.

2. Pervo, Richard I., *Women in Scripture* (Grand Rapids, MI/Cambridge, U.K., William B. Eerdman's Publishing Company, 2000), 150.

3. *The Abingdon Bible Commentary,* 1100.

4. Peter Menzel, Paul Kennedy, and Charles C. Mann, *Material World: A Global Family Portrait* (San Francisco, CA: Sierra Club Books, 1994), 7.

Notes

Notes

4

Hellenist Widows and Others

The women in this lesson appear over the next three chapters of Acts. The Hellenists, or Greek-speaking Jews, constituted a minority in the early Christian church, but were vocal enough to cause a whole new restructuring of the church in Jerusalem. Stephen, one of the seven Hellenists assigned to oversee the new system, also became a powerful preacher. After his stoning, the first great persecution of the church began.

In Acts 6, we encounter some of the problems caused by rapid growth of the church. As a result, a dispute arose between the Hellenists and the apostles. They claimed their **widows** were being overlooked in the daily distribution of food. This resulted in the formation of a separate group of seven men to take care of the community of goods and to administer the financial affairs. This structure was needed as a way to give the apostles the freedom to continue their witness through prayer, teaching, and preaching. As a result, there was another great increase in disciples, including even some of the priests of the Temple. Stephen, one of the seven, performed many signs and wonders among the people. The Jews from the synagogue of the Freedmen (Cyrenians, Alexandrians, and those from Cilicia and Asia) argued with him, stirred up the crowd and brought false witnesses before the Jewish council, who accused him of blasphemy. But they were confronted with the Spirit within him, and they could only see *"that his face was like the face of an angel"* (Acts 6:15).

> The Hellenists, or Greek-speaking Jews, constituted a minority in the early church, but were vocal enough to cause a whole restructuring of the church in Jerusalem.

Most of Acts 7 is taken up with Stephen's defense of his faith before the Jewish council. He recounts the history of the Jews, beginning with Abraham and tells the stories of Joseph and Moses. The **daughter of Pharaoh** is mentioned as part of the story of Moses being raised up to free God's people from the bondage of the Egyptians. Stephen goes on to remind them, in much the same way as Peter had before, of how their ancestors turned from God and opposed his laws for them.

He abruptly switches to his present audience and tells them that they also oppose the Holy Spirit and do the same things that their ancestors did. He accuses them of not keeping the Law. Of course, this enrages them. Near the end of his discourse, Stephen is shown a vision of Jesus *"standing at the right hand of God!"* (Acts 7:56). This is more than his listeners can stand, and they rush against him, drag him out of the city, and stone him to death. Stephen prays for and forgives his persecutors before his death.

Chapter 8 begins with the first great persecution of the Christians, when they are forced to scatter to all regions of the Empire. Many, including both **women** and men, are dragged from their homes, beaten, and imprisoned. And much of this persecution is carried out by none other than Saul of Tarsus, who continued his persecution all the way to Damascus by bringing both women and men back to Jerusalem for punishment. But this did not deter the people from continuing to witness their faith wherever they went. The Christian church began to grow beyond Jerusalem. (We will continue studying the growth of the Christian church in Lesson Five.)

📖 Read how the Holy Spirit continues to direct the apostles and all the disciples of the early church. Acts 6:3, 5, 10; 7:51, 55)

GOD'S CARE OF WIDOWS AND OTHERS

Au ll through the Bible, and especially in the Old Testament, God commands his people to take care of widows and other disadvantaged members of society.

The *Eerdman's Bible Dictionary* says of widows: "Together with the fatherless and the so-journers, the widows were members of a disadvantaged class in ancient Hebrew society."[1]

They were women without any visible means of support —without husbands or grown sons to care for them, or a brother of their dead husband to marry. As such, the Jewish people were mandated by the Hebrew Scriptures to take care of the widow, the orphan and the stranger in their midst because of their susceptibility to oppression, injustice and exploitation. The consequence of either curse or blessing by God was clearly tied to their Law and was taken very seriously.

There are many Old Testament scriptures about widows and the consequences of failure to follow the Law in taking care of them.

"You shall not wrong or oppress a resident alien, for you were aliens in the land of Egypt. You shall not abuse any widow or orphan. If you do abuse them, when they cry out to me, I will surely heed their cry; my wrath will

All through the Bible, and especially in the Old Testament, God commanded his people to take care of widows and other disadvantaged members of society.

burn, and I will kill you with the sword, and your wives shall become widows and your children orphans." (Exodus 22:21–24)

"Every third year you shall bring out the full tithe of your produce for that year, and store it within your towns; the Levites, because they have no allotment or inheritance with you, as well as the resident aliens, the orphans, and the widows in your towns, may come and eat their fill so that the Lord your God may bless you in all the work you undertake." (Deuteronomy 14:28–29)

Other verses in Deuteronomy (24:17, 19–21; 27:19) and from the prophets Isaiah (1:17; 10:2; Ezekiel 22:7; Jeremiah 7:5–7; 22:3; Zechariah 7:10; and Malachi 3:5) continue to warn against the mistreatment of the less fortunate of God's people. Even Job cries out curses for himself and others who abuse them (Job 24:21; 31:16–22).

📖 Look up some of these passages and note the similarities in how God protects these people.

_____

_____

_____

In the Psalms and other Old Testament passages, this group is seen as being especially protected and cared for by God Himself:

"Father of orphans and protector of widows is God in his holy habitation." (Psalms 68:5)

"The Lord watches over the strangers; he upholds the orphan and the widow, but the way of the wicked he brings to ruin." (Psalms 146:9)

"The Lord tears down the house of the proud, but maintains the widow's boundaries." (Proverbs 15:25)

"For the Lord your God...executes justice for the orphan and the widow, and who loves the strangers, providing them food and clothing." (Deuteronomy 10:17–18)

"Leave your orphans, and I will keep them alive; and let your widows trust in me." (Jeremiah 49:11)

📖 Look up these passages. How do you react to the compassion of God toward these groups?

_____

_____

_____

> **"The Lord watches over the strangers; he upholds the orphan and the widow, but the way of the wicked he brings to ruin."**
>
> **Psalms 146:9**

In the New Testament, both Mark and Luke say almost exactly the same thing about the consequences of taking advantage of widows. *"Beware of the scribes, who like to walk around in long robes, and love to be greeted with respect in the marketplaces, and to have the best seats in the synagogues and places of honor at banquets. They devour widows' houses and for the sake of appearances say long prayers. They will receive the greater condemnation"* (Luke 20:46–47; Mark 12:38–40).

Timothy goes on for several verses concerning widows and he ends with this: *"If any believing woman has relatives who are really widows, let her assist*

> "Religion that is pure and undefiled before God, the Father, is this: to care for orphans and widows in their distress, and to keep oneself unstained by the world."
>
> James 1:27

them; let the church not be burdened, so that it can assist those who are real widows" (1 Timothy 5:16).

And, finally, James clearly defines the responsibility toward widows and orphans of those who take their religion seriously: *"Religion that is pure and undefiled before God the Father, is this: to care for orphans and widows in their distress, and to keep oneself unstained by the world"* (James 1:27). Here we have the definition of "pure religion," which is always focused outward rather than inward.

📖 Read all of Timothy's (1 Timothy 5:3–16) message about widows. Write down your reaction to these mandates.

_____

_____

_____

_____

Jesus told stories about the generous heart of a poor widow and about the widow of Zarephath in the time of Elijah. He raised the widow of Nain's son. He told a parable about a widow and justice. There are many, many stories about widows, which indicate that they are very important to God and he expects all of his people to take care of them.

Hellenist Widows & Others

DAY TWO

> "Now during those days, when the disciples were increasing in number, the Hellenists complained against the Hebrews because their widows were being neglected in the daily distribution of food."
>
> Acts 6:1

BETTER SERVICE, PLEASE

Verse in Which the Women Appear: Acts 6:1
"Now during those days, when the disciples were increasing in number, the Hellenists complained against the Hebrews because their widows were being neglected in the daily distribution of food."

In this verse, there are two groups of Jewish women mentioned. There are the Hebrews, or Aramaic-speaking Jews, who were native to Palestine, and the Hellenists, or Greek-speaking Jews, who had been dispersed to different areas and had returned to Jerusalem for the festival of Pentecost. While in Jerusalem, many had converted to the new sect of Christianity and this had brought with it an increase in the population of widows.

The Hellenist widows fall into two of the categories that God's people were implored to take care of—widows and resident aliens or strangers. (See previous discussion on widows.)

And in a culture that allowed women little economic independence, widows, and especially those of immigrants, would be among the most disadvantaged portion of the population. This made the Greek widows as dependent on others for their needs as the Hebrew widows. Lucinda A. Brown, in *Women in Scripture*, adds: "The daily distribution of food is thereby understood as part of the church's charitable activity of contributing to the care of the poor."[2]

"Those days" (6:1) were the early days of the church in Jerusalem, when the explosive growth of the new faith made it hard for the church to keep up

with the needs and demands of everyone. The word "disciple" is first used in this passage in Acts to denote church membership. (Some interpreters believe that this refers only to the Greek-speaking converts living in Jerusalem.) The procedures that were in place for taking care of the increase in widows were proving to be inadequate.

William Barclay describes the way in which the Jewish Temple had always provided for their welfare:

> "In the synagogue, there was a routine custom. Two collectors went around the market and the private houses every Friday morning and made a collection for the needy, partly in money and partly in goods. Later in the day, this was distributed. Those who were temporarily in need received enough to enable them to carry on; and those who were permanently unable to support themselves received enough for fourteen meals, that is, enough for two meals a day for the week ahead. The fund from which this distribution was made was called the Kuppah or Basket. In addition to this, a house-to-house collection was made daily for those whose needs were more pressing. This was called the Tamhui, or Tray."[3]

This custom probably carried over to the church. In addition, as previously mentioned in Lesson Two, the people voluntarily brought money and goods to the apostles that they might distribute them to the needy among them.

 How is your church organized to provide such service?

_____

_____

_____

In spite of these customs, there was a complaint from the Hellenists that their widows were *"being neglected."* The translators of the *Interlinear Greek-English New Testament* chose the word "overlooked." Cultural, ethnic, and linguistic differences all play a part in this dispute. The conflict may have evolved out of social and cultural differences and spilled over into the daily distribution of food. And, the language barrier between them may explain in part why the practice of food distribution was impeded.

Another possible factor was that the Hebrews considered the Greeks to be inferior. It has been suggested that the "unequal" distribution was done deliberately. It is interesting to note that it was not the widows who complained, but rather the Hellenists who complained on *behalf* of their widows.

What role do the Greek widows have in this story? What is the role of the Hebrew widows?

_____

_____

_____

While all of these factors may play a part, the sheer size of the Christian community (at this point over eight thousand) seems to have been the major contributor to the uneven distribution, which was still being administered solely by the apostles. These men finally realized that they could not do it alone and this recognition led to the first formal organizational structure in the church. Ministries of the church were divided into two distinct categories: serving the Word and serving at table.

The procedures that were in place for taking care of the increased population of widows was proving to be inadequate.

The apostles finally realized that they could not continue to do everything themselves, and this recognition led to the first formal organization in the church.

The Solution: *"And the twelve called together the whole community of the disciples and said, 'It is not right that we should neglect the word of God in order to wait on tables."* (Acts 6:2)

The apostles felt that if they continued to be the sole providers of this service to widows and the poor, they would neglect that which they were called to do—spread the word of God. The phrase *"to wait on tables"* or *"to keep accounts"* is not considered to be a menial task in this case. It not only involves the ministry of serving, but also indicates that these leaders had a say in the flow of all of the resources of the community. Just as the disciples were in charge of distributing both goods and monies (the community of goods), discussed in Lesson Three, they are now handing over this task to a different group.

"Therefore, friends, select from among yourselves seven men of good standing, full of the Spirit and of wisdom, whom we may appoint to this task, while we, for our part, will devote ourselves to prayer and to serving the word." (Acts 6:3–4)

Here the disciples are very particular about the men they appoint to this task. First, the number seven is not arbitrary, but reflects the Jewish practice of selecting seven members to provide oversight to local congregations. And, the number seven is symbolic of completeness.

What are the three necessary attributes of the seven?

_____

_____

_____

_____

These are required in order to provide competent leadership and oversight within the church. The New Revised Standard Version commentary adds:

> "The participle translated 'good standing' suggests a good reputation that is based upon the favorable testimony of others; it is a crucial feature of leading others. The combination of 'full' with 'Spirit' denotes evidence of a candidate's mature faith and implies the capacity for prophetic ministry. . . . The final characteristic, 'wisdom,' may refer to an organizational talent; but in combination with the Holy Spirit it suggests spiritual authority."[4]

 How do you select mature and service-minded individuals for these tasks in your church?

_____

_____

"What they said pleased the whole community and they chose Stephen, a man full of faith and the Holy Spirit together with Philip, Prochorus, Nicanor, Timon, Parmenas, and Nicolas, a proselyte of Antioch. They had these men stand before the apostles, who prayed and laid their hands on them." (Acts 6:5)

All of the seven chosen have Greek names, consistent with their identification with the Hellenists. Only Stephen and Philip are mentioned as going on to other prophetic ministries. Nicolaus is identified as a proselyte, or convert, which may suggest that the others were born into Jewish families.

Sidebar

"Therefore, friends, select from among yourselves seven men of good standing, full of the Spirit and of wisdom, whom we may appoint to this task, while we, for our part, will devote ourselves to prayer and to serving the word."

Acts 6:3

There is much discussion, debate, and disagreement over whether these seven men were the forerunners of our modern-day deacons. Many commentators say that this delegation was not the establishment of an office, but rather a transferring of power by "the laying on of hands" by the apostles. The Greek noun, *diakonia,* translated here as the "daily distribution," and the verb, *diakoneo,* have a variety of ministerial connotations, including apostolic ministry, financial service, and testifying to the good news, as well as "one who serves."

The laying on of hands was actually a very common Jewish practice in which people believed that a transfer of certain qualities took place from one person to another. It was a ritual of empowerment and indicated religious authority to govern the community's internal life and sanction its decisions. The apostles, who were held in great respect by the people, were thought to have the leadership qualities that everyone needed. And they had the authority to transfer their power to others and, in this case, they did so to preserve the distinctive practices of both preaching the Word and taking care of the needs of people.

 It is interesting to note that the first such leaders were appointed to be of practical service to the poor. Does your church observe the laying on of hands when it ordains elders or deacons for service? Describe how it works and when it happens?

_____

_____

_____

PHARAOH'S DAUGHTER: AN ANCESTOR REMEMBERED

Verse in Which the Woman Appears: Acts 7:21 (Exodus 2:5–10; Hebrews 11:24)
". . . and when he was abandoned, **Pharaoh's daughter** *adopted him and brought him up as her own son"* (Acts 7:21)

Exodus 2:5–10:

> *"The daughter of Pharaoh came down to bathe at the river, while her attendants walked beside the river. She saw the basket among the reeds and sent her maid to bring it. When she opened it, she saw the child. He was crying, and she took pity on him, 'This must be one of the Hebrews' children,' she said. Then his sister said to Pharaoh's daughter, 'Shall I go and get you a nurse from the Hebrew women to nurse the child for you? Pharaoh's daughter said to her, 'Yes.' So the girl went and called the child's mother. Pharaoh's daughter said to her, 'Take this child and nurse it for me, and I will give you your wages.' So the woman took the child and nursed it. When the child grew up, she brought him to Pharaoh's daughter, and she took him as her son. She named him Moses, 'because,' she said, 'I drew him out of the water.'"*

> "And when he was abandoned, Pharaoh's daughter adopted him and brought him up as her own son."
> **Acts 7:21**

> *Pharaoh's daughter's character seems clearly that of someone whom God could use for His purposes. Here she acts without knowing of God's plan for Moses.*

In the Bible, we know her only as "Pharaoh's daughter." In the *Antiquities* of Josephus, she is called Thermouthis. She is also known as Merris or Mercis in *Artaphanes* (quoted by the church historian Eusebius), and by Myrrina in the *Alexandrian Chronicle*. Some even believe she was the feminist Queen Hatshepsut, half-sister of Thutmose III, who ruled Egypt in her own right; however, this does not support the biblical wording of a "daughter." Still others believe she was one of Rameses II's daughters. An inscription of the reign of Rameses II says that he had sixty sons and fifty-nine daughters. Among the names of these daughters is one called Meri, who may be this princess. Finally, others conjecture that the ruling Pharaoh at the time of Moses may not have been Rameses II, but either Aahames I or Seti I. The description, *"the daughter of Pharaoh,"* may even suggest that she was an *only* daughter. Regardless of her name, it is her pity and compassion for a Hebrew infant that stands out in this story.

Obviously, this woman was an Egyptian and a pagan who worshipped the sun. But in her action of rescuing the infant whom she named Moses, she revealed a maternal instinct stronger than the risk of disfavor from her own father, who, in his cruelty, had decreed the drowning of all Hebrew babies. Her character seems clearly to be that of someone whom God could use for his purposes. And she acts without knowing about God's plan for Moses.

The daughter of Pharaoh is mentioned in Stephen's defense before the Jewish Council. A large portion of his long discourse is taken up with the story of Moses, who was born at a time *"for the fulfillment of the promise God had made to Abraham"* (Acts 7:17). Stephen makes several parallels between Moses and Jesus to help the people understand. In his Gospel, Luke casts Jesus as a "prophet like Moses" who is also rejected by his own. The phrase, *"beautiful before God"* (verse 20) denotes something exceedingly beautiful, a sign of divine favor.

Why do you think Stephen even bothered to mention the daughter of Pharaoh?

_____

_____

_____

Moses was born when the Pharaoh, because of the great increase in the population of the Jews in Egypt, was ordering the deaths of Hebrew boys by throwing them into the Nile River to drown. Moses' parents, Amram and Jochebed of the House of Levi, knew of the king's cruel edict and hid their baby for three months. When they no longer felt it safe, the baby was put into an ark or small boat made of bulrushes and placed among the reeds where Pharaoh's daughter came to bathe. The ark was made from the long stems of Nile rush or papyrus, woven tightly together and "painted" with bitumen and pitch to make it watertight.

Various translations of the story say he was *"exposed"* (RSV, NEB), *"cast out"* (KJV), *"put out"* (TEV), *"placed outside"* (NIV) *and "abandoned"* (NRSV). He was *lovingly* placed inside the little boat and set upon the Nile in an attempt to save his life. And then we discover something surprising about this daughter. Her heart, unlike her father's, is not hard. When she sees the baby and hears his cry, she takes pity and shows compassion on him in her desire to save him. She names him Moses and takes him as her own son.

The name *Moses* is pronounced in Hebrew *Mosheh* and means "to draw out." The word is rare in Hebrew and it has been suggested that it may have originated from an Egyptian word meaning "son" or "child." The Egyptian word *mes*, or *mesu*, is similar in pronunciation to the Hebrew. Without her tenderness and compassion for the child, Moses would surely have been killed by an animal, died of exposure or drowned. God uses this pagan Princess of Egypt as his divine instrument—without her knowledge—to deliver Moses from death and to protect him throughout his time with her.

How does the story of Moses relate to the early church?

_____

_____

_____

_____

"So Moses was instructed in all the wisdom of the Egyptians and was powerful in his words and deeds." (Acts 7:22)

This daughter of Pharaoh had everything the ancient world could offer, and she gave it all to Moses. He was taken into the palace and knew its luxuries. He was given the finest education. The phrase, *"powerful in words and deeds,"* also describes Jesus, in a continuation of the parallels between them (Luke 24:19). A princess of Egypt, the Pharaoh's own daughter, saved one Hebrew baby that she named Moses. She played a far greater role in God's plan for His people and the shaping of the future of Israel than she could ever have imagined. The daughter of a king became the protector of a child who would be great in the history of the Jewish people. And she is being remembered in Stephen's speech before the Jews.

APPLY Does the story of one of your female ancestors have a direct impact on your life today? Write about them.

_____

_____

_____

_____

_____

> We discover something surprising about this daughter of Pharaoh. Her heart, unlike her father's, is not hard. When she sees the baby and hears his cry, she takes pity and shows compassion on him in her desire to save him.

EQUALITY IN ALL THINGS

Hellenist Widows & Others

DAY FOUR

Verses in Which the Women Appear: Acts 8:3; 9:1–2 (Acts 22:4–5, 19; 26:10–11; Galatians 1:13)

8:3: *"But Saul was ravaging the church by entering house after house; dragging off both men and* **women**, *he committed them to prison."*

9:1–2: *"Meanwhile Saul, still breathing threats and murder against the disciples of the Lord, went to the high priest and asked him for letters to the synagogues at Damascus, so that if he found any who belonged to the Way, men or* **women**, *he might bring them bound to Jerusalem.*

"But Saul was ravaging the church by entering house after house; dragging off both men and women, he committed them to prison."

Acts 8:3

Women have been present since the beginnings of the Christian church. They have heard the gospel, believed it and been baptized. They have received the Holy Spirit and helped spread the message—along with the men. And now they are being persecuted, along with the men. This is the first time others besides the apostles have been arrested, beaten, and thrown into prison.

Women are mentioned three times in the story of Saul's persecution of the Christian church (Acts 8:4; 9:1–2; 22:4), and are assumed to be included as the "saints" in Acts 26:10–11. In his letter to the Galatians, he also mentions them again (Galatians 1:13).

📖 Read the later passages in Acts (22:4 and 26:10–11) to see how Paul later referred to his persecution of the Christians. Write down any similarities.

_____

_____

_____

These passages emphasize that women were indeed present, and Luke makes *no* distinction between the way the women and the men were treated. They were all disciples of Christianity and were all enduring the *same* kind of persecution.

Jesus predicted this persecution in the Gospels (Matthew 5:10–12; 24:9–14; Luke 21:12–19; John 16:2). *"But before all this occurs, they will arrest you and persecute you; they will hand you over to synagogues and prisons, and you will be brought before kings and governors because of my name"* (Luke 21:12). And Timothy says, *"Indeed, all who want to live a godly life in Christ Jesus will be persecuted"* (2 Timothy 3:12).

APPLY Do you think it was right for Saul to treat women in the same manner as men? Did he care?

_____

_____

_____

_____

The *Eerdman's Bible Dictionary* defines persecution as *"The use of forcible means to inhibit the spread or practice of a religious faith."*[5] Persecution of the Jews has been common throughout history. And, from the time Christianity began to be preached, it too was persecuted. Peter and John were arrested first, then all the apostles, then Stephen and from there, all were subjected to arrest and prison, including the women. This persecution was the beginning of a continuous, yet sporadic, persecution of Christians by Jews and by many Roman emperors until the reign of Constantine.

The devout Jew, Saul of Tarsus, is the major figure in this persecution of the Christians. He witnessed and approved the stoning of Stephen. Eusebius, in *The Church History*, states *"Stephen's martyrdom was followed by the first and greatest persecution of the church in Jerusalem by the Jews."*[6]

Most scholars believe the initial persecution was probably only against the Hellenist or Greek-speaking Jews, since it immediately followed Stephen's murder. This group would have been angry and perhaps close to rioting and Saul may have initially tried to keep the peace among them.

Luke does not tell us specifically *how* the disciples were persecuted, but Barclay relates:

> "The Authorized Version [KJV], says 'made havoc' of the church and the word used in the Greek denotes a brutal cruelty. It is used of a wild boar ravaging a vineyard and of a wild animal savaging a body."[7]

If you want true equality, here it is! Other sources indicate that this persecution was merely a lashing like Saul himself received when he was known as the apostle Paul (2 Corinthians 11:24), in order to get the Christians to renounce Christianity. Paul's own words before King Agrippa at Caesarea (Acts 26:10), further describe his actions and motives behind them.

The words in Acts 9:1–2 fulfill Stephen's words in Acts 7:51–52. Saul was not pleased with the escape of many of the Christians to other areas, and in Acts 9:1–2, we read that he wants to go to Damascus to find anyone who belonged to the Way, bind them and bring them back to Jerusalem in chains. It is interesting to note that while on his way to Damascus to do this, he himself is converted to the faith. Then, he also begins to be persecuted for believing the Christian message. In Acts 22:4, Paul tells the Jewish Council what he had done. And, in his letter to the Galatians, he also mentions his "earlier" life in Jerusalem, and said, *"I was violently persecuting the church of God and was trying to destroy it"* (Galatians 1:13).

 If you were arrested under the charge of being a Christian, would there be enough evidence to convict you? Why or why not?

_____

_____

_____

As a result of this persecution, the disciples are forced to flee Jerusalem and are scattered throughout the countryside of Judea and Samaria. Saul's persecution gives all of the disciples new places in which to spread the gospel and fulfill Jesus' words to them in Acts 1:8.

FOR ME TO FOLLOW GOD

Life Principle for Lesson Four: The Ways of God
This lesson shows us the real interconnectedness and dependence we have on each other, not just as Christians, but as people who belong to God.

First, this week's lesson shows us how we either take care of or neglect each other in the body of Christ. It forces us to ask the question, are we about serving ourselves or serving others? The act of serving others should be a joyful task, not one of drudgery or work.

"Be hospitable to one another without complaining" (1 Peter 4:9).

"Jesus answered them, 'Do not complain among yourselves" (John 6:43).

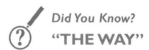

Did You Know?
"THE WAY"

"The Way" was a name Luke attached to the Christian faith. The Jewish leaders saw the followers of The Way as a suspicious sect of Judaism. It's followers agreed with all the basic tenets of Judiasm and saw God as their father, but also saw Christ as the fulfillment of Jewish law. They saw themselves as those who followed The Way of their Savior.

If you want true equality, here it is!

Hellenist Widows & Others
DAY FIVE

This lesson shows us the real inter-connectedness and dependence we have on each other, not just as Christians, but as people who belong to God.

In Paul's letter to the Colossians, he sums up what kind of countenance we are to present as Christians in our service to our fellow human beings:

"As God's chosen ones, holy and beloved, clothe yourselves with compassion, kindness, humility, meekness, and patience. Bear with one another and, if anyone has a complaint against another, forgive each other; just as the Lord has forgiven you, so you also must forgive. Above all, clothe yourselves with love, which binds everything together in perfect harmony. And let the peace of Christ rule in your hearts, to which indeed you were called in the one body." (Colossians 3:12–15)

 May God help us all not to complain so much about what we are not getting, but worry more about what we are not giving. How are you doing today at serving God's people and at being a true servant of God?

_____

_____

_____

Second, the lesson shows us the rich history of God's dealings with His people and how He can use all of us for His purposes, even when we don't think so. We are *all* important to the body of Christ. God provided a pagan adoptive mother for one of his greatest servants. All those who have gone before us have done something to help us be all we can be. Someone in our past has had compassion or pity or has been used by God for a great purpose and remains an example for us today. And God has overlooked our own sin and forgiven it, so that someone else can perhaps benefit from our example.

"The Lord will fulfill his purpose for me." (Psalms 138:8)

"The human mind may devise many plans, but it is the purpose of the Lord that will be established." (Proverbs 19:21)

"We know that all things work together for good for those who love God, who are called according to his purpose." (Romans 8:28)

 May God help us all to be mindful of the fact that He is working in everyone's life, so we can go about treating everyone we meet like children of God. What do you discern as your purpose from God?

_____

_____

_____

Third, the lesson shows us that others will not always accept us when we believe in Jesus Christ. There are still thousands of Christians in our world today that are persecuted for simply being Christian. We are called to take up our cross and follow Jesus Christ and also be ready to suffer because of his name. The response to persecution is clearly laid out in Scripture: *"Bless those who persecute you; bless and do not curse them"* (Romans 12:14).

"Blessed are you when people revile you and persecute you and utter all kinds of evil against you falsely on my account. Rejoice and be glad, for your reward is

great in heaven, for in the same way they persecuted the prophets who were before you" (Matthew 5:11–12).

"But I say to you, Love you enemies and pray for those who persecute you" (Matthew 5:44).

"I have said this to you, so that in me you may have peace. In the world, you face persecution. But take courage; I have conquered the world!" (John 16:33).

 May God give us the same strength and willingness of those early Christians to cling to Christ in all the situations we find ourselves faced with in life. Have you ever been persecuted harshly for what you believe in? Was it worth it?

_____

_____

_____

"Therefore take up the whole armor or God, so that you may be able to withstand on that evil day, and having done everything, to stand firm. Stand, therefore, and fasten the belt of truth around your waist, and put on the breastplate of righteousness. As shoes for your feet put on whatever will make you ready to proclaim the gospel of peace. With all of these, take the shield of faith, with which you will be able to quench all the flaming arrows of the evil one. Take the helmet of salvation, and the sword of the Spirit, which is the word of God." (Ephesians 6:13–17)

With God's help, we can serve our best, live with His purpose in mind, and withstand anything.

 Lord of service, teach us better how to serve You, Your church and Your world. Help us to forget our selfish ways and continually strive to be like You. Lord of purpose, plant Your purposes in our hearts that they may grow into the fullness of Your will for each of our lives. Lord of courage, keep us safe in our walk with You, that we might always be bold in our witness wherever we are and in whatever situations we find ourselves. In Your Name we pray, Amen.

Works Cited

1. Allen C. Myers, Revision Editor, *The Eerdman's Bible Dictionary* (Grand Rapids, MI: William B. Eerdman's Publishing Company, 1987), 1056.

2. Carol Meyers, General Editor; Toni Craven and Ross S. Kraemer, Associate Editors, *Women in Scripture* (Grand Rapids, MI/Cambridge, UK: William B. Eerdman's Publishing Company, 2000), 458.

3. William Barclay, *The New Daily Study Bible, The Acts of the Apostles* (Louisville, London: Westminster John Knox Press, The William Barclay Estate, 1975, 2003), 58.

4. Leander E. Keck, Convener, *The New Interpreter's Bible, A Commentary in Twelve Volumes, Volume X, The Acts of the Apostles, Introduction to Epistolary Literature, The Letter to the Romans, The First Letter to the Corinthians* (Nashville, TN: Abingdon Press, 2002), 113.

5. *The Eerdman's Bible Dictionary,* 814

6. Paul Maier, *Eusebius, The Church History, A New Translation with Commentary* (Grand Rapids, MI: Kregel Publications, 1999), 59. Used by permission of the publisher. All rights reserved

7. Barclay, p. 73

Notes

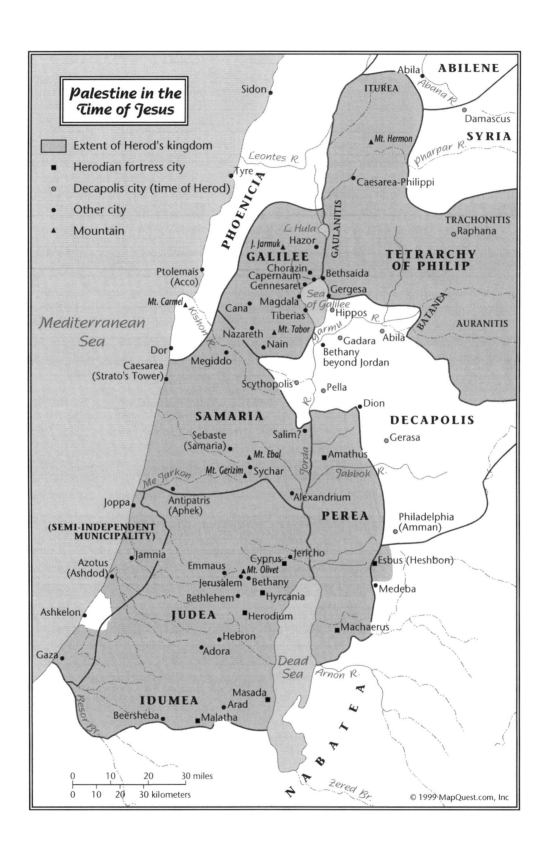

Palestine in the Time of Jesus

Extent of Herod's kingdom
■ Herodian fortress city
◉ Decapolis city (time of Herod)
• Other city
▲ Mountain

ABILENE
Abila
ITUREA
Sidon
Abana R.
Damascus
SYRIA
▲ *Mt. Hermon*
Caesarea-Philippi
Leontes R.
Pharpar R.
PHOENICIA
Tyre
TRACHONITIS
Raphana
L. Hula
GAULANITIS
Hazor
J. Jarmuk ▲
GALILEE
TETRARCHY
OF PHILIP
Ptolemais
(Acco)
Chorazin
Capernaum
Bethsaida
Gennesaret
Gergesa
Sea of Galilee
BATANEA
Mt. Carmel ▲
Kishon R.
Cana
Magdala
Hippos
AURANITIS
Tiberias
R.
Jarmuk R.
Nazareth ▲ *Mt. Tabor*
Abila
Mediterranean
Sea
Nain
Gadara
Dor
Bethany
beyond Jordan
Caesarea
(Strato's Tower)
Megiddo
Scythopolis
Pella
R.
Dion
SAMARIA
DECAPOLIS
Sebaste
(Samaria)
Salim?
Gerasa
▲ *Mt. Ebal*
Amathus
Me Jarkon
▲ *Mt. Gerizim*
Sychar
Jordan
Jabbok R.
Joppa
Antipatris
(Aphek)
Alexandrium
PEREA
Philadelphia
(Amman)
(SEMI-INDEPENDENT
MUNICIPALITY)
Azotus
(Ashdod)
Jamnia
Cyprus ■
Jericho
Esbus (Heshbon) ■
Emmaus
▲ *Mt. Olivet*
Jerusalem
Bethany
Medeba
Bethlehem
Hyrcania ■
Ashkelon
Herodium ■
Machaerus ■
JUDEA
Gaza
Hebron
Adora
*Dead
Sea*
Arnon R.
Besor R.
IDUMEA
Masada ■
Arad
Beersheba
Malatha ■
NABATEA
Zered Br.

0   10   20   30 miles
0   10   20   30 kilometers

© 1999 MapQuest.com, Inc

5

Samaritan Women and an Ethiopian Queen

God never leaves anybody out. All are given the opportunity to respond to the gospel message. In this lesson, we see how the words of Jesus in Acts 1:8 are coming to pass in the witness to the Samaritans and all the way to the land of Ethiopia, then called Nubia. The gospel was and is and will forever be for the whole world—a faith for all people in all times and all places.

Following the dispersion of the Jews from Jerusalem, Chapter 8 continues with the ministry of Philip the Evangelist, one of the seven (not the apostle Philip). The chapter begins in Samaria, where he proclaims the gospel, heals the sick and demon-possessed, and baptizes many, *"both men and women."* Included in this group is Simon the magician, who previously amazed the people with his magic, but now even he believes and is baptized. The apostles Peter and John are sent to Samaria to lay their hands on the people that they might receive the Holy Spirit. When Simon sees the way the Spirit is given, he offers to buy this power for himself. Peter warns him that his heart is not right before God and Simon asks for prayer and release from his wickedness. While on their way back to Jerusalem, Peter and John also proclaim the good news *"to many villages of the Samaritans"* (Acts 8:25).

Philip is sent by an angel of the Lord to a road near Gaza, where he meets an Ethiopian eunuch of the court of the Candace, who is in charge of her entire treasury. He reads from Isaiah and asks Philip who the prophet is talking about. Philip explains it to him

> **The gospel was and is and will forever be for the whole world—a faith for all people in all times and places.**

and proclaims to him the good news of Jesus Christ. The eunuch is baptized and goes *"on his way rejoicing"* (Acts 8:39). Then Philip is taken to Azotus, where he continues his witness to many other towns all the way up the coast to his home in Caesarea.

📖 Look up the "Spirit" verses in chapter 8 (8:15–19; 29, 39) and see how directly he is involved in these stories, especially with the eunuch.

*Samaritan Women &
an Ethiopian Queen*

DAY ONE

Samaria has a long history in the Bible, being mentioned over one hundred times in the Old Testament alone.

SAMARITAN WOMEN: BEYOND JERUSALEM

The Holy Spirit is on the move. Just as Jesus predicted, the gospel is going out from Jerusalem to Judea, Samaria and to the ends of the earth, indicating that God is including all people, even the "unclean Samaritans" and those from Ethiopia, then called Nubia, in his plan of salvation for the whole world.

Samaria has a long history in the Bible, being mentioned over one hundred times in the Old Testament alone. And most are familiar with the stories in the New Testament about the Good Samaritan and the Samaritan woman at the well, to whom Jesus revealed his Messiahship.

Samaria was originally established as the capital of the Northern Kingdom of Israel by King Omri (1 Kings 16:24). The Assyrians then conquered it in 772 BC (2 Kings 17:6). At that time, the name "Samaria" was applied to the whole territory of the former northern kingdom (1 Kings 21:1, 13:32; 2 Kings 1:3; 23:19). The Assyrians transported a large part of their population into the Northern Kingdom and, as a result, the Jews who were left there began to intermarry with them, thus becoming a mixed race and no longer "pure" Jews. This intermarriage caused a bitter hatred between the Jews and the Samaritans, which continued throughout biblical history. Jews had no dealings with the Samaritans at all. They looked down on them and considered them a degraded ethnic class—half-Jew, half-Gentile.

In the Old Testament book of Nehemiah, there is a reference to the intermarriage of Jews to foreign women:

> *"In those days also I saw Jews who had married women of Ashdod, Ammon, and Moab; and half of their children spoke the language of Ashdod, and they could not speak the language of Judah, but spoke the language of various peoples. And I contended with them and cursed them and beat some of them and pulled out their hair; and I made them take an oath in the name of God, saying, 'You shall not give your daughters to their sons, or take their daughters for your sons or for yourselves... Shall we then listen to you and do all this great evil and act treacherously against our God by marrying foreign women?'"* (Nehemiah 13:23–25, 27)

 I have known both young women and young men who have been punished by their parents or others for marrying either outside their faith or their race. How do you feel about marriage between different faiths/races?

_____

_____

Samaria experienced many different rules over the centuries, and the city was rebuilt under Roman rule in 57 BC. In 30 BC it became part of the kingdom of Herod the Great and remained a Gentile city. The Samaria of the New Testament is the name for an area located in the central hill country, and extends east to the Jordan river, south to the valley of Aijalon and Joppa, west to Caesarea Maritima and north to the valley of Jezreel. Look on the map on page 64 and locate the Samaria of the New Testament.

In contrast to the Jews' hatred of Samaritans, Jesus does not reject them. It may seem, at first, that he does because when He is instructing his disciples on their initial witness, he says: *"Go nowhere among the Gentiles, and enter no towns of the Samaritans, but go rather to the lost sheep of Israel"* (Matthew 10:5–6). The initial purpose of Jesus' coming was to gather the Jews, God's lost people, to Himself. But as the story unfolds, both in the Gospels and in Acts, we see that salvation has been extended to all. And he, again, lays the groundwork for the transcendence between the division and disagreement of the two groups.

📖 In several Gospel stories, Jesus shows the Samaritans respect, acceptance, and love. He witnesses to them (John 4:40–42). Read these verses and see how the witness of the Samaritan woman transfers to Jesus. Does this discount her testimony at all?

_____

_____

_____

_____

📖 He heals ten lepers, and the only one who thanks Him is a Samaritan (Luke 17:16). Read this story in Luke 17:11–19. How was the Samaritan healed?

_____

_____

_____

📖 Jesus tells the very familiar parable about a Samaritan who takes pity on a man robbed and beaten and left on the road for dead (Luke 10:33). Read this whole story in Luke 10:30–37. Why do you think the Samaritan was a more compassionate person?

_____

_____

_____

📖 And finally, he reveals himself to be the Messiah to a Samaritan *woman* (John 4:26). Read the whole story in John 4:7–26. Record the reaction of the disciples to this.

_____

_____

_____

The Samaria of the New Testament is the name for an area located in the central hill country, and extends east to the Jordan River, south to the valley of Aijalon and Joppa, west to Caesarea Maritima and north to the valley of Jezreel.

Jesus defines Samaritans, both women and men, as good enough for His kingdom. As we turn to the witness to the Samaritans in Acts, look for some similarities between the stories of the Gospels and the Samaritan's response in Acts.

THE "GOOD" SAMARITANS

As previously stated, Samaritans are not new to the stories of the Gospels. Those stories are examples of how Jesus raised the status of all He met, including and especially women, regardless of ethic make-up or position in society. And as the church is now expanding out of Jerusalem, all of the disciples are obeying the command of Jesus "*. . . you will be my witnesses in . . . Samaria...*"

Since Samaritans are of a mixed ethnic background, half of which is Jewish, the mission to Samaria can be seen as a symbolic transitional place to bring the Christian message of reconciliation.

Since Samaritans are of a mixed ethnic background, half of which is Jewish, the mission to Samaria can be seen as a symbolic transitional place to bring the Christian message of reconciliation. In spite of the "disobedience" of intermarriage and sin, God is saying to everyone that restoration can occur.

Luke's purpose in relating Philip's work in Samaria is to show that everything has changed through Jesus' resurrection and the giving of the Holy Spirit. The Samaritans, considered ethnically inferior by the Jews, are now *accepted* into the kingdom of God. And because of Jesus' attitudes toward them, the disciples also proclaim His message to them. The *Abingdon Bible Commentary* adds:

> "the religious experience of these early disciples of Jesus had tempered their race prejudices. Luke has not introduced into his narrative a single note of surprise that Philip, a Jew, should thus fellowship with the people of Samaria."[1]

The message of the gospel has now breached cultural and ethnic divisions and separations, because this is *God's* plan.

The Verse in Which the Women Appear:
Acts 8:12: *"But when they believed Philip, who was proclaiming the good news about the kingdom of God and the name of Jesus Christ, they were baptized, both men and* **women***."*

"But when they believed Philip, who was proclaiming the good news about the kingdom of God and the name of Jesus Christ, they were baptized, both men and women."

Acts 8:12

The mission to the Samaritans opens up a new section of Acts. The first seven chapters show how the church was started, first among the Jews, and how it grew in Jerusalem. The next five chapters tell how the Gospel is preached beyond Jerusalem and becomes a faith for the whole world. *"Now those who were scattered went from place to place, proclaiming the word"* (Acts 8:4). When the Jews were scattered, some traveled as far as Phoenicia, Cyprus, and Antioch and like Philip, they brought the gospel to all they met.

📖 Read Acts 8:6–8 and write down the responses of the Samaritans to the gospel.

_____

_____

Philip, full of the Holy Spirit, is the first to preach the gospel in Samaria. The eagerness of the crowd is almost palpable in the text. They are excited; they are receptive; they are anxious—for words of hope and healing. Many of the Samaritans were possessed by unclean spirits, were paralyzed or lame or had other diseases. Philip not only proclaims the word to them, but he also heals their infirmities. There is a restoration to wholeness, not only of body and mind, but of spirit. And there is joy. In fact, there is *"great joy"* (Acts 8:8).

 Joy is a key component of the fruit of the Spirit. What are the others (Galatians 5:22)? Which ones have you experienced?

_____

_____

_____

_____

There is a restoration to wholeness, not only of body and mind, but of spirit.

Joy causes them to want to be baptized, both *women* and men. Luke's representation of Samaritan believers as women and men is consistent with his regular portrait of early Christians and parallels his representation of new believers elsewhere in Acts, whether Jew or Gentile. Luke uses the phrase, *"both men and women"* several times. Arlandson says, in this case:

> ". . . Luke duplicates the location of the reference to the Samaritan in Luke 17:16 and thereby makes the women stand out all the more... we the readers are now required to go back over all the great signs, wonders, and blessings recorded in verses six through eight and understand that women took equal part."[2]

The apostles hear about the Samaritans accepting the word of God and being baptized, so they send Peter and John to pray for them that they might receive the Holy Spirit. Here is another reference to prayer preceding the giving of the Holy Spirit, as it has in all of the other cases before this. And this time, the physical act of the laying on of hands by the apostles is used to give them the Holy Spirit.

In yet another filling of the Spirit, *all of them* receive it. There is no reason to conclude that the Holy Spirit differentiated between women and men here, since it has included both sexes in every case thus far. *Both* women and men were baptized, *both* women and men received the Spirit, and *both* women and men have been forgiven, freed, and restored.

The mission to Samaria is expanded as Peter and John also proclaim the gospel to the Samaritans on their way back to Jerusalem. And from a later reference in Acts, we find that this was a very successful mission indeed. *"Meanwhile the church throughout Judea, Galilee and Samaria had peace and was built up. Living in the fear of the Lord and in the comfort of the Holy Spirit, it increased in numbers"* (Acts 9:31).

 Why do you think the mission to the Samaritans was so successful?

_____

_____

_____

Are there parts of our world today that are more receptive to the Gospel than others? Where?

_____

_____

_____

Samaritan Women & an Ethiopian Queen

DAY THREE

Ethiopia, or Nubia, as it was called at that time, was considered to be an area that the Greeks viewed as the farthest regions of mankind, thus encompassing areas that Jesus was referring to as "the ends of the earth" in Acts 1:8.

AN ETHIOPIAN QUEEN: TO THE ENDS OF THE EARTH

Ethiopia, or Nubia, as it was called at that time, was an area that the Greeks viewed as the farthest reaches of mankind, thus encompassing areas that Jesus was referring to as *"the ends of the earth"* in Acts 1:8. Ethiopia is mentioned over twenty times in the Old Testament, also under the name Cush, because the descendants of Cush settled it. The *Eerdman's Bible Dictionary* states, "In the Old Testament period "Ethiopia" appears to have been synonymous with 'Cush.'"[3] In Bible genealogy, Cush was the son of Ham and the father of Nimrod (see Genesis 10:6–8; 1 Chronicles 1:8–10).

This ancient land is not to be confused with modern Ethiopia, which was then called Abyssinia. The Ethiopia in the story in Acts is in Africa, (modern Sudan) south of Egypt. The area depended on the Nile River for its survival, and Nubia was a major center of commercial travel between Africa and the south of Asia and became famous for its wealth. *"The wealth of Egypt and the merchandise of Ethiopia. . . "* (Isaiah 45:14).

In the same way as the Samaritans, some of the Israelites intermarried with the Hamitic Ethiopians. Of note, Moses took a Cushite wife, a black woman named Zippora. (Exodus 2:21; 4:25; 18:2). Miriam, his sister, became "white as snow" with leprosy and shut out of the camp for seven days after criticizing him for it. *"While they were at Hazeroth, Miriam and Aaron spoke against Moses because of the Cushite woman whom he had married (for he indeed married a Cushite woman)"* (Numbers 12:1).

📖 Read the whole story of Miriam and Aaron in Numbers 12 to see how God is defending Moses' decision.

Several Bible characters in the Old Testament are Ethiopian. Read Jeremiah 38:7–13. In this story, Ebed-melek the Ethiopian is a eunuch in King Zedekiah's house who appeals to the king to save Jeremiah from the cistern he has been thrown into. There are also Ethiopian kings, including Zerah (2 Chronicles 14:9); and Tirhaqah (2 Kings 19:9; Isaiah 37:9).

The prophet Amos mentions the Ethiopians as examples of God's universal concern for all people: *"Are you not like the Ethiopians* [Nubians] *to me, O people of Israel? says the Lord"* (Amos 9:7).

Notice that Ebed-melek is a eunuch, like the treasurer to the Queen in the Acts story. Eunuchs were commonly placed in the king's household (see Esther 2:3, 14). But eunuchs were, like the despised Samaritans, considered outcasts by Israel. The law forbade them to enter the Israelite assembly (Deuteronomy. 23:1). And, scholars differ as to whether a eunuch could even be a Jew. But God had a plan, as always. Following the restoration of Israel, eunuchs and foreigners would become full members of the community.

> *"Do not let the foreigner joined to the Lord say, 'The Lord will surely separate me from his people'; and do not let the eunuch say, 'I am just a dry tree.' For thus says the Lord: To the eunuchs who keep my sabbaths, who choose the things that please me and hold fast my covenant, I will give, in my house and within my walls, a monument and a name better than sons and daughters; I will give them an everlasting name that shall not be cut off"* (Isaiah 56:4–5).

 So, in the same way that God accepted the Samaritans, Ethiopians [foreigners], and eunuchs will also receive the promise of God. How does this give us all the hope of salvation?

_____

_____

_____

Which groups of people in our world today that are considered outcasts might be included in God's *universal* plan of salvation for all?

_____

_____

_____

ETHIOPIAN QUEEN: FAITH BY ASSOCIATION

It is necessary to tell the story of the eunuch because of his relationship to, and perhaps his influence, on this Ethiopian Queen. It appears that God has used these two unlikely people—one a foreign woman in very high position—to bring his word to *"the ends of the earth."*

Verse in Which the Woman Appears: Acts 8:27:
"…Now there was an Ethiopian eunuch, a court official of the **Candace***, queen of the Ethiopians, in charge of her entire treasury."*

Greek: Kandake, meaning either "queen" or "queen mother."

Candace was not the name of the queen, but rather a title applied to the ruling Queens of Meroe, the capital of the country called Nubia (south of Egypt) that later became the kingdom of Ethiopia. Candace was a hereditary title by which all of the dark-skinned queens of Ethiopia were called, just as the term "Pharaoh" or "Caesar" was a dynastic name or title. The government of Ethiopia was in the hands of women, who for several successions, assumed this title.[4] It is not possible to identify this particular queen from the story in Acts, since Luke does not give us her name.

In the same way that God accepted the Samaritans, Ethiopians [foreigners] and eunuchs will also receive the promise of God.

Samaritan Women & an Ethiopian Queen

DAY FOUR

"Now there was an Ethiopian eunuch, a court official of the Candace, queen of the Ethiopians, in charge of her entire treasure."

Acts 8:27

It was supposed at this time that a certain form of Judaism had taken root in Ethiopia, and the Queen as well as the eunuch were somewhat familiar with the Messianic idea and desired more knowledge of it.

And because Philip followed the prompting of the Spirit, he was able to tell the story of Jesus Christ to a high-standing official from a far-off land.

The Candace is mentioned in relationship to the eunuch, who is a high-ranking official or chamberlain of her court, in charge of her entire treasury. His position as a court official in charge of the queen's entire treasury was common in this area of the world. Eunuchs served in many different capacities. Whether the eunuch was a disapora Jew, a Jewish proselyte—someone who accepted Judaism and was circumcised, or a "God-fearer"—a Gentile who read the Jewish scriptures and attended the synagogue, is not known for sure. It was supposed that at this time a certain form of Judaism had taken root in Ethiopia and the Queen as well as the eunuch were somewhat familiar with the messianic idea and desired more knowledge of it.[5]

William Barclay states that "in those days, the world was full of people who were weary of the many gods and the loose morals of the nations."[6] Many came to Judaism and found the one God *and* the moral standards that gave life meaning. As a result, the eunuch could have gone to Jerusalem for the Jewish festival or simply for the opportunity to worship at the temple. Most likely he was allowed to worship in the outer court in the "Court of the Gentiles."

The story begins immediately after Philip's Samaritan mission. God gets *directly* involved in the next piece of Philip's witness and sends an angel, who instructs him where to go next. And while the road from Jerusalem to Gaza was not that far away, the witness involves someone who is from the land of Nubia, which is very far away from Jerusalem. The eunuch's conversion signals the fulfillment of the promise to all those who are *"far away"* (Acts 2:39), and the instruction from Jesus is again being fulfilled *"to the ends of the earth."*

The Holy Spirit is really the major figure in this story—not Philip, not the eunuch, not the Queen. And because Philip followed the prompting of the Spirit, he was able to tell the story of Jesus Christ to a high-standing official from a far-off land. The Spirit has not only taken him to meet the eunuch, he has set up the scene so perfectly that he is able to proclaim the gospel in such a way that the eunuch is converted right then and there!

Read the first part of the story from Acts 8:27b–33. How does the Spirit continue to be involved in this story?

_____

_____

_____

There are two significant questions in this section. First, Philip asks, *"Do you understand what you are reading?"* And the eunuch answers with another, *"How can I, unless someone guides me?"*

Read the next part of the story in Acts 8:34–39.

The questions by the eunuch show several things. One, he accepts the fact that he needs guidance and explanation (8:31); two, he asks questions about the text in Isaiah in regard to its meaning (8:34); and three, he recognizes his own need for repentance and baptism (8:36).

 Why are these questions so important for our own understanding of Scripture and our need for repentance and baptism?

_____

_____

The eunuch is so excited at his new-found faith that he is baptized right there on the road and experiences the joy of knowing Jesus Christ. He then *"went on his way rejoicing"* (Acts 8:39).

There's that fruit of the Spirit again that shows up when we have received Christ into our lives. The other thing that happens is that you want to tell everyone around you about it. And I suspect that as soon as he got back home, he was busy witnessing his faith.

Eusebius, the early church historian, speaks of this convert, the first Gentile to receive the word from Philip, returning to his native country and preaching the knowledge of God and the saving grace of Jesus Christ to his people. There is an Ethiopian tradition, naming the eunuch as Judiah and representing him as propagating the gospel in Ethiopia and of bringing the Candace herself to the faith.[7]

 How do you think the eunuch related his experience with Philip to the Candace?

_____

_____

_____

Tradition tells us that it is probable that the Candace was the first person in high circles in Ethiopia to hear the triumphant message of Jesus Christ, and her conversion may have caused her to use her office to promote Christianity in Ethiopia and the surrounding countries.[8]

Maier, in *First Christians,* tells us that

> "More is involved in this episode than the extraordinary conversion of a colorful person at a bizarre corner of Palestine. African mission work started here. The names, the places, and the connections have been lost to history, but a curiously strong Christian church developed in Nubia. Such a conversion also foreshadowed the inclusive or universal direction of the future faith in contrast to the exclusivity of its parent Judaism. People of another nation, another color, another race were clearly welcome as full members of the church, even if they were physically maimed."[9]

Through Philip, the eunuch, and the Candace, the prophecy concerning Ethiopia in Psalms 68:31 was fulfilled: *". . . let Ethiopia hasten to stretch out its hands to God."* The New International Version translates this sentence as: *"Cush will submit herself to God."*

FOR ME TO FOLLOW GOD

Life Principle for Lesson Five: A Faith For All People

Being accepted is an important thing for most people and I think people sometimes allow others to manipulate them into being something different than God intended for them. It can happen very easily to someone through control, intimidation, or abuse. But be assured that God

Tradition tells us that it is probable that the Candace was the first person in high circles in Ethiopia to hear the triumphant message of Jesus Christ and her conversion caused her to use her office to promote Christianity in Ethiopia and the surrounding countries.

Samaritan Women & an Ethiopian Queen

DAY FIVE

disapproves of all of these methods. He accepts us, as we are, where we are, and most importantly, where he wants to lead us to be.

 How is God directing your life to bring you closer to Him?

_____

_____

_____

The Samaritans had a label put on them by God's own people—*unacceptable*. They didn't fit into the culture; they were half-breeds; they didn't believe the right things; they just plain weren't good enough. But God thought otherwise. And he made it possible for them to be accepted and loved and healed and saved and free and full of joy. Later in Acts, when the Christian mission is expanding to the Gentiles, Peter has a vision about them and says: *"but God has shown me that I should not call anyone profane or unclean."* I believe God expects the same of us.

I think the Samaritans were so enthusiastic and open about Christianity because they finally felt *accepted* and included. We learn in this lesson that the despised Samaritans and the outcast castrate were told that the gospel of Jesus Christ was also for *them*. The unclean and rejected were made clean and acceptable. The Holy Spirit makes it very clear in Acts that Christ is for *all* people, no matter who they are, what they look like, where they are from or what they have done.

 Do you feel accepted and loved by God? Why or why not?

_____

_____

_____

The Holy Spirit makes it very clear in Acts that Christ is for all people, no matter who they are, what they look like, where they are from or what they have done.

We are not only accepted in Christ, but we are temples of the Holy Spirit (1 Corinthians 6:19); we are new creatures (2 Corinthians 5:17); we are reconciled to God (2 Corinthians 5:18); we are no longer condemned (Romans 8:1); we have eternal life (John 6:47); we have peace (Philippians 4:7); we are set free (John 8:31–33); we are healed (1 Peter 2:24); we are chosen (1 Thessalonians 1:4); we have conquered the world (1 John 5:4).

 Write down your favorite verse of all of these and tell how you will begin to live by it.

_____

_____

_____

_____

It was fortunate for the Candace that she was associated with this eunuch because it may have changed her life for the better. If she did hear the gospel from him and encouraged the spread of Christianity in her country, it was a good association, indeed. Many proverbs tell us who we *shouldn't* associate with:

"A gossip reveals secrets; therefore do not associate with a babbler" (Proverbs 20:19).

"Make no friends with those given to anger, and do not associate with hotheads" (Proverbs 22:24).

And from 1 Corinthians:

"I wrote to you in my letter not to associate with sexually immoral persons" (1 Corinthians 5:9).

"But now I am writing to you not to associate with anyone who bears the name of brother or sister who is sexually immoral or greedy, or is an idolater, reviler, drunkard or robber. Do not even eat with such a one" (1 Corinthians 5:11).

"Do not be deceived: 'Bad company ruins good morals' " (1 Corinthians 15:33). Who you associate yourself with in life can change your very soul for the better or for the worse.

And, in turn, we are to associate with these: *"Live in harmony with one another; do not be haughty, but associate with the lowly"* (Romans 12:16).

 I would say, above all, associate with those who know Christ and live in him, through him, and with him in everything. Are those you associate with building you up or bringing you down? How can you change this?

_____

_____

_____

The Jews of the dispersion, and in this case Philip the Evangelist, one of the seven, became ambassadors for Christianity wherever they went. Maier, in *First Christians,* says, "These scattered Christians were never quiet about their beliefs but shared them enthusiastically."[10] That is how the church kept growing and expanding. In the same way, if we can share our faith enthusiastically and associate with other Christians and show our joy, our churches today will also keep growing and going.

 How do you share your faith? How does your church share the gospel (evangelism)?

_____

_____

_____

 Is there someone in your life who shared their faith with you?

_____

_____

_____

Lord of all the peoples of the earth, help us listen eagerly to your message for us. Give us the wisdom of the Holy Spirit to proclaim your Gospel to all those we meet, both near and far, that all may hear your good news of hope, healing, and redemption. Above all, let our joy in you shine through us, that others may see it and believe. In Jesus' name we pray, Amen.

> ## Who you associate with in life can change your very soul for the better or for the worse.

Works Cited

1. Frederick Carl Eiselen, Edwin Lewis, and David G. Downey, Editors, *The Abingdon Bible Commentary* (New York, Nashville: Abingdon Press, 1929), 1104.

2. James Malcolm Arlandson, *Women, Class and Society in Early Christianity, Models From Luke-Acts,* (Peabody, MA: Hendrickson Publishers, Inc., 1997), 178.

3. Allen C. Myers, Revision Editor, *The Eerdman's Bible Dictionary* (Grand Rapids, MI, William B. Eerdman's Publishing Company, 1987), 354.

4. Edith Deen, *All the Women of the Bible* (New York, NY: Harper & Brothers, 1955), 257.

5. Herbert Lockyer, *All the Kings and Queens of the Bible* (Grand Rapids, MI: Zondervan Publishing Co., 1961), 219.

6. William Barclay, *The New Daily Study Bible: The Acts of the Apostles* (Louisville, KY: Westminster John Knox Press, 2004).

7. Lockyer, *All the Kings and Queens of the Bible,* 219.

8. Deen, *All of the Women of the Bible,* 257.

9. Paul L., Maier, *First Christians, Pentecost and the Spread of Christianity* (New York, NY: Harper & Row Publishers, 1976), 37.

10. Ibid, p. 38.

Notes

Notes

6

Dorcas, Mary the Mother of John Mark, and Rhoda

In this lesson, we meet three women whose lives are completely dedicated to serving the early church. Their faith is not without works to back it up and those works are clearly manifested in three of the fruits of the Spirit—kindness, generosity and joy. It is a lesson about taking care of each other and protecting each other. It is also about God blessing their work and leadership in ways that only He can do. Dorcas' service was very important to the early church in Joppa. When she died, God raised her from the dead, and we can presume that she resumed her "good works and acts of charity."

Chapter 9 stands out in the Book of Acts, mainly due to its account of the dramatic conversion of Saul of Tarsus as he makes his way to Damascus to continue his persecution of Christians. In this familiar story, he receives a heavenly vision from God, is blinded and then healed. Subsequently, he is filled with the Holy Spirit, renamed Paul, and begins to proclaim the gospel in the synagogues. The first plot to kill Paul is made known to him, and he escapes to Jerusalem (where he joins the other believers), but the people do not believe the change in him. So Barnabas takes Paul to the apostles and tells them of his conversion. Paul preaches Jesus in Jerusalem, where another plot to kill him by the Hellenists is revealed. The believers learn of it and take him to Caesarea and on to Tarsus. It is interesting to note that Paul spent several years preaching in various places before his ministry began through the missionary journeys

> *Dorcas' service to the church in Joppa was very important. When she died, God raised her from the dead, and we can presume that she resumed her "good works and acts of charity."*

reported in Acts (see Galatians 1:18—2:1). It is Barnabas who goes to Tarsus to look for him and take him to Antioch in Syria to begin his ministry there (Acts 11:25).

The church continues to be built up, and Peter continues his preaching in many places. He is at Lydda, visiting the saints there when he restores a cripple by the name of Aeneas. Because of this, *"all the residents of Lydda and Sharon saw him and turned to the Lord"* (Acts 9:35). We are introduced to **Dorcas,** whose life was *"devoted to good works and acts of charity"* (Acts 9:36). She dies in the midst of her fruitful life, and Peter is called to Joppa, where he raises her from the dead.

The Holy Spirit is mentioned twice in this chapter, in Acts 9:17, when Saul is filled with the Spirit and in Acts 9:31, when the Spirit is referred to as a comforter for the very first time.

This is what Dorcas did—she clothed herself with kindness so she was able to clothe others with what they physically needed.

DORCAS: A LIFE OF KINDNESS

Kindness is listed as one of the fruits of the Spirit in Galatians 5:22. By this and the others listed, we can see the Holy Spirit at work in someone. The book of Proverbs says, *"Whoever pursues righteousness and kindness will find life and honor"* (Proverbs 21:21). The prophet Micah lists kindness as one of three things that the Lord requires of us: *"and what does the Lord require of you but to do justice, and to love kindness, and to walk humbly with your God?"* (Micah 6:8). And Colossians 3:12 says to *"clothe yourselves with compassion, kindness, humility, meekness, and patience."* This is what Dorcas did—she clothed herself with kindness so she was able to clothe others with what they physically needed.

 Have you known anyone who exhibited great kindness? If so, how did it manifest itself in helping others?

_____

_____

_____

"Now in Joppa there was a disciple whose name was Tabitha, which in Greek is Dorcas."

Acts 9:36

The story of Dorcas and the widows of Joppa takes place in a town roughly thirty-eight miles northwest of Jerusalem at the port of Joppa, which was an important Christian center. Philip had established a Christian church there in his continuing witness up the Mediterranean coast to Caesarea (Acts 8:40). This church was known for its evangelistic activities and well-organized social services. It was likely that Dorcas became a Christian here in Joppa.

Verse in Which the Woman Appears: Acts 9:36
*"Now in Joppa there was a disciple whose name was **Tabitha**, which in Greek is **Dorcas**. She was devoted to good works and acts of charity."*

Pronounced (dor'kuhs), (Greek, *Dorkas*)
The word "disciple" or "disciples" occurs many times in the Book of Acts when referring to the women and men who joined the Christian movement. Four of the five times it is used to introduce an individual person, and it follows this pattern: *"Now there was a disciple . . . named . . ."* But

Dorcas is the only named *woman* in Scripture specifically referred to as a disciple, and the feminine form of the Greek word for disciple (*mathetria*) is found only this once in the Greek New Testament.

Dorcas may be singled out in this way because her life was so totally given up to serving the poor and destitute.

📖 Look up the other references to disciple as an introduction:

Acts 9:10: Ananias (different from Ananias in 5:1)

Acts 9:26: Saul

Acts 16:1: Timothy

Acts 21:16: Mnason of Cyprus

What are the similarities?

_____

_____

_____

Dorcas is introduced not only by her Aramaic name, Tabitha, but also by its Greek translation. This could be because she was so widely known for her good works among both the Aramaic and Greek-speaking populations of Joppa. Who is the other major character in Acts who was known by two names?

_____

_____

_____

There are several thoughts among scholars as to her larger identity. Some say she may have been a wealthy widow herself or belonged to a group of widows who provided their services to other widows and the poor. Women were in the forefront in the early church in providing these kinds of services. Joyce Hollyday in *Clothed with the Sun* adds:

> "Evidence suggests that there was an early order of widows who dedicated themselves to the service of the church. . . . It is likely that the widows who gathered around Dorcas were the beginnings of such an order. And from such orders came some of the most outstanding women in the church."[1]

Timothy, in his lengthy discourse on widows, says that a widow *"must be well attested for her good works, . . . shown hospitality, washed the saint's feet, helped the afflicted, and devoted herself to doing good in every way"* (1 Timothy 5:10).

Some suggest that Dorcas was a philanthropist and supported the needy and other widows out of her own resources. In the Greco-Roman world of the first century, some widows were self-sufficient through the return of dowries, the inheritance of property or wealth from their husbands, or from their own businesses. Dorcas appears to be one of these widows. Regardless of which characterization is correct, she is held up by Luke as being *"devoted to good works and acts of charity,"* both of which were commended as virtues in the ancient Mediterranean world.

Dorcas is the only named woman in Scripture who is specifically referred to as a disciple, and the feminine form of the Greek word for disciple (mathetria) occurs only once in the New Testament.

*Dorcas, Mary
and Rhoda*

DAY TWO

Many families in this coastal city depended on the sea for a living, and many men died in boat accidents as a result of the rocky coastline and the violent storms along this area of the Mediterranean. The hazards of seafaring left many widows and needy children. The women would search the shore for rags that washed up so they would have something to wear.[2] This is where Dorcas comes in.

Her "good works and acts of charity" included making coats and other clothing for the needy of her church and community. "Acts of charity" is translated as alms or alms deeds in the Greek, and this term, along with "good works" is used only this once in Acts, for the purpose of describing the activities of Dorcas. She took Jesus' words, *"I was naked and you gave me clothing"* (Matthew 25:36) seriously and showed her faith in a very practical way. She made new clothes for them, and was loved by everyone.

DORCAS: A LIFE RESTORED

"At that time she became ill and died. When they had washed her, they laid her in a room upstairs." (Acts 9:36)

Dorcas becomes ill in the midst of her fruitful life and dies. Lucinda A. Brown in *Women in Scripture*, says:

> "Tabitha's death would have been a tragic loss to the church at Joppa - not because of her contributions to the economic well-being of its members, but because of her role as a devout and faithful member, perhaps even leader, of the early Christian community. . . . Indeed a close reading of the story supports the idea that women took an active leadership role within the early church."[3]

The grief of the people of Joppa is great. The widows prepare her body, lay her in *"a room upstairs"* and stand around her and mourn. By this time, widows were associated with the act of mourning and so this scene describing the widows standing around her bed weeping is not unusual.

Peter was preaching the good news of the Gospel in Lydda, about ten miles from Joppa. He had already performed the miracle there of healing the cripple, Aeneas. In this section, we have an example of Luke's pairing of female and male characters; in one case, a healing, and in Dorcas' case, a resurrection from the dead. The people send two men to get Peter. The Scriptures tell us that Peter had been present on all three occasions recorded in the Gospels when Jesus raised individuals from the dead (Matthew 9:25; Luke 7:11–17; John 11:1–44).

📖 Read these three passages and write down the similarities.

_____

_____

_____

_____

It is in this section that we hear to what extent Dorcas had provided for the poor. The widows show Peter and the others the garments that she has made. Peter makes his way to the room upstairs, dismisses the mourners at her bedside, kneels down and prays over Dorcas's body. You will notice that before he speaks to her, he prays. But, most importantly, it is not his own power that he depends upon, but the power of God through the Holy Spirit. He does not assume that he can perform a miracle himself. He prays for help—the kind of help that only God can provide.

The raising of Dorcas is the first such miracle in Acts. And Dorcas is the only woman recorded in Acts to have been raised from the dead. How significant is this?

_____

_____

_____

The raising of Dorcas has a two-fold effect. First, the miracle comforts the widows to whom she has given so much. And second, when the people of Joppa learn of it, *"many believed in the Lord"* (Acts 9:42). This story is only one of the many miracle stories in Acts that helps facilitate the growth of the early church. Similarly, after Jesus raised Lazurus from the dead, we read that many Jews believed. (John 11:45)

Hers was such an important ministry that it needed a miracle so it could continue. How might Dorcas' ministry have changed after she was raised from the dead?

_____

_____

_____

William Barclay adds some interesting commentary about the reference to the Christians as saints, both at Lydda and Joppa as well as in Jerusalem:

> "The Greek word is *hagios,* and it has far-reaching associations. It is sometimes translated as 'holy'; but the root meaning of it is 'different.' . . . we who are Christians are not different from others in that we are chosen for greater honour on this earth; we are different in that we are chosen for a greater service. We are saved to serve."[4]

In this story, God uses the resurrection of a woman as a way to show us all that service is at the heart of being Christian.

We learn from Dorcas that she had that spirit of service within her and we can see just how well she used it. She saw a need and met it with her own individual gift of the Spirit. She simply did what needed to be done in the church—she saw a need and met it instead of worrying so much about how or if her own needs were being met. And in turn, *God* met her need in her raising according to *His* will to continue the upbuilding of His church.

Nothing is said of Dorcas after she is restored to life, but we can imagine that she promptly re-started her ministry to the poor. Her legacy reaches across the centuries, and her name today is synonymous with acts of charity.

The raising of Dorcas is the first such miracle in Acts.

In this story, God uses the resurrection of a woman as a way to show us all that service is at the heart of being Christian.

Even today, the Dorcas Sewing Societies are known worldwide. Because of it, millions of needy people are still clothed.

 Is there a sewing or knitting group in your church that helps the poor? Are you a part of it? What impact has it had on you or others who might benefit from it?

_____

_____

_____

Transition–Chapters 10 and 11

Chapter 10 opens with the introduction of Cornelius, who is a devout man who prays and gives generously. He is visited by an angel of God, who tells him to send for Peter, who is still in Joppa. In the meantime, Peter goes up to the roof of the house where he is staying to pray and has a vision of a large sheet descending from heaven with all kinds of animals in it. A voice speaks to him and tells him, *"What God has made clean, you must not call profane"* (Acts 10:15).

Peter is greatly puzzled about this vision's meaning. Just then, the men sent by Cornelius arrive and ask for Peter. They tell Peter of Cornelius' vision of an angel from God telling Cornelius that God has accepted his generosity. They ask Peter to go with them to meet Cornelius. When Peter arrives in Caesarea, the meaning of the rooftop vision becomes clear to him as Cornelius explains his own experience. Peter speaks to them about the message of the gospel, about Jesus, and about the fact that God shows no partiality, *"but in every nation anyone who fears him and does what is right is acceptable to him"* (Acts 10:35). The Holy Spirit falls upon all those who hear Him, Jews and Gentiles alike, and the Gentiles speak in tongues and praise God. Peter baptizes them all.

Chapter 11 opens with word reaching the apostles and the believers in Judea about the Spirit's infilling of the Gentiles. When Peter returns to Jerusalem, he receives criticism for associating with Gentiles. Peter tells his critics about his vision and his understanding that God has given the gift of the Spirit to all whom He chooses and calls to Himself. They are silenced and praise God, saying, *"Then God has given even to the Gentiles the repentance that leads to life"* (Acts 11:18). As the result of the dispersion and witness to both Jews and Gentiles, in this case Hellenists, a church at Antioch in Syria is formed and grows rapidly. When the news reaches Jerusalem, Barnabas is sent to help them. After his initial witness, he goes to Tarsus and finds Saul and brings him to Antioch to help him. They stay for a year, teaching the people and building up the church there. At Antioch, the disciples are first called "Christians." Many prophets come to Antioch, including Agabus, who predicts a great famine. The disciples there send relief and supplies to the believers in Judea by way of Saul and Barnabas.

The Holy Spirit is very active in these two chapters. Look up all of the Spirit verses to see how the Spirit is given to the Gentiles. (Acts 10:19, 38, 44, 45, 47; 11:12, 15, 16, 24, 28).

Chapter 12 begins with Herod Agrippa I beginning his persecution of the church. He has the apostle James killed and Peter put into prison. But an angel of the Lord comes to Peter and frees him on the eve of his trial. The angel leads him out of the city and Peter realizes this is not a vision. He goes to the home of **Mary, mother of John Mark,** where the community of faith has been praying for him and where he knows he will be safe. **Rhoda, Mary's maid**, answers Peter's knocking, but instead of opening the door at her recognition of his voice, she excitedly runs upstairs and tells everyone that Peter is there. She is ridiculed, but insistent, and finally they all go to the door and see Peter, much to their amazement. Herod orders the execution of the soldiers who were guarding Peter. Herod then speaks to the people of Tyre and Sidon, with whom he is angry. They appeal for reconciliation so the king agrees to talk to them. But because he does not give glory to God, an angel strikes him dead. The Word of God continues to spread and gain disciples. Barnabas and Saul return to Jerusalem with John Mark. There are no verses in chapter 12 that mention the Holy Spirit.

MARY, MOTHER OF JOHN MARK: A LIFE OF GENEROSITY

Verse in Which the Woman Appears: Acts 12:12
"As soon as he [Peter] realized this, he went to the house of **Mary, the mother of John** *whose other name was Mark, where many had gathered and were praying."*

We are introduced to this Mary by only twenty-nine words. She is identified as being the mother of John Mark (not the apostle John), who may have written the second Gospel and was a co-worker with Paul and Barnabas. Peter called him "my son, Mark" (1 Peter 5:13). This is not a literal parentage, but a spiritual one. Church tradition says that Mark was the first Christian preacher in Alexandria and that he founded the church in that Jewish-Greek city. The family of John Mark was very important not only to the early church in Jerusalem, but far beyond it as well.

In Colossians 4:10, it states that John Mark and Barnabas are cousins, so Mary was most likely the aunt of Barnabas, though other sources list her as his sister. Barnabas was a prophet and teacher in the primitive church in Jerusalem. We first met him prior to the story of Sapphira and Ananias, as he is singled out for his generosity with the early church. This characteristic seems to run in the family. Mary herself is an independent woman, perhaps a wealthy widow, as evidenced by her ownership of a house large enough to host church meetings and by the fact that she employs a maidservant.

Some historians consider Mary's house to have been the center or headquarters of the Jerusalem church and perhaps the very first "house church." It may have been the largest of the house churches at the time, and Mary did not hesitate to offer it as a place of worship and prayer. Edith Deen in *All of the Women of the Bible* indicates its location: "It was said to have been on the south end of the western hill of Mt. Zion, a residential section of Jerusalem at the time of Jesus. Here may have taken place that overwhelming event known as Pentecost."[5]

Traditional accounts tell us that Mary's house was not only the house of Pentecost, but also the location of the Last Supper and the resurrection appearances of Jesus, but this cannot definitely be confirmed. House churches were also provided by Lydia, Priscilla, and Nympha, among others. In addition, in

> **"As soon as he realized this, he went to the house of Mary, the mother of John whose other name was Mark, where many had gathered and were praying"**
>
> **Acts 12:12**
>
> **Some historians consider Mary's house have been the center or head-quarters of the Jerusalem church and perhaps the very first "house church."**

the several cases in Acts where an "entire household" is baptized, these groups or families may have formed the basis of other house churches.

📖 Look up the other women in the New Testament who are specifically mentioned as having "house churches" (Acts 16:15, 40; Romans 16:5; 1 Corinthians 16:19; Colossians 4:15; Philemon 2).

House churches were essential to the early Christian movement. They were private homes where the disciples could pray, listen to the Gospel, and participate in the Lord's Supper. They also provided refuge in times of persecution, as in Mary's case. Wealthy and prominent members of the community, both women and men, provided many of the earliest houses. However, the early churches are identified as meeting in the homes of women *more often* than in the homes of men.

Wealthy widows (such as Mary the mother of John Mark) provided many of the homes. Joyce Hollyday, in *Clothed with the Sun,* reminds us that "The early Christian widows were known for their hospitality, generosity and compassion."[6] During the mounting opposition in Jerusalem to the Christian movement, Mary's prayer meetings are evidence that Luke is portraying one woman's courageous contribution to the community of faith. Why was Mary's contribution so important?

_____

_____

_____

Many scholars believe that Mary was the leader of the church family that met in her house. Barbara J. MacHaffie in *Her Story, Women in Christian Tradition,* says: "Although we cannot be sure of the role women played in the worship and administration of house churches, leadership roles would not have been surprising. The churches conceived of themselves as households of God. In the New Testament, women are not only described as the patronesses of house churches but also as their leaders."[7]

 Many offer their homes for Bible study today, but would you be courageous enough in the face of persecution to offer your home as a safe haven? Why or why not?

_____

_____

> **House churches were essential to the early Christian movement. They were private homes where the disciples could pray, listen to the gospel and participate in the Lord's supper.**

Dorcas, Mary and Rhoda

DAY FOUR

RHODA: A MANIFESTATION OF JOY

Verse in Which the Woman Appears: Acts 12:13
*"When he [Peter] knocked at the outer gate, a maid named **Rhoda** came to answer."*

Pronounced (roh'duh); Greek: *Rhode,* meaning "rose"

Rhoda probably had the lowest status of any of the men and women in the prayer meeting, but is the first to believe in the miracle of Peter's release from prison. She has a major role in this story, and she is among the very few women who speak in Acts narrative, though indirectly.

"While Peter was kept in prison, the church prayed fervently to God for him." (Acts 12:5)

After Peter is released from prison, he heads straight for Mary's house, where he knows the believers are gathered and where he knows he will be welcomed and safe. Notice the activity in which the believers are engaged—that of prayer, which again stands out as one of the primary activities of the early disciples.

"When he knocked at the outer gate, a maid named Rhoda came to answer. On recognizing Peter's voice, she was so overjoyed that, instead of opening the gate, she ran in and announced that Peter was standing at the gate." (Acts 12:13–14)

Other translations read that Peter was knocking at *"the door of the gateway"* (RSV); *"the door of the gate"* (KJV); *"the outer door"* (NEB); *"the outside door"* (TEV); *"the outer entrance"* (NIV). Only the J. B. Phillips version says simply, *"at the door."* In the *Parallel New Testament in Greek and English,* it is translated *"the door of the porch."* Clearly, this was not the main entrance to the house. The larger houses had open courtyards that separated the house from the street and outer walls in which this door or gate was probably located. These prayer groups in the time of the early church usually met in upstairs guest rooms reached by an outside stairway leading up from a walled court.

Sue and Larry Richards in *Women of the Bible* further describe the construction of first-century homes: "In Jerusalem, houses were set side by side with their outside walls facing the street. The doors in these walls were kept closed, ensuring the family's privacy and safety. The door had no windows or peepholes. Instead, the doorkeeper was expected to recognize the voice of family friends and open the door only for friends."[8]

It is probably about midnight when Peter knocks at the door of Mary's house. Peter not only knocks, but he speaks, and we read that Rhoda recognizes his voice. But, she is so stunned and overwhelmed at the answer to the believer's prayers that she fails to draw the bolts and admit him. Knowing that it is Peter, it is her duty as the maid to open the door. But she is momentarily thoughtless. She forgets herself, and instead of performing her duty, she runs in to tell everyone that Peter is at the door.

 Rhoda is so excited, so overcome with joy, so anxious to tell everyone the "good news" of Peter's release from prison that she forgets herself. The joy of answered prayer transcends everything else. Have you ever been so excited about something that you have "lost your senses?"

_____

_____

_____

When have you experienced the joy of answered prayer?

_____

_____

_____

_____

"When he knocked at the outer gate, a maid named Rhoda came to answer"
Acts 12:13

Rhoda has a major role in this story, and she is one of the very few women who speak in the Acts narrative, though indirectly.

Rhoda is so excited, so overcome with joy, so anxious to tell everyone the good news of Peter's release from prison that she forgets herself. The joy of answered prayer transcends everything else.

The words, "overjoyed," "joy," "gladness," and "happy," used by various translations, may indicate she was also among those disciples in that upper room who knew the joy of believing in Jesus Christ. God promised that He would pour out His Spirit *"even upon my slaves."* Here we have a slave being used as a carrier of good news.

What important purpose does Rhoda play in this story? What does it say about God's use of women in servant (or slave) roles?

_____

_____

_____

"They said to her, 'You are out of your mind!' But she insisted that it was so. They said, 'It is his angel.'" (Acts 12:15)

But those inside mock her and scorn her and call her mad and crazy. The Greek is translated, *"Thou ravest."* The prophet Hosea speaks about the spiritual man being mad: *"The prophet is a fool, the man of the spirit is mad!"* (Hosea 9:7). And Festus speaks of Paul when he is witnessing before him, *"You are out of your mind, Paul!"* (Acts 26:24). And remember that the people are accused of being drunk after the Spirit falls upon them (Acts 2:13).

Being told that she has lost her senses does not deter Rhoda from the repetition of what she knows to be true. When we know something is true, we are not easily convinced otherwise. The Greek is translated *"emphatically asserted."* They continue to mock her when they say, *"It is his angel."* They treat her as if her message is from the dead. Jews believed that everyone had a guardian angel and that each person's angel closely resembled him or her. If Rhoda really heard Peter's voice, perhaps it was Peter's angel speaking rather than Peter himself.

"Meanwhile, Peter continued knocking; and when they opened the gate, they saw him and were amazed." (Acts 12:16)

When the knocking does not stop, the others run and open the door, see Peter, and are astonished. They had been praying for Peter for hours, yet when Peter stood at the door they did not believe it. They were surprised by the miracle, and they finally believe Rhoda's joy, belief and persistence—but *only* when they themselves saw Peter. It reminds us of the story of Thomas, who would not believe in the resurrection until he saw Jesus' hands and side for himself.

The parallels that Arlandson draws to the resurrection story are interesting: "Rhoda . . . plays a role that has a curious resonance with the role played by the women in the Easter narrative:

(1) Jesus is placed in the tomb by the Roman authorities; Peter is thrown into prison by the Roman authorities,

(2) Jesus is resurrected ('released') with angels present; Peter is released by an angel.

(3) At first, there are somewhat unclear tokens of Jesus' resurrection; Peter knocks on the door out of Rhoda's sight,

(4) The women hurriedly run back to the eleven to announce Jesus' resurrection; Rhoda runs back to the prayer meeting in Mary's house to announce Peter's release,

Being told that she has lost her senses does not deter Rhoda from the repetition of what she knows to be true.

(5) The women's report is called foolish; Rhoda is called mad,

(6) Peter runs to the tomb; the praying but unbelieving disciples go to the door where Peter is standing,

(7) Jesus appears to the men; Peter 'appears' to the praying disciples,

(8) The women's and Rhoda's reports are now believed."[9]

FOR ME TO FOLLOW GOD

Life Principle for Lesson Five: Fruits of the Spirit—Kindness, Generosity, Joy

In Galatians 5:22, we read about the fruits of the Spirit: *"By contrast, the fruit of the Spirit is love,* **joy***, peace, patience,* **kindness***,* **generosity***, faithfulness, gentleness and self-control. . . . If we live by the Spirit, let us also be guided by the Spirit"* (emphasis added).

The women in this lesson lived by the Spirit and, as a group, manifested three of these fruits in their lives. These stories teach us what it means to *live out* our faith in Christ.

Dorcas is one of the best examples in all of Scripture of someone who really *practiced* her faith. Hers is visible, service-oriented, other-centered and extremely productive. James tells us that *"faith without works is dead"* (James 2.26). That is not Dorcas' problem! Her faith is so alive that she devotes her *whole life* to good works. She manifests the fruit of kindness.

These stories teach us what it means to live out our faith in Christ.

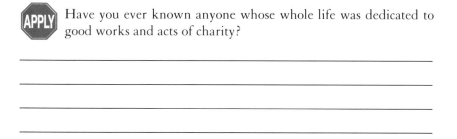 Have you ever known anyone whose whole life was dedicated to good works and acts of charity?

_____

_____

_____

_____

Jesus talked about *visible* faith, faith that is like light. He said: *"You are the light of the world. . . . let your light shine before others, so that they may see your good works and give glory to your Father in heaven"* (Matthew 5:14– 15).

Not only is Jesus the light of the world, He tells us that *we* are lights. We are to be like Him in such a way that we bring His light to others, so that *God* can be glorified. Our works done in His name are the lights we are to shine forth, so that others may be helped and know the tangible love of God in their lives.

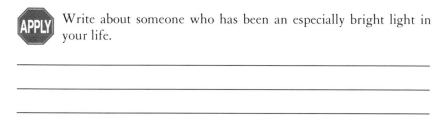 Write about someone who has been an especially bright light in your life.

_____

_____

_____

_____

Mary's faith manifests itself in generosity. Proverbs tells us: *"A generous person will be enriched, and one who gives water will get water"* (Proverbs 11:25). Generous hearts receive generosity back. And to know God is to practice generosity: *"Every generous act of giving, with every perfect gift, is from above"* (James 1:17).

APPLY It is God who gives the gifts; it is we who are responsible for using them for His glory. How has someone enriched your life with generosity?

_____

_____

_____

Her generosity is made manifest in providing her home as a meeting place for the early Christians in Jerusalem, so they can practice their faith through prayer, worship, the breaking of bread and fellowship. Mary's faith shines very brightly in that house in Jerusalem, even in the midst of the darkness of persecution and fear.

APPLY Tell how you bring the light of your faith in Christ to others.

_____

_____

_____

Mary's faith also shines brightly through her son John Mark, who became a co-missionary of Paul and Barnabas, and who may have written the second Gospel. If she had not been faithful to Christ, he might not even have known about him.

And finally, Rhoda, in her faith, exhibits joy. Joy is the one fruit of the Holy Spirit that literally *shows* our faith to others. It comes from deep within us. It shows on our faces and in our lives when we truly know Jesus Christ. Rhoda is the one who freely and excitedly shouts for joy when the glory of God is revealed to her in Peter's release from prison. And she is the one who is also mocked for being so overjoyed.

APPLY Have you ever been mocked for exhibiting unrestrained joy?

_____

_____

_____

The words "joy," "joyful," "joyfully," "joyfulness," "joyous," "joyously," "joys," "overjoyed," "jubilant," "jubilation," "rejoice," "rejoiced," "rejoicing," and "rejoices" appear over three hundred times in the Bible. I think we're supposed to have joy. God wants us to have *His* joy. The Psalms and Isaiah contain the greatest number of verses on expressing our joy to God for His great goodness and mercy.

📖 Look up Psalms 5:11; 32:11; 47:1; 63:7; 71:23 and 126:2 and feel the joy! It doesn't matter if you are a master or a servant, sing for joy to the Lord. Write you own psalm of joy to the Lord.

_____

_____

_____

_____

 Lord of kindness, give us hearts of kindness and love for all those in special need, that they might be fed, clothed and cared for. Help us love them like You love them. Lord of generosity, give us generous hearts for everyone we meet, for the sake of Your gospel and Your glory. Lord of joy, give us the joy of knowing You. Manifest your Spirit in all of us in Your own way that we may have new strength, new courage and new determination to be Your hands and feet wherever we find ourselves. In Jesus' name, Amen.

Works Cited

1. Joyce Hollyday, *Clothed With the Sun, Biblical Women, Social Justice & Us* (Louisville, KY, Westminster John Knox Press, 1994), 177.

2. Edith Deen, *All of the Women of the Bible* (New York, Harper & Brothers, 1955), 219.

3. Lucinda A Brown, quoted in *Women in Scripture,* Carol Meyers, General Editor (Grand Rapids, MI/Cambridge, U.K., William B. Eerdman's Publishing Company, 2000), 160.

4. William Barclay, *The New Daily Study Bible, The Acts of the Apostles* (Louisville, London, Westminster John Knox Press, The William Barclay Estate, 1975, 2003), 90.

5. Deen, *All of the Women of the Bible*.

6. Hollyday, 180.

7. Barbara J. MacHaffie, *Her Story, Second Edition, Women in Christian Tradition* (Minneapolis, Fortress Press, 2006), 10.

8. Sue Poorman Richards, and O. Lawrence, *Women of the Bible, The Life and Times of Every Woman in the Bible* (Nashville, TN, Nelson Reference and Electronic, a Division of Thomas Nelson Publishers, 2003), 190.

9. James Malcolm Arlandson, *Women, Class and Society in Early Christianity, Models From Luke-Acts,* (Peabody, MS, Hendrickson Publishers, Inc., 1997), 195–196.

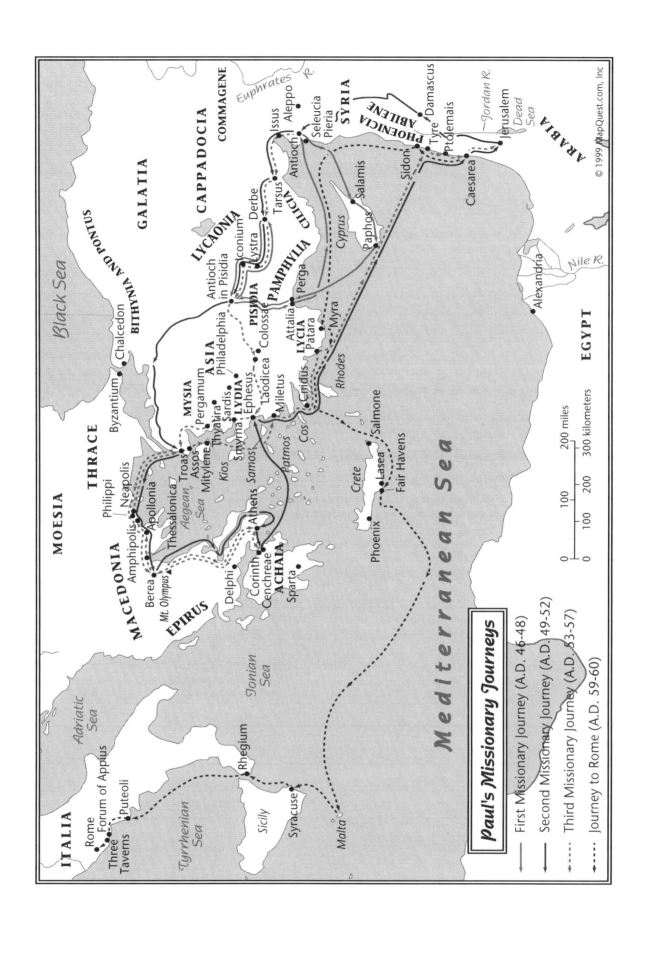

Paul's Missionary Journeys

First Missionary Journey (A.D. 46-48)
Second Missionary Journey (A.D. 49-52)
Third Missionary Journey (A.D. 53-57)
Journey to Rome (A.D. 59-60)

© 1999 MapQuest.com, Inc

7

Devout Women of Antioch and Timothy's Mother

*I*n this lesson we learn that being faithful can mean different things. Traveling with Paul on his first missionary journey, we meet women who are faithful, not to Christ, but to the Jewish religion and the rabbis. We also meet Timothy's mother, who is faithful in teaching him the Hebrew Scriptures as a child, but who later, along with Timothy, become faithful to the way of Christ.

Chapter 13 is a transitional point. From this chapter on, the focus leaves Judea, Samaria and the coastal areas and turns to the wider Greek and Roman world. Paul begins his missionary journeys, and he and his associates now travel in an empire where Roman law and Greek culture have created conditions very different from those encountered thus far. Antioch in Syria has replaced Jerusalem as the center of church mission, and Paul and Barnabas have replaced Peter and John as the principal pair of prophetic witnesses.

Paul and Barnabas are set apart by the Holy Spirit for special service. The church in Antioch commissions them by the laying on of hands and sends them off. They travel first to Cyprus, along with John Mark, and preach the gospel to the Jews in the synagogues. There is opposition from a Jewish false prophet as well as acceptance, by the proconsul Sergius Paulus. Paul and Barnabas travel on to Perga in Pamphylia, and then to Antioch in Pisidia, where Paul preaches a sermon in the synagogue on the Jewish Messiah. The message is well received, and many

In this lesson, we learn that being faithful can mean different things.

Jews and devout converts to Judiasm accept it. Paul is invited back the next Sabbath to preach again, when he is greeted by a very large crowd, "... *almost the whole city.* ..." The Jewish authorities become jealous and contradict him, so Paul then preaches to the Gentiles. Many Gentiles become believers, and the word is spread throughout the region. The Jewish leaders incite the crowd against them, and some **devout women of high standing** assist in driving them out of the region.

📖 Read how the Spirit is involved in the commissioning of Paul and Barnabas: Acts 13:2, 4, 9, 52

Women of Antioch & Timothy's Mother

DAY ONE

Paul has a bad reputation in regard to the place of women in the church, due to the misrepresentation of only a handful of Bible verses.

PERSECUTION OR FAITH: PAUL AND WOMEN

Paul has a bad reputation in regard to the roles of women in the church and home, due to the misrepresentation of only a *handful* of Bible verses, most notably, 1 Corinthians 14:34–36, Ephesians 5:22–24, Colossians 3:18–19, 1 Timothy 2:8–15, and Titus 2:3–5. These are some of the most hotly contested verses in all of the Bible, and volumes have been written about them. It is not my purpose to comment on these passages here, but instead, to note the fact that in all of Paul's writings about women, there is a context, both culturally and socially, in which he attempts to equalize the situation by calling us all, both women and men alike, to be more Christlike in our thoughts and actions toward each other. He is, in fact, calling for a radical transformation of ourselves and all of our relationships. And he always makes the point that women as well as men are to take part in this transformation. Because Paul believed that in Christ and through the Holy Spirit we are *all* new creations (2 Corinthians 5:17), he was convinced that the gospel message transcended the barriers mentioned in Galatians 3:28— those of race, sex, and class.

📖 Read and study 2 Corinthians 5:16–21. What does it really say about change in Christ?

_____

_____

_____

Paul believed in the equality of all believers. I don't know how he could believe anything less about women and be a true disciple of Jesus Christ. Jesus' attitudes and actions toward women were compassionate and empowering. Women were invited into his inner circle, they were his friends, they were taught by him and commissioned by him. And not in the least, he revealed himself as the Messiah to a woman first (John 4:26) and appeared to women first upon his resurrection (Mark 16:9).

Paul carried these attitudes through all of his travels, in spite of tremendous setbacks and problems in the world in which he lived.

As in the situation with the Jews (see Lesson One), the early Christian church was in an environment that was oftentimes hostile to its beliefs. These outside forces, coupled with struggles within the church itself meant that women and men were sometimes caught up in rules and restrictions that were contrary to the teachings of Jesus.

According to Elizabeth Achtemeier, writing in the *Oxford Companion to the Bible,* even Paul could be caught up in them: "When Paul was faced with the misuse of Christian freedom in his churches, . . . he could revert to his Pharisaic background to silence both contentious men and women in his congregations (1 Corinthians 14:28, 33–36)."[1] Paul and those with him dealt with tremendous problems, among them idol worship and the influence of paganism within the church, not to mention dangerous Gnostic doctrines. In addition, we read throughout all of Acts how he continuously ran into strict Jewish laws that contradicted and attempted to constrain the freeing message of the gospel for both women and men. The patriarchal society was not going to give up so easily.

There is a great complexity in the interpretation of everything Paul said in regard to the place of women in the church and it is subject to many factors, some of which are ignored when we want it our way instead of God's way.

But, in fact, Paul regarded women as his *full* and *equal* partners in the spread of the gospel. James Carroll, in his book, *Practicing Catholic,* puts it this way: ". . . when the norms and assumptions of the Jesus community are being written down, the ongoing equal status of women is reflected in the letters of St. Paul (c. AD 60), who names women as full partners—*his* partners—in the Christian project.. . . ."[2]

The evidence is in favor of women having held *major* leadership roles, from missionaries to apostles, in the creation of the church. The tragic thing about the Christian movement is that the patriarchal society has been a *curse* and a *contradiction* to Christian teaching throughout its history. Eventually, the freedom and importance of women to God and His church in the first three centuries of Christianity were diminished by *human* forces that led to the formation of a church with a male hierarchy. These forces are still adversely affecting the church today.

I believe we must always go back to the Spirit. The power of the Holy Spirit is what transforms individuals and even the whole *structure* of human relationships—and the church—into the image of Christ. That is what the Holy Spirit did on Pentecost—it not only transformed everyone, it gave *everyone* the ability to proclaim the Gospel, each according to the gifts of God. The Good News is such good news for women because it is the Spirit who defines and empowers them for the kingdom. The Spirit, like Jesus, restored them, transformed them, lifted them *and* commissioned them to be carriers of that good news wherever and in whatever circumstances they found themselves. And, as stated in Acts 8:4, when the Christians were scattered from Jerusalem, "[they] *went from place to place, proclaiming the word."* Paul may have founded several churches in the larger cities, some with the help of women, but it was the ordinary women and men of faith, whose witness to their own transformation in Christ by the Holy Spirit, who took the gospel further into the countryside and rural areas. Paul could not do it by himself. Men cannot do it by themselves. And, women cannot do it by themselves. We have been made to work *together* in the body of Christ, so that the entire world may hear the gospel.

> The tragic thing about the Christian movement is that the patriarchal society has been a curse and a contradiction to Christian teaching throughout its history.

> The Good News is such good news for women because it is the Spirit who defines and empowers them for the kingdom.

Sidebar (left column)

We would do well for the church if we could start to emphasize the positive teachings of Paul for women instead of the negative and restrictive, which are, more often than not, reflective of our own prejudices and limitations.

Women of Antioch & Timothy's Mother

"But the Jews incited the devout women of high standing and the leading men of the city, and stirred up persecution against Paul and Barnabas, and drove them out of their region."

Acts 13:50

Main column

 How can women and men work together in the church for the sake of the gospel?

_____

_____

_____

So, let's meet Paul all over again and try to see past his humanity into the soul who was called to proclaim the Gospel. And let's study the real relationships he had with the women who helped him spread that Gospel.

As we travel with Paul, you will be introduced to some of the important women in his life and in the life of the rapidly growing Christian church. And I think you will see for yourselves that Paul loved and depended on women because he was full of the Holy Spirit himself, and because he accepted and *understood* the message of Jesus Christ so completely. Women worked side by side with him, traveled with him, and ministered to him as he ministered to them. Paul was a great proponent of the shared leadership of men and women, and he regarded women as essential to the spread of Christianity. Garry Wills, in *What Paul Meant,* says:

> "But the important thing is to notice that Paul gives every kind of honor to the women he works with—as emissaries, as prophets, as attendants *(diakonoi).* They are not second-class citizens in the gatherings he knows or in the ideals he holds up for them."[3]

We would do well for the church if we could start to emphasize the *positive* teachings of Paul for women instead of the negative and restrictive, which are, more often than not, reflective of our own prejudices and limitations and I would argue, less negative and restrictive than they appear upon a quick reading and often taken out of context.

BEING FAITHFUL, BUT NOT TO CHRIST

The Verse in Which the Women Appear: Acts 13:50
"But the Jews incited the **devout women of high standing** *and the leading men of the city, and stirred up persecution against Paul and Barnabas, and drove them out of their region."*

At this stage in Acts, Paul and Barnabas are in Antioch in Pisidia, which is now central Turkey. This city was founded by one of Alexander the Great's successors about 300 BC, and it became a Roman colony in 6 BC. It is described as a lively and volatile city with a very mixed population, including a large population of Jews, Greeks and Romans as well as the native Phrygians.

Paul arrives and does what he always does. He goes to the synagogue and preaches Jesus to the Jews. This is Paul's first speech in the Book of Acts and is reminiscent of the earlier ones of Peter and Stephen. And for the first time, the theme of Jewish rejection of the gospel is tied to that of the Gentile mission, and Paul preaches to many Gentiles here. Note the very familiar verse: *"I have set you to be a light for the Gentiles, so that you may bring salvation to the ends of the earth"* (Acts 13:47).

The message is well received, and many Jews and devout converts to Judaism are brought to Christ. Paul is invited to preach again the following week, a good sign for a preacher! This time almost the entire city shows up. The Jews' jealousy is taken a step further, and they incite both these women as well as "the leading men of the city" against him.

At this time, the Jewish religion had a special attraction for women because of the pagan culture's lack of morals and the general debasement of Greek and Roman society, especially in the breakdown of the family. And, like today, some of the worst sufferers were women. The Jewish religion preached a higher moral position, and many women eagerly responded to this and became converts to Judaism. There were also non-Jewish devotees of the God of Israel, who were called God-fearers or God-worshippers. Ample evidence from the Roman period demonstrates that some of these women and men also attended the Jewish synagogues and observed various Jewish practices, but without formally converting to Judaism.[4]

These women are referred to in other translations as *"devout and honorable women,"* (KJV), *"women of standing who were worshippers,"* (NEB), *"Gentile women of high social standing who worshipped God,"* (TEV), *"God-fearing women of high standing,"* (NIV) and *"religious and respectable women."* (JBP) and were devoted to Judaism. The Greek translates the words, *"the worshipping women—honorable."*

As for their high standing, Luke hints that they are wealthy women, perhaps landowners, since the primary source of wealth at that time was land. In the Roman world, it was much more common for women to hold wealth in their own right. Wealthy women in the Greek East also had a high measure of political power and social prestige, thus they were able to assist in decision-making, as they perhaps did here by cooperating in the expulsion of Paul and Barnabas from Antioch.

📖 Read this entire speech in Acts 13:16–41. Write down why the Jews became so upset.

_____

_____

_____

_____

The one thing that infuriated the Jews more than anything else was that God's privileges could also be extended to the uncircumcised Gentiles. The Jews were intent on keeping their privileges to themselves. When the Jewish leaders sought to stop the preaching of the Christian message, these women cooperated with them. They seem to hold equal power with the men, appearing in public with them as well as taking part in the decision to run Paul out of town. And this time, they are mentioned first in the passage.

Why do you think these women rejected the message of Christ?

_____

_____

_____

> **The one thing that infuriated the Jews more than anything else was that that God's privileges could also be extended to the uncircumcised Gentiles.**

The devout
Antiochene women
succeed in helping
to drive Paul and
Barnabas out of
Antioch, but they
do not succeed in
blocking the large
Gentile response.

The Jews persuade them, along with some leading men of the city, to take steps against Paul. And they muster enough clout to oppose the gospel and drive the "socially deprived" apostle out of the region.

It is a different part of the world; it is a different social class, and it is a different reaction. Instead of embracing Christianity like so many before them, these women remain loyal to Judaism. They succeed in helping drive Paul and Barnabas out of Antioch, but they do not succeed in blocking the large Gentile response.

It is interesting to note that Paul and Barnabas *"shook the dust off their feet in protest against them, . . ."* (Acts 13:51). This is the very advice that Jesus gave to his disciples in three of the Gospels:

"If anyone will not welcome you or listen to your words, shake off the dust from your feet as you leave that house or town" (Matthew 10:14).

"If any place will not welcome you and they refuse to hear you, as you leave, shake off the dust that is on your feet as a testimony against them" (Mark. 6:11).

"Whenever they do not welcome you, as you are leaving that town shake the dust off your feet as a testimony against them" (Luke 9:5). And to the seventy that he commissioned:

"But whenever you enter a town and they do not welcome you, go out into its streets and say, 'Even the dust of your town that clings to our feet, we wipe off in protest against you" (Luke 10:10–11).

APPLY Paul and Barnabas return to Antioch in Pisidia at a later date without incident. Have you ever known a pastor or a missionary who was run out of town, due to disagreements with the "women of high standing" or "the leading men of the city" or the "powers that be?"

_____

_____

_____

_____

Write down how you reacted to this and how it affected your faith or membership in a church.

_____

_____

_____

Have you ever known anyone who has actively spoken against the Christian faith? If so, how did you respond?

_____

_____

_____

OTHER PERSECUTORS OF PAUL: DIFFERENT TOWNS, SAME RESPONSE

Transition: Chapter 14

After Paul and Barnabas are run out of town, they continue their first missionary journey and go to Iconium, a town approximately ninety miles from Antioch, where the same thing happens. First, a great many Jews and Greeks become believers, including undoubtedly, many women as well as men.

Then, *"But the unbelieving Jews stirred up the Gentiles and poisoned their minds against the brothers"* (Acts 14:2). The population at that time consisted of Greeks, Roman officials and veterans and Jews. But instead of leaving immediately, as in Antioch, Paul and Barnabas stay a long time, speak boldly for the Lord, and do many signs and wonders among the people.

In spite of this, the city becomes divided, some siding with the Jews and some with Paul and Barnabas. The people, along with their rulers (could be the same as the leading men in Antioch) launch a full-scale attempt to mistreat and stone them. Paul's team learns of the plan and flees once again, this time to Lystra and Derbe. Did they shake the dust off their feet this time, too? It does not say so in the text, but I can picture them doing it for the same reasons.

As we follow Paul on this first missionary journey, we find him in the towns of Lystra and Derbe, still further south in Lycaonia, where they continue to proclaim the Gospel. This first major mission to the Gentiles is fraught with danger as well as joy. It follows the pattern of Peter in his witness to the Jews and Philip in his witness to Samaria and beyond, with its share of trials as well as successes.

In Lystra, Paul heals a cripple, and the people mistake he and Barnabas for the gods, Zeus and Hermes and they prepare to make sacrifices to them in the temple. Paul quickly seeks to correct them and tells them about the one true God.

But some Jews from Antioch and Iconium cannot leave them alone. They follow Paul to Lystra and turn the crowds against him there as well. This time, they succeed in physically dragging Paul out of town, stone him and leave him for dead. But the disciples protect him by surrounding him and the next day he and Barnabas escape to Derbe.

Paul and Barnabas continue to draw great numbers of both Jews and Greeks to the gospel without incident there. Following the pattern, there are undoubtedly many women among them. They continue the first missionary journey by returning to Lystra, Iconium, and Antioch, where they strengthen the souls of the new disciples and encourage them in the faith.

The two men appoint elders in each church along the way. Since the beginning of the church in Antioch in Syria, there were elders appointed in the church. Paul and Barnabas finish their journey by passing through

This first major mission to the Gentiles is fraught with danger as well as joy.

Peter reminds them that God has made no distinction between Jews and Gentiles and that salvation comes through the grace of the Lord Jesus Christ.

Pisidia, Pamphylia, Perga, and Attalia, returning finally back to Syrian Antioch, where Paul calls the church together to tell them about the Gentile mission. No verses in chapter 14 mention the Holy Spirit.

Transition: Chapter Fifteen
There appears to be dissention in the church about whether the Gentiles need to be circumcised in order to be saved. Several from the church in Antioch, including Paul and Barnabas, are appointed to go to Jerusalem to meet with the apostles and elders. While they are there, Peter reminds them that God has made no distinction between Jews and Gentiles and that salvation comes through the grace of the Lord Jesus Christ.

📖 Read Acts 15:6–11. What criteria does God use for salvation?

_____

_____

_____

_____

Paul and Barnabas tell the council of all the signs and wonders God has done through the Gentiles and James tells of how the prophet Amos had predicted their conversion (see Amos 9:11–12). The conclusion is that the Gentiles need not be circumcised, but they must abide by only a few activities of Jewish Law.

Two representatives of the council, Judas and Silas, are appointed along with Paul and Barnabas to take a letter to the various churches about the council's decision. The church at Antioch (in Syria) receives the news with joy. Paul and Barnabas continue their teaching and proclamation of the word and decide to embark upon a second missionary journey to strengthen the churches. They disagree about whether John Mark should accompany them and it is decided that Barnabas will go with John Mark to Cyprus while Paul and Silas will go through Syria and Cilicia in Asia Minor.

Read how the Holy Spirit is given to the Gentiles in Acts 15:8 and how the Spirit directs the mind of Peter to tell the Jerusalem Council that God does not impose requirements on those whom he saves. He saves by His grace alone. (The Holy Spirit is also mentioned in 15:28.)

📖 Read several verses in the letters of Paul about the grace of God: Romans 3:24, 6:14; Ephesians 2:8; Titus 3:7. Also Acts 15:11. How does it feel to you to know that the grace of God alone is your salvation?

_____

_____

_____

_____

_____

_____

Timothy's Mother: A Faithful Mother

Verse in Which the Woman Appears: Acts 16:1
"Paul went on also to Derbe and to Lystra, where there was a disciple named Timothy, the son of **a Jewish woman** *who was a believer; but his father was a Greek."*

Timothy's mother (and grandmother) are named in 2 Timothy 1:5: *"I am reminded of your sincere faith, a faith that lived first in your grandmother Lois and your mother* **Eunice** *and now, I am sure, lives in you."*

Eunice: Greek *Eunike,* **meaning 'good victory'**

While in Lystra on his second missionary journey with Silas, Paul meets Timothy. Timothy's mother is not named in this passage, but we learn in 2 Timothy 1:5 that her name is Eunice and that his grandmother's name is Lois. She is mentioned first before his father, is identified as Jewish, and is a believer. We discover that Timothy is of a mixed faith family. Evidence seems to point to the fact that Lois, Eunice, and Timothy were converted to Christianity by Paul during his first missionary journey to Lystra, about five years earlier.

Timothy's father's name is not mentioned anywhere, which is unusual in Scripture. It says only that he is a Greek. Luke *implies* that he may not be a Christian because he is not identified as a believer, like his mother. And, as we have seen in Scripture how Samaritans were treated, Jews looked down upon intermarriage, especially strict Jews who refused to accept the non-Jewish partner.

What difficulties do you think Eunice (and Lois, his grandmother) faced in raising Timothy in a mixed faith marriage in the first century?

_____

_____

_____

It is to Eunice's (and Lois') credit that the people of Lystra and Iconium attest to Timothy's good character. She is the one who taught him the Jewish faith. Paul writes to him: *". . . and how from childhood you have known the sacred writings that are able to instruct you for salvation through faith in Christ Jesus"* (2 Timothy 3:15).

 It was the responsibility of the mother, especially in Jewish tradition, to pass the faith on to the children in the home. The mother was in charge of the son until he was thirteen years of age. From whom did you receive your faith training? Tell how this person shared their faith with you and what impact it has had on your life. Look up Proverbs 22:6.

_____

_____

_____

_____

"Paul went on also to Derbe and to Lystra, where there was a disciple named Timothy, the son of a Jewish woman who was a believer; but his father was a Greek."

Acts 16:1

It was the responsibility of the mother, especially in Jewish tradition, to pass the faith on to the children in the home.

Paul sent Timothy on the prickliest misssions and put him over important churches.

As a result of this faithful nurturing, Timothy becomes one of Paul's most trusted associates. Paul is looking for a replacement for John Mark, who went on to accompany Barnabas to Cyprus. Timothy is associated with Paul during a longer period than any of Paul's other colleagues. Paul refers to him as *"my loyal child in the faith"* (1 Timothy 1:2). He sends Timothy on the prickliest of missions and puts him over important churches.

📖 Read both letters of Paul to Timothy and discover just how much Paul loves and trusts him. Write the verses down where Paul is complimenting Timothy.

_____

_____

_____

The faithful nurturing of his mother and grandmother helps Timothy become a respected leader. Edith Deen states in *All of the Women in the Bible* that: "Timothy the son, Eunice the mother, and Lois the grandmother represent the strongest spiritual trio stemming from the maternal line of any family group in the New Testament."[5]

Paul is so impressed with Timothy's faith that he accepts him as a fellow Jew. According to rabbinic tradition, the son of a Jewish mother is considered to be Jewish. But Paul is worried that other Jews will not accept Timothy because of his mixed heritage, so Paul has him circumcised in order to "restore" his Jewish identity. This was to help him avoid offending the Jews and also to maintain good relations between the Jews and the Gentiles in the churches. In this action, Paul manages to break down national barriers between Jew and Greek and to insure harmony between them in the church. This brings to mind the phrase in Galatians 3:28, *"There is no longer Jew or Greek."* This proves to have been the right thing for Paul to do, since the churches *"increased in numbers daily"* (Acts 16:5).

 Do you know any women today in mixed faith marriages who are raising their children as Christians? Write about any difficulties they might be having.

_____

_____

_____

Being Faithful

DAY FIVE

FOR ME TO FOLLOW GOD

Life Principle for Lesson Seven: Being Faithful

If God is anything, He is faithful. We can always trust Him for everything. In 1 Corinthians 1:9, it says: *"God is faithful; by him you were called into the fellowship of his Son, Jesus Christ our Lord."* (See also 1 Thessalonians 5:24; 2 Thessalonians 3:3; 1 John 1:9.) How is God faithful to us? (See Psalms 31:23; 37:28; 69:13; 85:8; 97:10; 101:6; and 148:14) Write a definition of faithfulness.

_____

_____

_____

_____

And He calls us to be faithful as well. How are you faithful to God?

_____

_____

_____

But as we have seen in this lesson, faithfulness means different things to different people. The Antiochene women in this lesson had faith—they were *faithful* to what they believed in. They were called *"devout"* in their own way of worshiping God. They were loyal to the Jewish religion and submitted themselves to the rabbis. And while they did not embrace the new Christian movement, and in fact, helped stir up persecution against it, their own faith in God was real.

APPLY Describe how your faith is real to you.

_____

_____

_____

But despite their success in expelling Paul and his associates from Antioch, they could not squelch the conversion of many Jews and Gentiles to Christianity. Even a negative impact on some cannot stop the conversion of others.

And while tolerance is important in respecting the faith of all, we as Christians are called to *live out* our faith every day in every circumstance so that others will see it and believe. Our witness, like Paul's, can make all the difference in someone's life, but *only* if we are willing to be laughed at, mocked, or thrown out of town, as he was.

Paul said: *"It is through many persecutions that we must enter the kingdom of God"* (Acts 14:22). Sometimes it is not easy to be faithful.

APPLY Have you ever experienced any kind of persecution for your faith?

_____

_____

_____

_____

Timothy's mother's faith was also real. She raised Timothy as a Jew and taught him the Hebrew Scriptures. He became a Christian as an adult and had such a good reputation among the people that Paul wanted him as an associate. Timothy became a giant in his witness for Christ. Eunice passed on her religious heritage to her son, Timothy, in spite of the fact that she was married to a Greek.

APPLY How do you pass on your faith to others, especially your children?

_____

_____

_____

I don't think there are any more important people in life than those who teach us faith. Some receive it as children, like Timothy, and some as adults. Sometimes it is not your parents who teach it to you. In Timothy's case, it is just one parent and a grandparent. Other times, it is not a family member at all. In all cases, it is those whose faith is *visible* that teach us the best. Sometimes the palpable joy or the intense commitment that dominates a person's attitudes or activities is enough to make you want to know more about the faith that they profess.

I have been fortunate in knowing many different people of faith. As a child, I had a grandmother, like Timothy did, whose faith was very real to me. Her faith shone like a light to me until the day she died and her faith helped me become faithful. I also had an extended family whose faith made a lasting impression on my life. In addition, I have known pastors and pastor's wives, church members, friends, and colleagues whose faith was so real that I had no doubt at all that God loved *me*. I have been truly blessed to have had so many faithful people in my life.

 APPLY Write your own psalm about how God is faithful to you and how you express your faithfulness to Him.

_____

_____

_____

_____

_____

Lord of faith, give us faith for our whole lives. Increase it daily, that we might not only be bold in our proclamation of it, but also sure in our defense of it. Help us teach it to our children, that they might also have the gift of life in You. Give us an outer manifestation of faith that others may see You in us. Thank You for Your great faithfulness to all of us. Through Jesus Christ our Lord we pray, Amen.

Works Cited

1. Bruce M. Metzger, Michael D. Coogan, eds., *The Oxford Companion to the Bible* (New York, Oxford: Oxford University Press, 1993), 807.

2. James Carroll, *Practicing Catholic* (Boston, New York; Houghton Mifflin Harcourt, 2009), 154. Used by permission of the author.

3. Garry Willis, *What Paul Meant* (New York: Viking, Published by the Penguin Group, 2006), 98.

Sometimes the palpable joy or the intense commitment that dominates a person's attitudes or activities is enough to make you want to know more about the faith that they profess.

4. Carol Meyers, Toni Craven, and Ross S. Kraemer, eds., *Women in Scripture: A Dictionary of Named and Unnamed Women in the Hebrew Bible, the Apocryphal/Deuterocanonical Books, and the New Testament* (Grand Rapids, MI: Wm. B. Eerdmans Publishing Co., 2001), 462.

5. Edith Deen, *All the Women of the Bible* (New York: Harper & Brothers, 1955), 238.

Notes

8

Lydia and a Slave Girl

Lesson Eight introduces us to Lydia, one of the most well-known women in the Book of Acts, and to an anonymous slave girl, who is part of a well-known story about the silversmiths of Ephesus. These two women could not be more different. Lydia is from the top end of the social scale, while the slave girl is from the bottom. And yet God, in his transforming love, calls each of them to himself to become more than they ever dreamed they could be—major characters in the story of His church.

Chapter 16 continues with Paul having a vision of a man from Macedonia, asking him to *"come and help us"* (Acts 16:9–10). Through this vision, the Holy Spirit calls Paul to an area to meet a woman who will help him start one of the leading New Testament churches. He obeys the Spirit and sets sail for Philippi, a leading city in Macedonia and a Roman colony. After several days, he and his companions go outside the city gate to a riverbank, where the people met for prayer because there was no synagogue. He meets a group of women, including one named **Lydia, a dealer in purple cloth**. She listens eagerly to his message, and she and her household are baptized. She offers her home as a place for Paul and his traveling team to stay.

Another day, on his way to the place of prayer, Paul meets a **slave girl** who has a spirit of divination, who is being used by her owners to make money from fortune telling. She begins to follow Paul and Silas around and shouts, *"These men are slaves of*

These two women could not be more different. One is from the top end of the social scale and the other is from the bottom.

the Most High God, who proclaim to you a way of salvation" (Acts 16:17). This becomes an annoyance and Paul orders the spirit to come out of her. Paul and Silas are arrested, beaten and put into prison.

God sends an earthquake to free all of the prisoners. The prison guard is so upset that he is going to kill himself, but Paul tells him that they are still all there. The guard, trembling, asks them what he needs to do to be saved. Paul tells him to believe on the Lord Jesus Christ, and, through doing so, he and his household will be saved. The authorities discover that Paul and his associates are Roman citizens, apologize to them, and ask them to leave the city. They go to **Lydia's** house to encourage the believers before they leave.

📖 Read in this chapter how the Holy Spirit is directly involved in these stories: Acts 16:6–7

PHILIPPIAN WOMEN: THE HOLY SPIRIT'S LEADING TO PHILIPPI

Lydia and a Slave Girl

DAY ONE

The Holy Spirit's every act enables the continuation of Jesus' work on earth. It is not only the power by which everything is accomplished, it is encourager, comforter, teacher and companion.

We have seen from the beginning of Acts how the Holy Spirit has been the guiding force for the early Christians in the creation of the church. The Spirit is not only poured out on all the believers at Pentecost, it is continuously poured out on all of them from Jerusalem to Rome. A series of "mini-Pentecosts" can be found all through the book.

📖 Look up the following passages and see the Spirit enabling believers everywhere to proclaim the good news of the gospel. Acts 4:31; 8:15–17; 10:44; 11:15; 19:5–6

What are the similarities between these verses?

_____

_____

_____

_____

The Holy Spirit's every act enables the continuation of Jesus' work on earth. It is not only the power by which everything is accomplished; it is encourager, comforter, teacher, and companion. This fellowship of the Spirit brings to mind Jesus' words: *"And remember, I am with you always, to the end of the age"* (Matthew 28:20). And the Spirit of God is *direct*. We have already seen in Acts 8:29 how the Spirit speaks *directly* to Philip and tells him to join the Ethiopian eunuch in his chariot. And then, how the Spirit supernaturally snatches Philip away from the eunuch and puts him in the next place he is to witness (Acts 8:39–40).

We have seen how the Spirit speaks *directly* to Peter to tell him three men are searching for him to go to Caesarea and meet Cornelius (Acts 10:19; 11:12). And finally, we have seen the Spirit *directly* intervene and set Barnabas and Saul apart for work among the Gentiles (Acts 13:2).

In the same way, preceding the next story of Lydia and the Philippian women, the Spirit gets very *direct* with Paul and Silas. Paul had the plan all worked out for his second missionary journey. He was going to go through areas in Asia and Bithynia, but the Spirit has other ideas.

📖 Read Acts 16:6–10. How does the Holy Spirit direct this journey?

_____

_____

_____

_____

Paul barely begins his second missionary journey when it is interrupted with a vision of a man standing and pleading with him to go to Macedonia (Acts 16:9). The Holy Spirit is leading him to different areas than he planned and also preventing him from going to other places. The Spirit is opening the door to Europe. The Holy Spirit calls Paul to the Roman colony of Philippi and directs him there because He has something important for Paul to do, but more importantly, He has *someone* important for Paul to meet, whose home will usher in the initial development of Christianity in that place. Many scholars believe that the church at Philippi was Paul's favorite church. In his letter, he calls it *"his joy and crown"* (Philippians 4:1).

Philippi became a Roman colony in 42 BC and was named for King Philip II of Macedonia. It was an important outpost on the Egnation Way. The gospel message was so needed in a place like Philippi, which was a rancid, pagan city full of many false teachers who, after the church was established, tried to sway Christians away from the belief that salvation is based on the death, burial, and resurrection of Jesus. So Paul begins his European ministry here. The text says: *"On the sabbath day we went outside the gate by the river, where we supposed there was a place of prayer; and we sat down and spoke to the women who had gathered there"* (Acts 17:13).

As we have seen over and over, it was Paul's normal pattern to go to the synagogue to preach the gospel, but because of the small Jewish population in Philippi, there was no synagogue. In this case, it was the practice, usually taken on by women, to establish a place of prayer by a river. The Greek word, *proseuche,* in this passage is translated "place of prayer." There was a river outside the Roman gate at Philippi named the Gangites (the modern Angista). And, the fact that Luke refers to the women meeting on the Sabbath indicates they were probably Gentiles who worshiped the one God of the Jews, though not full converts to Judaism.

 Prayer groups are fairly common in the church today. If you are part of one, where do you meet? Is your group made up of only women or a combination of both sexes?

_____

_____

_____

Among Paul's first conversations with anyone in Philippi were with women—by God's design and by the *direct* intervention of His Spirit. As related in Paul's letter to the Philippians, this new church, started by the

Did You Know?

THE EGNATION WAY

The Egnation Way was a Roman highway that connected the Adriatic and Aegean Seas and became the most important east-west route in the Roman Empire, making possible easy passage from Rome to Asia Minor. It was built in 146 BC after the conquest of Greece. This route also provided the way for Paul to establish three important churches during his second missionary journey—Philippi, Thessalonica and Berea.

Among Paul's first conversations with anyone in Philippi were with women—by God's design and by the direct intervention of His Spirit.

generosity and hospitality of the Philippian women, carried on in the midst of *"a crooked and perverse generation"* (Philippians 2:14). But one of the features of Paul's letter to the Philippian Christians is the expression of joy in spite of the circumstances.

📖 Read Paul's letter to the Philippians to learn some more of the characteristics of this new church and how they coped in spite of the "perverse generation." Write some of them down.

_____

_____

_____

_____

Lydia and a Slave Girl

DAY TWO

LYDIA: AN EAGER LISTENER

We are not told who comprised this group other than a woman named Lydia, but some suggest that they could have been Lydia's slaves (her household in verse 15), her business associates (people of the same trade associated with each other) or simply other women, along with Lydia, who were God-worshippers or God-fearers. Most of those called God-worshippers were Gentiles who came from the wealthy class, studied the Jewish scriptures, worshiped the one God of the Jews, but had not yet heard of Jesus.

In Paul's letter to the Philippians, he mentions the names of two women, Euodia and Syntyche, and says that they *"have struggled beside me in the work of the gospel, together with Clement and the rest of my co-workers, whose names are in the book of life"* (Philippians 4:2–3). Some interpreters suggest that they were among the women on the riverbank in Philippi, co-founded the church at Philippi, and became leaders, perhaps deaconesses, in it. Others say they were a missionary pair who may have traveled with Paul. In any case, Paul adds that their names are in the book of life, suggesting that they, too, are spiritual laborers called by God.

What does the term "spiritual laborer" mean to you?

_____

_____

_____

> *That Paul, Silas, Timothy, and possibly Luke himself, would sit down and talk to a group of Philippian women by a riverside dramatically shows the counter-cultural effect of Christianity.*

That Paul, Silas, Timothy and possibly Luke himself would sit down and talk to a group of Philippian women by a riverside dramatically shows the counter-cultural effect of Christianity. The *New Interpreter's Bible Commentary* adds: "His (Luke's) depiction of the easy relations between a male religious leader and a female outsider symbolizes a counterculture that remains impressive even for our modern liberal democracies."[1] The message of the gospel does away with social barriers as well as gender barriers between people. It is the most affirming message for women that the world has ever known. And in Paul's easy acceptance of these women, it shows that *he* has crossed this cultural divide and we are reminded again that this transforming power is for all people and for all the world.

The Verse in which the Woman Appears: Acts 16:14
"A certain woman named **Lydia***, a worshipper of God, was listening to us; she was from the city of Thyatira and a dealer in purple cloth."*

Lydia is the only one in the group given a name. She is introduced without reference to a husband, which could mean two things: that she never married or that she is a widow. She is further defined as being a "worshiper of God." (See above.)

Lydia was originally from the town of Thyatira in the territory of Lydia in Asia Minor. It was a city of many guilds, one of which was the dyer's guild, where they used a unique dye from the murex shellfish that turned cloth into luxurious shades of purple. An old inscription bearing the words, 'Dyer's Guild,' was discovered in the ruins of Thyatira. Lydia probably trained in her craft there and took her knowledge to Philippi.

Purple clothing was a luxury item consumed by the rulers and other wealthy patrons in the major cities throughout the Roman Empire. In Luke's Gospel, Jesus tells a story about a rich man and a poor man: *"There was a rich man who was dressed in purple and fine linen"* (Luke 16:19). And in Mark's Gospel, when Jesus is being mocked as king of the Jews, *"And they clothed him in a purple cloak"* (Mark 15:17). And in the book of Exodus, when God is explaining to Moses how to build the tabernacle, there are more than twenty-five references to the fact that the curtains and vestments were to include the color *purple*.

How does the church use purple today? (i.e., in vestments, hangings, liturgical seasons, etc.)

_____

_____

Purple merchants had to be wealthy even to enter the business, and as a dealer in purple, Lydia would have made a good living for herself. She is an example of the comparatively independent position that some women attained in Asia Minor.

"The Lord opened her heart to listen eagerly to what was said by Paul" (Acts 16:14).

The Spirit not only led Paul to Philippi, to the riverbank, and to a group of women, but the Lord also opened Lydia's heart to *"listen eagerly."* Just as the disciples, after the resurrection, had experienced the Spirit's opening of their minds to fully understand the meaning of the Scriptures (Luke 24:45), Lydia's heart was opened by God to respond to the gospel. The Greek intimates that Lydia is singled out in the hearing and in the opening of her heart.

Where else in Acts have we heard that the people "listened eagerly" or responded with joy to the gospel message? What does this tell us about someone's need for God?

_____

_____

_____

"A certain woman named Lydia, a worshiper of God, was listening to us; she was from the city of Thyatira and a dealer in purple cloth."
Acts 16:14

Lydia is an example of the comparatively independent position that some women attained in Asia Minor.

Jesus closes out many of His parables in Matthew, Mark and Luke with the phrase, *"Let anyone with ears to hear listen!"* (Matthew 13:9, 43; Mark 4:9, 23; Luke 8:8; 14:35). Look up these references and "listen" to the message for you. We are all to be eager listeners. How does Lydia's eager listening compare with your own experience?

_____

_____

_____

Lydia and a Slave Girl

DAY THREE

> **"When she and her household were baptized, she urged us, saying, 'If you have judged me to be faithful to the Lord, come and stay at my home.' And she prevailed upon us."**
>
> **Acts 16:15**

And from the minute she opens her home to them, she not only ministers to Paul, but ministers with him as well.

LYDIA: A NEW CHURCH "HOME"

"When she and her household were baptized, she urged us, saying, 'If you have judged me to be faithful to the Lord, come and stay at my home.' And she prevailed upon us." (Acts 16:15)

Lydia is the first to respond to Paul's message and be baptized. The immediacy of her response to the gospel message brings to mind the eagerness of the Ethiopian eunuch to be baptized. This "newness of heart" is a sure sign that Christ has entered into it.

Lydia has the distinction of becoming the first Christian convert in Europe and her entire household is baptized. This could suggest that the other women with her were members of her household, i.e., servants or slaves.

And, she is *immediately* led to action. Her joy in Jesus Christ must surely have shown as brightly on her face as it did in her heart. The phrase, *"If you have judged me to be faithful to the Lord. . . ."* indicates an *eagerness* to do what she can to help the Christian cause. The fact that she is a wealthy merchant indicates that she has a home large enough to host Paul and his sometimes-large traveling team. *"She prevailed upon us."* Other translation words used include: she *constrained* (KJV), she *insisted* (NEB), and she *persuaded* (NIV) us to go. She wouldn't take "no" for an answer. Paul's acceptance of her hospitality indicates that he is convinced of the genuineness of her heart. And from the minute she opens her home to them, she not only ministers *to* Paul, but she ministers *with* him as well.

Her hospitality is part of the Christian character that Paul refers to in Romans 12:13, *"extend hospitality to strangers,"* and when Peter is telling new converts to Christ to *"Be hospitable to one another without complaining"* (1 Peter 4:9). And, perhaps the most well known verse on hospitality, from Hebrews 13:2, *"Do not neglect to show hospitality to strangers, for by doing that some have entertained angels without knowing it."*

 APPLY How does your church show hospitality to strangers? How do you do it individually?

_____

_____

_____

Lydia proves herself to be hospitable, and she shares her resources with them. She symbolizes this invaluable gift given by Christian women throughout history.

As a result, Paul establishes one of the leading New Testament churches with a group of women. The *New Interpreter's Bible Commentary* concludes: "Indeed it is her home that becomes the spiritual center for the entire city, and the story's presumption is that she becomes its spiritual leader."[2]

Lydia's story is one that most refutes the idea that Paul had a poor opinion of women. His relationship with her and the women of Philippi strongly contradicts that impression. We see through these women just how much he needs them in Philippi and how vital a part they play in the initial spreading of the gospel in Europe. Women seem to have played a major role in the Philippian church and it grew because women as well as men were *fully involved*.

Paul believed that the Holy Spirit had re-directed him to Philippi partly because these women needed to hear the gospel and partly because *he* needed what these women had to offer him. It is an example of the true *partnership* of women and men that God intended.

What other female-male "partnerships for the gospel" from Scripture can you think of?

_____

_____

_____

_____

In Paul's letter to the Philippians, he indicates that this church was the *only* one in the early days of his preaching the gospel that provided him with offerings to help support him in his travels (Philippians 4:15–18). And, Lydia may have been one of the wealthy widows who supported him, just as there were also wealthy women who supported Jesus' ministry.

The founding mothers of the church at Philippi had partnered with him from the beginning. In the beginning verses of his letter to the Philippians, Paul thanks God for those who shared the gospel *"from the first day until now,"* possibly referring to that group of women, among others. Far from demeaning women, Paul is actually declaring them *essential* for the spread of the gospel. God used Lydia in an incredible way. Her influence as a member of the top end of the social scale could be good for the gospel, from those wealthy members of her own community who bought her purple cloth all the way to the royals, who wore her purple cloth on state occasions. God definitely knows what He is doing when He causes the heart of a prominent, wealthy and influential *woman* to be changed for His glory!

How do you think Lydia's business might have been affected after she became a Christian?

_____

_____

_____

_____

Paul believed that the Holy Spirit had re-directed him to Philippi partly because these women needed to hear the gospel and partly because he needed what these women had to offer him. It is an example of the true partnership between women and men that God intended.

How might her wealthy customers have seen her after her conversion?

_____

_____

_____

Hostilities continue to plague Paul and Silas and they are imprisoned once again. When they are released, it is to Lydia's house that they go, like Peter did to Mary's house in Jerusalem. He encourages the brothers and sisters there before he departs (Acts 16:40).

"One day, as we were going to the place of prayer, we met a slave girl who had a spirit of divination and brought her owners a great deal of money by fortune-telling."

Acts 16:16

SLAVE GIRL OF PHILIPPI: POSSESSED BY A SPIRIT, FREED BY THE HOLY SPIRIT

Verse in Which the Woman Appears: Acts 16:16
*"One day, as we were going to the place of prayer, we met a **slave girl** who had a spirit of divination and brought her owners a great deal of money by fortune-telling."*

Greek *paidiske*, diminutive of *pais*, or "girl"

Paul and Silas proclaim the gospel in Philippi for many days. The place of prayer in this instance could be Lydia's house, previously established as the new meeting place for Christians. Or it could be that Paul, on each Sabbath day, continued to go to the riverbank to meet others.

Just as Lydia is at the top of the social scale, the slave girl of Philippi is at the bottom. Richard I. Pervo, in *Women in Scripture,* says: "This anonymous 'slave girl' . . . may be the most marginalized person in the New Testament: a demon-possessed, exploited, 'pagan' female slave."[3]

"Spirit of divination" (Greek *pneuma pythonos*) means literally, "the spirit of a Python," which is associated with the Delphic oracle. In Greek mythology, a serpent by the name of Python guarded an oracle on Mt. Parnassus. The serpent was slain by Apollo, who was then called Pythius, or the God of divination. William Barclay adds: "She was what was called a Pytho, that is, a person who could give oracles to guide people about the future. She was insane and the ancient world had a strange respect for such people because, they said, the gods had taken away their wits in order to put the mind of the gods into them."[4]

Slaves in the Roman Empire had no right to choose what was best for them. This girl has fallen into the hands of dishonest men who use her misfortune for their own gain. She has to do whatever her owners think is best for *them,* with no regard for *her* at all. Her owners are delighted by her affliction, since it earns them a great deal of money.

"While she followed Paul and us, she would cry out, 'These men are slaves of the Most High God, who proclaim to you a way of salvation.' She kept doing this for many days." (Acts 16:17)

While Paul and Silas are proclaiming the gospel in Philippi, a spirit takes possession of the slave girl's faculties so that she is forced to follow them. As she does, the spirit shouts out through her. Herbert Lockyer in *"All the Women of the Bible,"* describes her actions in more detail: "When caught up by the demon, the girl's wild cries were received as oracles, and her masters traded on her supposed inspiration and made her answer those who sought guidance for their lives. Luke recognized in her phenomena that was identical with those of the priestess of Delphi—the wild distortions, the shrill cries, the madness of evil inspiration."[5]

In this passage, the spirit refers to Paul and his companions as "slaves of the Most High God." This term is also used in the worship of Zeus. She *seems* to be supporting Paul's message, but in both the Gospels and Acts, spirit beings are sensitive to the presence of an inspired person.

 In Mark's Gospel, they tell Jesus who he is (Mark 1:24; 3:11). And the unclean spirit uses almost identical language in Mark 5:7. Look up these three passages and note the similarities.

_____

_____

_____

_____

"But Paul, very much annoyed, turned and said to the spirit, 'I order you in the name of Jesus Christ to come out of her.' And it came out that very hour." (Acts 16:18)

Paul, finally becoming irritated at the continuous shouting over many days, commands the spirit to come out of her. This is a demonstration that the Holy Spirit of God is more powerful than the spirit within the girl. In his exorcising of the spirit, Paul is telling us that Jesus has the ultimate power, even over Zeus and all the other gods of the ancient world. It also demonstrates to us that Jesus Christ has the ultimate victory over *all* the powers of this world.

APPLY Paul only needs to speak the name of Jesus, and the spirit flees, according to various translations, *"there and then,"* (NEB) *"at that very moment,"* (TEV) *and "immediately"* (JBP). How have you achieved victory over some of the "powers of this world" that control you?

_____

_____

_____

Have you ever consulted your horoscope or had your palm read? How has this distracted you from the gospel?

_____

_____

_____

"But when her owners saw that their hope of making money was gone, they seized Paul and Silas and dragged them into the marketplace before the authorities." (Acts 16:19)

> The slave girl's owners were delighted by her affliction, since it earned them a great deal of money.

> In his exorcizing of the Spirit, Paul is telling us that Jesus has the ultimate power, even over Zeus and all the other gods of the ancient world. It also demonstrates to us that Jesus Christ has the ultimate victory over powers of this world that would control us.

This is ultimately a story about a battle for power and the exploitation of a slave girl. When the spirit is cast out, the girl no longer has any value to her owners. They are angry that their source of revenue is gone and seize Paul and Silas and drag them off to the authorities. Paul and Silas are beaten and cast into prison. We do not know what happened to this girl after her release from the power of the spirit. Perhaps Lydia took her into her home and took care of her for a time. Perhaps she becomes a Christian and continues her witness—this time, with fullness of mind and faculties—and of *equal* rank with everyone else in the church.

Lydia's need was for spiritual completeness.

FOR ME TO FOLLOW GOD

Life Principle for Lesson Eight: Wholeness

Lydia and the slave girl of Philippi each had a need. Lydia's need was for spiritual completeness. She was wealthy in worldly things, but she needed the true wealth of knowing Jesus. And when she was touched by the Spirit of God, her need was met.

APPLY What is your need?

_____

_____

_____

_____

Lydia was baptized, and as a result of her need being met, the needs of *others* were met. First, her household was baptized, and then she offered hospitality—*without hesitation*. Lydia offered her home for the beginnings of the new church at Philippi, which would become one of Paul's most influential churches.

APPLY How have you helped meet the needs of others?

_____

_____

_____

By opening our ears and our hearts and responding eagerly, God can and will meet our true needs. In Paul's letter to the Philippians, he speaks about our true needs. And at the end of the letter, he gives us the assurance: *"And my God will fully satisfy every need of yours according to his riches in glory in Christ Jesus"* (Philippians 4:19). There are no needs that we have that God cannot meet, physically, mentally, emotionally or spiritually.

APPLY How has God met your needs?

_____

_____

_____

The slave girl's need was twofold: first, to be freed from being possessed by a spirit that controlled her and second, to be freed from those who would exploit her for their own gain. Both her needs were met when God, through Paul, exorcized the spirit from her, which then resulted in freeing her from those who used her. I remember the old saying, "Whatever *possessed* you to do that or to say that?"

APPLY Are we in our "right mind" when we do or say something we don't mean to say or do? What possesses you? Whatever it is, does it control your life in a positive or negative way?

_____

_____

_____

Even Paul struggled with such issues. He writes in his letter to the Romans: *"I do not understand my own actions. For I do not do what I want, but I do the very thing I hate"* (Romans 7:15). But he also wrote in Romans 8:37: *"No, in all these things we are more than conquerors through him who loved us."* We can, with Christ, conquer all the things that might possess us or hold us in bondage of some sort. The power of this world cannot compare with the power of Jesus Christ. The *only* thing that will set any of us free is the power of the gospel message.

It has the power to change all our lives for the better—and forever. Its power will give you a joy-filled and *full*-filled life. It will be your greatest "possession."

Like Lydia, do you believe that God exists but do not have Christ within you? Like the slave girl, does some kind of demon or ungodly thing rule your existence? Are you a "slave" to someone besides Christ or a "slave" to worldly things and pursuits? If so, ask God to restore you to wholeness in Jesus Christ. Jesus tells us in John's Gospel (15:11; 16:24; 17:13) that our joy is complete in *Him,* that He is all we need to be completely free.

APPLY How have you been made whole in Him?

_____

_____

_____

Have you ever known anyone who was a "slave" to someone else in the sense that they were being used for that person's personal or professional gain? Tell about them. What can we do as Christians to help women or men who are "slaves" in that someone else is controlling them?

_____

_____

_____

_____

📖 Read stories from the Old Testament about women who were victims of male abuse: Dinah (Genesis 34); Tamar (2 Samuel 13:22); The Levite's Concubine (Judges 20:4–6); Jephthah's Daughter (Judges 11:39–40); Samson's Wife (Judges 14); and the Women of Midian (Numbers 31).

> **The slave-girl's need was twofold: first, to be freed from being possessed by a spirit that controlled her, and second, to be freed from those who would exploit her for their own gain.**

> **The only thing that will set any of us free is the power of the Gospel message.**

Lord of all social classes, help us see Your face in everyone we meet. Keep us mindful that you have made us all in your image and that we all belong to Your kingdom. Teach our hearts to listen for the message You have for each of us and help us act to help those who are possessed by something other than Your Holy Spirit. Above all, teach us to trust You for all of our living. In Jesus' name we pray, Amen.

Works Cited

1. Leander E Keck, Convener, *The New Interpreter's Bible, A Commentary in Twelve Volumes, Volume X, The Acts of the Apostles, Introduction to Epistolary Literature, The Letter to the Romans, The First Letter to the Corinthians* (Nashville, TN: Abingdon Press, 2002), 235.

2. Ibid, p. 235

3. Carol Meyers, General Editor, *Women in Scripture* (Grand Rapids, MI; Cambridge, UK: William B. Eerdman's Publishing Company, 2000), 464.

4. William Barclay, *The New Daily Study Bible, The Acts of the Apostles* (Louisville, London: Westminster John Knox Press, The William Barclay Estate, 1975, 2003), 145.

5. Herbert Lockyer, *All the Women of the Bible* (Grand Rapids, MI: Zondervan, 1967), 242.

9

Leading Women and Damaris

In contrast to the harassment that Paul and his team received in Antioch of Pisidia and Iconium, he is now greeted with a more positive response from the Greek women in Thessalonica and Berea and enjoys limited success in Athens. The Jews are still after him, but the women in these places make a bold decision for Christ.

Chapter 17 has Paul leaving Philippi and continuing on to Thessalonica, where there is a Jewish synagogue. He preaches for three Sabbath days and some of the Jews and *"a great many of the devout Greeks and not a few of the leading women"* (Acts 17:4) become believers. But the Jews become jealous and incite the crowds against him. They cannot find him, so they assault the house of Jason, where he is staying, and drag him and some other believers before the authorities. The believers help Paul and Silas escape to Berea. Paul preaches at the synagogue there and the Bereans are more receptive and welcome the message very eagerly. *"Many of them therefore believed, including not a few Greek women and men of high standing."* (Acts 17:12). But the Jews in Thessalonica hear of it, and they come and incite crowds against them. The believers save Paul's neck again and send him to the coast, where he sails for Athens.

Paul argues with the Athenians in both the synagogue and the marketplace. He is challenged by two groups of philosophers, the Epicureans and the Stoics, who accuse him of babbling. But, when asked to speak about this strange new teaching, he stands

In contrast to the harassment that Paul and his team received in Antioch of Pisidia and Iconium, he now receives a more positive response from the Greek women in Thessalonica and Berea, and even limited success in Athens.

before the Areopagus, or high court of Athens, and delivers one of his most famous "sermons." Paul tells them about the one true God—that He is not made with human hands, and that He has been working since creation to redeem the whole world to himself. Paul gets a mixed reaction: some scoff; some delay, and a few join him, including Dionysius the Areopagite and a woman named **Damaris**. The Holy Spirit is not specifically mentioned in this chapter.

The Holy Spirit's directing of Paul and his team on to Thessalonica, a distance of over one hundred miles from Philippi, indicates the importance of preaching the gospel there.

LEADING WOMEN BELIEVE: THE SPREAD OF CHRISTIANITY IN EUROPE AND GREECE

The Holy Spirit's directing of Paul and his team on to Thessalonica, a distance from Philippi of over one hundred miles, indicates the importance of preaching the gospel there. As noted, this was the route that God intended for Paul to take.

Thessalonica was a seaport of about 200,000 people, located on the Thermaic Gulf. Its main street was part of the great Roman road, the Egnation Way (see Lesson Eight). This major Roman artery made it very easy for Christianity to spread to these regions. Paul had already traveled it from Neapolis to Philippi, then through Amphipolis and Apollonia to Thessalonica. After Christianity was planted in Thessalonica, it could in turn, easily spread in every direction.

What kinds of major roads are there in your area that make it possible for you to travel easily from place to place? Write how you travel some of them to go to Bible studies and other gatherings. How does your church's mission travel to other areas near or far to help people?

_____

_____

_____

In Paul's letters to the Thessalonians, he writes about how the people of this area spread the word of the Lord: *"For the word of the Lord has sounded forth from you not only in Macedonia and Achaia, but in every place your faith in God has become known, so that we have no need to speak about it"* (1 Thessalonians 1:8). This verse indicates just how all the early Christians helped Paul in planting the Christian faith in every place, even to the point of him not even having to speak about it any more.

How do you think women were involved in this "sounding forth" of the gospel?

_____

_____

_____

Thessalonica was an important trade and communication center and also the capital of the Roman province of Macedonia. And, unlike Philippi, it had a Jewish synagogue that made it easier for Paul to immediately come into contact with a significant number of the Jews. In order for the gospel to take a strong hold there, Paul later sent Timothy to help and encourage them. And his letters to them also encourage and build them up and tell them not to "quench the Spirit" who first brought him there and not to weary in "doing what is right." Read these two short letters of Paul to the Thessalonians and see how he continually encourages them to stay strong in their faith.

Write some of your favorite verses down.

_____

_____

_____

APPLY How does your church encourage you and its other members?

_____

_____

In spite of Paul's bold testimony, he is forced out of town by the Jews of Thessalonica. The believers take Paul and Silas to Berea, another major city in Macedonia, about fifty miles from Thessalonica. Berea was a prosperous center for artisans, farmers, and stonecutters. He follows his regular pattern of preaching to the Jews at the synagogue. But the Jews from Thessalonica come there and force him to flee once again. He is taken to the coast and sails another three hundred miles south to Athens. From Philippi to Athens, he has covered over 450 miles. Have you ever moved to a different area because of negative factors? What were they? Are there reasons you might have left a church?

_____

_____

_____

_____

Athens, of course, we have heard of. It was the chief city of ancient Greece and the cultural capital of the ancient world. It was full of idols, intellectuals, and philosophers, as well as art and architecture. Famous temples, parts of which still stand, and shrines to the gods and goddesses dominated the city. What cities in our modern world can compare with Athens?

_____

_____

_____

Interestingly, Athens was not a part of Paul's major missionary activity. He did preach there with very limited success, but amidst mockery and cynicism, he finally just left the city. He was very distressed to see all the idols and spoke against them. One of the better-known verses from his address to them includes: *"For 'in him we live and move and have our being'"* (Acts 17:28).

> **"For the word of the Lord has sounded forth from you not only in Macedonia and Achaia, but in every place your faith in God has become known, so that we have no need to speak about it."**
>
> **I Thessalonians 1:8**

> *"For 'In him we live and move and have our being.'"*
>
> **Acts 17:28**

 APPLY How do you live in Christ? Are there "idols" from which you need to be freed?

_____

_____

_____

As is God's way, even amidst persecution and idol-worship, there are those whom He calls to Himself. And, in all three of these places, from Thessalonica to Berea to Athens, there are women and men who join the Christian movement and assist in making sure it prospered and grew. Let's meet some of them.

Leading Women and Damaris

DAY TWO

LEADING WOMEN BELIEVE: THE LEADING THESSALONIAN WOMEN

> *"Some of them were persuaded and joined Paul and Silas, as did a great many of the devout Greeks and not a few of the leading women."*
>
> **Acts 17:4**

Verse in Which the Women Appear: Acts 17:4
"Some of them were persuaded and joined Paul and Silas, as did a great many of the devout Greeks and not a few of the **leading women**.*"*

As previously noted, the recurring pattern in Acts is that Paul arrives in a city, goes to preach at the Jewish synagogue (or place of prayer if there is none), converts some to Christianity and experiences rejection and/or persecution from others, usually jealous Jews. Many times he is forced to flee to another city. But in Thessalonica and Berea, Luke includes some women who are more receptive to the gospel message.

In this verse, there are really three different groups who become believers. First, there are **"some of them,"** who are the Jews who belong to the synagogue. Second, there are a great many **"devout Greeks"** (Gentiles). And third, there are not a few of the **"leading women."** The latter two groups could have been connected to the synagogue in some way, as God-fearers or worshipers, like Lydia, but were not yet full converts to Judaism.

The actions of these women are different. Instead of assisting the Jews in *ejecting* Paul, some of them are persuaded by the message of Christ and *join* Paul and Silas. Their status, however, is similar to the Antiochene women. In Antioch, they were the *"devout women of high standing."* In Thessalonica, it is "not a few of the *leading women*." The phrase, "leading women," is literally translated, "first women." In both cases, they are probably wealthy landowners, since the primary source of wealth was land, or that they hold influential positions in society. They may even have had some political power or held public office.

One important fact of ancient social history was that wealthy women could, as benefactors, attain power and prestige otherwise not available to them. Religion was one sphere in which women made many philanthropic efforts. Phoebe, mentioned at the end of the book of Romans, is identified as a benefactor (Romans 16:2). And, some of the women who followed Jesus provided for Him and the others out of their resources (Luke 8:3). Do you think such efforts have the appearance that they were "buying" their position?" How does their aid assist in the spread of the gospel?

_____

_____

_____

The general image of these women in Acts supports the historical evidence. Inscriptions have been found honoring such women for their many public good deeds *and* their services as high-ranking *religious* officials. In fact, the word *benefice* is defined as "an endowed church office providing a living for a vicar, rector, etc."[1] Women in Thessalonica had the resources and personal autonomy to join the Christian movement, possibly as leaders. This does not necessarily assume, however, that these women (or men) automatically received church leadership roles after they joined the church. Neither does it assume that they were kept *from* them because of wealth.

While some of the scriptures tell us that women did hold high positions in the church, Luke does not indicate it, except to say "leading women." Perhaps it is because that is not what the kingdom of God is about. The rich and the poor are included *equally* into the church and receive the same honor as children of God. It is Jesus Christ and the gift of eternal life He offers that makes us wealthy. Because He changes our *hearts*, our religious good deeds become actions of love and joy. How do you think these "leading women" served the church *after* they believed in Christ?

_____

_____

_____

The gospel message is breaking down social and class barriers even further, and including more of those from the top end of society. Everyone is welcome in the kingdom of God, *even* those with high levels of wealth, status and power.

Are there any "high-standing" or "leading women" of the community in your church? What do they and others understand their "positions" in the church to be?

_____

_____

_____

Even with the converts, the Jews do the same thing to Paul and Silas as they did in Antioch. They again stir up the crowds against them. This time, they form a mob and *"set the city in an uproar."* Their actions appear to take on a more vicious tone. When they can't find them, they attack the house of Jason, a fellow Christian (could be the same Jason in Romans 16:21, a "kinsman" of Paul) and drag him and some other believers into the street because they had been entertaining them as guests. They define Paul and Silas as *"Those people who have been turning the world upside down. . ."* (Acts 17:6). The leading women of Thessalonica are also now defined this way. We are also supposed to be turning the world upside down with our witness! How do you think these new female converts reacted to the intense jealousy of some of the Jews? How would you respond if you saw someone in your

> *One important fact of ancient social history was that wealthy women could, as benefactors, receive power and prestige otherwise not available to them. Religion was one sphere in which women made many philanthropic efforts.*

> *Inscriptions have been found honoring such women for their many public good deeds and their services as high-ranking religious officials.*

church "dragged before the city authorities" simply for associating themselves with the gospel?

_____

_____

_____

Luke does not list women here as assisting in the persecution. The believers find Paul and Silas and under cover of darkness, send them safely to Berea.

LEADING WOMEN BELIEVE: THE GREEK WOMEN OF BEREA

Verse in Which the Women Appear: Acts 17:12
"Many of them therefore believed, including not a few **Greek women** and men of high standing."

"**Many of them therefore believed, including not a few Greek women and men of high standing.**"

Acts 17:12

As we have just seen, the leading women of Thessalonica are _"persuaded"_ by Paul and become believers. Now in Berea, _"not a few Greek women"_ are said to have believed. In Berea, as in Thessalonica, the converts include both women and men. Many other translations include one or more additional descriptive words for the women: _"a number of prominent Greek women"_ (NIV); _"women of standing"_ (NEB); _"many Greek women of high social standing"_ (TEV); _"a number of Greek women of social standing"_ (JBP); _"also of honorable women which were Greeks"_ (KJV). The earliest Greek manuscripts indeed contain the word translated "honorable" in the King James Version. So, the Berean women are described in much the same way as those in Thessalonica. And here, Luke mentions the women first in the passage. Also, more information is given here about the response of the ones who became believers.

"These Jews were more receptive than those in Thessalonica, for they welcomed the message very eagerly and examined the scriptures every day to see whether these things were so." (Acts 17:11)

This must have been quite a relief to Paul after he had been run out of both Antioch in Pisidia and Thessalonica. There doesn't seem to be the intense jealousy or anger here. It is interesting to note that in both of these places, there are many conversions, both Jews and Gentiles, _before_ the Jews get jealous and angry. Perhaps what made them so angry was the massive crowd of people that Paul was attracting _away_ from them and their own understanding of the Jewish Messiah.

In contrast, here in Berea, the Jews are "more receptive" and "welcomed the message very eagerly." This verse sounds similar to how the Samaritans reacted to the gospel message in Acts 8:6: _"The crowds with one accord listened eagerly to what was said by Philip."_

Why, if they are the same kind of people, Greek elite men and women, do you think they were more receptive? What would be so different here?

_____

_____

_____

Some scholars suggest that the Bereans were of a "more noble character." This could be attributed to the difference in the identity of the population. Thessalonica was a much larger city, a bustling commercial seaport, whereas Berea was smaller and made up of artisans and farmers. Perhaps we can describe them as less stressed! What differences do you see, if any, in people from different areas of our country? Are some calmer and more polite than others?

_____

_____

_____

The Bereans seem to be much more interested in what the Scriptures say about the Messiah. Like the Ethiopian eunuch, they wanted to understand what the Old Testament prophets said about him. As the eunuch said, *"How can I* [understand], *unless someone guides me?"* (Acts 8:30). And, they were *eager* like Lydia, and welcomed Paul and his message about Jesus Christ. So they held a Bible study!

And of course, there is God, who is opening the hearts of people like Lydia. Jesus said, *"So I say to you, ask, and it will be given you; search, and you will find; knock, and the door will be opened"* (Luke 11:9). The Bereans were *searching and examining the Scriptures,* and they found what they needed and wanted—a new life in Christ. Psalms 146:8 tells us that it is the Lord who opens the eyes of the blind and He who loves the righteous.

What character type are you? Are you open to the possibility that God can change your life?

_____

_____

_____

It has been suggested that women were so receptive to the gospel message because it proclaimed freedom, equality and expanded roles for them as human beings. We have seen over and over again that Jesus Christ opens the door for everyone who believes in Him to come through, regardless of nationality, position, or gender.

The Jews from Thessalonica, on the other hand, were intent on stopping the message under all circumstances. They chase Paul to Berea when they hear of his great success there. This has a kind of eerie parallel to when Paul (then Saul of Tarsus) followed the Christians to Damascus to bring them back to Jerusalem for persecution. It also parallels the way the Jews incited the crowds in Jerusalem and other places to demand that Jesus be stopped from preaching his message.

Fortunately for Paul, the believers protect him once again and send him to the coast, where he sails for Athens. How would you feel if you had to keep moving from place to place to avoid those who persecuted you?

"The Jews were more receptive than those in Thessalonica, for they welcomed the message very eagerly and examined the scriptures every day to see whether these things were so."

Acts 17:11

The Bereans were searching and examining the Scriptures, and they found what they needed and wanted—a new life in Christ.

DAMARIS OF ATHENS

Verse in Which the Woman Appears: Acts 17:34
"But some of them joined him and became believers, including Dionysius the Areopagite and a woman named Damaris, and others with them."

Pronounced (dam' uh ris), meaning possibly "wife" or a variant of Damalis, meaning "heifer.

The reality is, as in lesson one, that we do not know the identity of this woman, other than her name. Damaris is presumably a Greek woman, singled out by name, who believed the message of Paul. There are different ideas about her identity. The fact that she is singled out with Dionysius, who is one of the court judges, indicates some kind of distinction, either personal or social. She could be an aristocratic landowner.

Edith Deen suggests: "In all probability she was one of the Hetairai, constituting a highly intellectual class of women who associated with philosophers and statesmen. . . . the Hetairai were the only free women in Athens."[2]

Chrysostom, among others, believed her to be the wife of Dionysius, but there is no real evidence of this. Greek wives lived in seclusion. If she had been his wife, she probably would have been referred to as such, or her name omitted completely. Others suggest she could have been a mother of one of the philosophers.

William Barclay offers still another interpretation: "The position of women in Athens was very restricted. It is unlikely that any respectable woman would have been in the market square at all. The likelihood is that she turned from a way of shame to a way of life."[3] This interpretation draws on the stereotype that "respectable women" did not appear in public. What do you sense in the difference between the descriptions of her possible identity?

_____
_____
_____

Perhaps she was someone with whom Paul had previously talked either at the synagogue or in the marketplace (Acts 17:17). She could be one of the "devout persons," or God-fearing Gentiles who was present at the synagogue.

Still others have suggested that she was a foreign educated woman, thus being allowed to be present at a public meeting. The text tells us that there were foreigners living there (17:21).

Richard I. Pervo in *Women in Scripture* says: "Some ancient manuscripts ascribe to her the epithet 'of high standing' [compare Acts 13:50; 17:12]; others delete the reference to her, perhaps to suppress recognition of independent women."[4] Again, the guesses at who she might be suggest that men describing her think of her as being less important. This is similar to the comment by Ross S. Kraemer mentioned in lesson two about Mary Magdalene being omit-

---

"But some of them joined him and became believers, including Dionysius the Areopagite and a woman named Damaris, and others with them."
Acts 17:34

The fact that she is singled out with Dionysius, who was one of the court judges, indicates some kind of distinction, either personal or social.

ted from the list of women present at Pentecost. In the case of Damaris, perhaps Luke mentions only her name because he doesn't want to offend his male audience. What is your reaction to this?

_____

_____

_____

But here is her most important definition as a person. She is now a believer in Jesus Christ, which means, no matter who or what she may have been in life, she is now a *new person* with the promise of eternal life. She can now live by verse twenty-eight where Paul utters one of his most life-giving definitions of what it means to know God: *"For 'In him we live and move and have our being'; . . . "* (Acts 17:28). She is free, transformed and brand new. And in 2 Corinthians 5:17, we are told what this means: *"So if anyone is in Christ, there is a new creation: everything old has passed away; see, everything has become new!"*

"When they heard of the resurrection of the dead, some scoffed; but others said, 'We will hear you again about this.' At that point Paul left them." (Acts 17:32–33)

I include these two verses because they lead up to the reaction to Paul's speaking to the Athenians about the Christian story. The story of Paul's mission in Athens is one of mixed success.

Paul preaches on Mars Hill in front of the Aeropagus—the distinguished high court of judges in Athens. He preaches to a group composed mostly of those who worship idols and are too "intellectual" to be receptive enough to receive his message. Paul encounters two groups: the Epicureans, who are materialists and atheists and believe in nothing eternal; and the Stoics, whose philosophy advocated virtue based on knowledge, self-sufficiency, reason and devotion to duty. To these men, new ideas were welcomed, but not easily embraced. And the introduction of foreign gods was frowned upon. Have you known any people like the Athenians?

_____

_____

_____

They debate and argue with him. They call him "a babbler," but yet still invite him to speak further. In this well-known sermon, Paul covers every essential element of the Christian faith and tells them about the one true God. Read Paul's speech in Acts 17:22-31 and note each element of our faith. Note also how Paul goes about his witness to a group of mostly unreceptive people. What can this teach us about our own witnessing?

_____

_____

_____

They scoff and doubt and delay their decision, except for a few. I can picture Paul shaking the dust from his feet as he did before and going to a place where the people are more receptive.

As for Dionysius, according to Eusebius, *"Dionysius the Areopagite, who was converted by the apostle Paul, as reported in Acts, was the first to be appointed Bishop of Athens."*

But here is Damaris's most important definition as a person. She is now a believer in Jesus Christ, which means, no matter who or what she may have been in life, she is now a new person with the promise of eternal life.

What challenges do you think Damaris, Dionysius and the others faced in keeping faith alive in a city like Athens, full of idols and intellectual pride?

_____

_____

_____

How do you participate in keeping your own faith alive today, both in your church and your community?

_____

_____

_____

The stories of these women and men in Acts 17 are about the conversion of Jews and Greeks to Christianity because of the powerful witness of Paul and his associates.

FOR ME TO FOLLOW GOD

Life Principle for Lesson Nine: A Decision for Christ
Prominent Female Thessalonians & Bereans—Positive Response

The stories of these women and men in Acts 17 are about the conversion of Jews and Greeks to Christianity because of the powerful witness and faith of Paul and his associates. Read 1 Thessalonians 1:2–9. Write down how the Thessalonians responded to Paul's witness and how they themselves became powerful messengers for Christ.

_____

_____

_____

_____

We are messengers for Christ in our world today. Read 2 Timothy 4:1–5 to see what Paul told Timothy about being a messenger to the Thessalonians. What are some of the characteristics of being a good messenger?

_____

_____

_____

_____

We must always be sure that we are true messengers, in that *we* are not the focus. We are never to try to convince people of *our* way; we are always to try to convince people of *God's* way. Our way is nothing; God's way is everything. Our way is death; God's way is life. And I think that we need not worry so much about how many are converted or even if we don't have great success in numbers, as long as our message is God's message. It is God who does the saving, not us.

How are you at being a good messenger of Christ?

_____

_____

_____

Write a letter of encouragement to the Bereans and then to your own church.

_____

_____

_____

_____

_____

_____

We must always be sure that we are true messengers, in that we are not the focus.

Damaris of Athens
The Athenians were harder to convince than the Thessalonians and Bereans. They were more into intellectual pursuits and wanted to debate and argue their own perspective on things. They were not as *spiritually* receptive. Paul talked and argued with them in the synagogue, in the marketplace and on Mars Hill. He finally got tired of arguing, so what did he do? *"At that point, Paul left them"* (Acts 17:33). But not before Damaris and a few others were convinced. Being in the minority, both as a woman in Greek culture and in those responding positively to Paul's message, she represents a rare receptivity and courage that probably had an influence after Paul left Athens.

What might Damaris have done in her own society to further convince others to believe in the message of the gospel?

_____

_____

_____

How is your church doing at teaching the gospel? What are you personally doing?

_____

_____

_____

_____

The one thing that Paul noticed in Athens and was deeply distressed about was *"that the city was full of idols"* (Acts 17:16). What are some of the idols in our modern cities? How should the church respond to them?

_____

_____

_____

_____

_____

_____

Paul did not write a letter to the Athenians. Write what you think "Paul's Letter to the Athenians" might have said based on the character descriptions in Acts 17:21.

_____

_____

_____

_____

_____

_____

_____

Now write a letter to your own city.

_____

_____

_____

_____

_____

_____

_____

 Lord of life everywhere, no matter what our position or place, help us respond eagerly to Your word, that our hearts and minds may be willing to serve only You. Search our hearts to find and rid us of anything that interferes with believing the gospel message. Help us give up the idols of this world that would control us, that we might find new and eternal life in Your son, Jesus Christ, in whose name we pray, Amen

Works Cited

1. _Webster's New World Dictionary of the American Language_ (Nashville, TN: The Southwestern Company, 1965), 69.

2. Edith Deen, _All of the Women of the Bible_ (New York, NY: Harper & Brothers, 1955), 259.

3. William Barclay, _The New Daily Study Bible, The Acts of the Apostles_ (Louisville, London: Westminster John Knox Press, The William Barclay Estate), 156.

4. Carol Meyers, General Editor; Toni Craven and Ross S. Kraemer, Associate Editors; _Women in Scripture, A Dictionary of Named and Unnamed Women in the Hebrew Bible, The Apocryphal/Deuterocanonical Books, and the New Testament_ (Grand Rapids, MI/Cambridge, U.K.: William B. Eerdman's Publishing Company, 2000), 65.

5. Paul Maier, _Eusebius, the Church History: A New Translation with Commentary_ (Grand Rapids, MI: Kregel Publications, 1999), 159.

Notes

Notes

10

Priscilla of Rome

*J*ust as the slave girl of Philippi may be the most marginalized woman in the New Testament, Priscilla may have been the most powerful woman in the early church. She was a true partner in faith, not only to her husband, but to Paul, more than equal to the task of proclaiming Christ and enduring the hardships of discipleship.

Chapter 18 has Paul arriving in Corinth, where he meets **Priscilla** and Aquila, two Christians who had settled there after Claudius expelled all the Jews from Rome. Paul is of the same trade, that of tentmaker, so he lodges with them. He preaches in the synagogue on the Sabbath, trying to convince both Jews and Greeks. But they are opposed to the idea that Jesus is their Messiah. Paul then proceeds to preach to the Gentiles, and many of the Corinthians become believers and are baptized, including Crispus, the official of the synagogue, along with his entire household. A vision of the Lord tells Paul to stay in Corinth, for there is much work to be done there. He stays for eighteen months.

But the Jews succeed in having Paul arrested and brought before the tribunal in front of Gallio, the proconsul of Achaia. But he is not interested in this internal war of words and frees Paul. The Jews then seize Sosthenes, the official of the synagogue (possibly the successor to Crispus after he became a Christian), and beat him.

> She was a true partner in faith, not only to her husband, but to Paul, more than equal to the task of proclaiming Christ and enduring the hardships of discipleship.

After his time in Corinth, Paul sails for Ephesus, accompanied by Priscilla and Aquila. He ends his second missionary journey by greeting the churches in Jerusalem and Antioch in Syria. He then goes through the regions of Galatia and Phrygia to encourage the disciples. While Paul is away from Ephesus, a Jew named Apollos arrives and speaks in the synagogue. He teaches about Jesus, but knows only the baptism of John. Priscilla and Aquila take him aside to explain the way of God more accurately. He then crosses over to Achaia and greatly helps the believers. There are no "Spirit" verses mentioned in chapter 18.

Priscilla of Rome

DAY ONE

A disciple is many things—a student, a teacher and a believer in a certain doctrine or teaching.

WHAT IS TRUE DISCIPLESHIP?

A disciple is many things—a student, a teacher, and a believer in a certain doctrine or teaching. The word "disciple" was applied to the Twelve that Jesus called to assist Him in His ministry. The word "disciple" was also synonymous with believer or Christian in the early church. But the most important definition of the word disciple is *follower*. What is your definition of a disciple?

_____

_____

Perhaps the most trouble we have with the word *follower* is that it means we are not the leader! But Jesus himself was a *follower* of the will of his father. He did what God told him to do. The transfiguration that took place on the mountain was to show His disciples that He was chosen by God for His purposes. The *Eerdman's Bible Dictionary* adds: ". . . it [the transfiguration of Jesus] clearly declared the identity of Jesus as the Messiah and Son of God, and provided assurance for the disciples that the path Jesus had chosen was indeed sanctioned by God."[1] The word "transfiguration" literally means to transform or *change* in form, as Jesus was transfigured—*changed*—before His disciples. It was revealed to them that Jesus was *following* what God had willed for Him. In the same way, we are followers of Christ when we do the things that He teaches.

In general, to follow Jesus means to be *changed* from within so that there is a visible *change* in the outer lifestyle. There's that "C" word that none of us likes to apply to ourselves! But there is a change—a transformation or transfiguration—that needs to take place. The Holy Spirit is transforming us all into the image of Christ when we *follow* Jesus (2 Corinthians 3:18). And our part is this: *"Do not be conformed to this world, but be transformed by the renewing of your minds, so that you may discern what is the will of God—what is good and acceptable and perfect."* (Romans 12:2).

APPLY What does being a follower of Jesus mean to you? Do you think you are living out God's will for your life?

_____

_____

_____

_____

Jesus Himself gave us many definitions and descriptions of what it means to be *His* follower. Maybe the most important one is found in John 13:35: *"By this everyone will know that you are my disciples, if you have love for one another."* This was His commandment: *". . . that you love one another as I have loved you"* (John 15:12).

But our human love for one other is always imperfect and often hurtful. But we are to strive daily to *change* that into something that looks more like the love of God for us through Jesus Christ. What does that look like and how do we do it? The following is only the tip of the iceberg:

> We love our enemies
> We do good to those who hate us
> We bless those who curse us
> We pray for those who abuse us
> We expect nothing in return for what we give
> We act mercifully toward one other
> We don't judge
> We do to others as we would have them do to us
> We forgive
> We pray for God's will to be done in our lives

📖 Read the beginning of the Sermon on the Mount, called the Beatitudes, in Matthew 5:1–11. (Read all of chapters five, six, and seven in Matthew for the full sermon). From these passages, what other ways can we love each other like Jesus loved us?

_____

_____

_____

Another way to be a disciple is to be *like* the teacher. *"A disciple is not above the teacher, but everyone who is fully qualified will be like the teacher"* (Luke 6:40). How do we even begin to be like Jesus? *Follow* Him, allow Him to *change* us in every way, and then begin to *act* like Him.

But we often fail, so Jesus asked, *"Why do you call me 'Lord, Lord,' and do not do what I tell you? I will show you what someone is like who comes to me, hears my words, and acts on them"* (Luke 6:46–47). He then proceeds to tell the story of the man who builds his house on a strong foundation, on rock, and the one who builds his house without a foundation, on sand (Luke 6:46–49; Matthew 7:24–27).

📖 Read these verses and write down what this parable means to you.

_____

_____

_____

_____

The man who builds on rock is the one who understands the lifestyle of Jesus Christ, proceeds to change more into His likeness, and begins to act like him. The one who builds on sand is the one who does not understand, therefore, does not think change is necessary. He or she may call Jesus *Lord*, but still not do what he tells them to do.

"By this everyone will know that you are my disciples, if you have love for one another."

John 13:35

How do we even begin to be like Jesus? Follow Him, allow Him to change us in every way, and then begin to act like Him.

Another way to be a disciple of Jesus is to learn everything about who He was while He walked this earth, what He taught and how He lived. To be a disciple is to know the Word of God. *"If you continue in my word, you are truly my disciples; and you will know the truth, and the truth will make you free"* (John 8:31–32). Finally, to be a disciple is to teach others everything that he commanded. (Matthew 28:19–20) What else is necessary to become a true disciple of Jesus Christ?

_____

_____

_____

When we are followers of *Jesus,* we are made stronger than any earthly leader. We are able to lead with the characteristics of *Jesus*, and that is *true* leadership and discipleship.

APPLY   How are you living like a true disciple of Jesus Christ?

_____

_____

_____

_____

Priscilla of Rome

DAY TWO

"After this Paul left Athens and went to Corinth. There he found a Jew named Aquila, a native of Pontus, who had recently come from Italy with his wife Priscilla, because Claudius had ordered all Jews to leave Rome."

Acts 18:1–2

A TRUE MARRIAGE PARTNERSHIP

Verse in Which the Woman Appears: Acts 18:1–2
"After this Paul left Athens and went to Corinth. There he found a Jew named Aquila, a native of Pontus, who had recently come from Italy with his wife **Priscilla***, because Claudius had ordered all Jews to leave Rome."*

Greek, *Priska, Priskilla***, meaning "worthy."**

Even though we are told that Aquila is from Pontus, Scripture does not tell us Priscilla's origins, but scholars suggest that she was connected with the gens Prisca, a noble Roman family. The name Prisca is found as a family name in the earliest Roman annals and is given prominence in Roman inscriptions and legends.

Priscilla or Prisca is mentioned six times in the New Testament, always with her husband, Aquila. She is one of the major female figures in Acts and is mentioned there three times and another three times in other letters (Romans 16:3; 1 Corinthians 16:19; 2 Timothy 4:19).

Read these other references to Priscilla. What do these passages tell us about her importance to Paul and the church?

_____

_____

_____

_____

Not only is Priscilla identified by name, but her name appears first in four of the six times they are mentioned, which inverts the usual practice. This may indicate either the more prominent or active role of Priscilla in the church or her higher social position. Garry Wills, in *What Paul Meant,* adds, "Some opine that she preceded her husband in baptism and helped instruct him, or took the lead in their evangelizing activities; Luke puts Barnabas before Paul in the early days of their evangelizing, which may indicate that Paul was the junior partner at that point (Acts 11:30; 12:25; 13:2)."[2] She was clearly considered an equal by both her husband and Paul and was granted the status of coworker by the apostle (Romans 16:3).

The church in Rome existed before Paul arrived, as it did in other places he visited. Priscilla and Aquila were among the first Jewish Christians in Rome, where scholars say they established a house church and probably taught in the synagogue as well. The *New International Version* (NIV) *Study Bible* adds in its notes: "Since no mention is made of a conversion and since a partnership is established in work, it is likely that they were already Christians. They may have been converted in Rome by those returning from Pentecost or by others at a later time."[3]

Jouette M. Bassler in *Women in Scripture,* states, "Thus it appears that they were already active as missionaries for Christ in Rome before their encounter with Paul."[4] However, there are other scholars who believe they did not become Christians until they met Paul in Corinth.

Priscilla and Aquila were forced to flee in the year AD 49 when Claudius ejected all Jews from Rome. According to the Roman historian Suetonius, fighting among the believing and nonbelieving Jews over the proclamation of Jesus Christ caused this expulsion. How does this compare with how the Jews reacted every time Paul preached to them?

_____

_____

_____

That Priscilla and Aquila are always mentioned together gives credence to the partnership they had, both in their marriage and in their work for the gospel. In their marriage, they appear to have one of those new relationships as a couple that gives us insight into the changed status of women in Christianity.

Jewish wives were subject to their husbands. But Priscilla and Aquila were models of the new order of things, in which gender became irrelevant. God Himself had first created male and female that way: *"So God created humankind in his image, in the image of God he created them; male and female he created them"* (Genesis 1:27).

I think it is interesting to note that often we don't hear the whole verse in Genesis, which refers to Eve being a *partner* to Adam. The whole verse says: *"Then the Lord God said, 'It is not good that the man should be alone; I will make him a helper as his partner"* (Genesis 2:18). Various translations use only *partner* (NEB), or a *suitable companion* to help him (TEV).

What is your interpretation of this Genesis passage?

_____

_____

She is one of the major female figures in Acts, and is mentioned there three times and another three times in Paul's letters (Romans 16:3; 1 Corinthians 16:19; 2 Timothy 4:19).

In their marriage, they appear to have one of those new relationships as a couple that gives us insight into the changed status of women in Christianity.

We often hear that women are simply "helpmeets," inferring that this is a lesser position. But, helper, in this case, is not a demeaning position. Its fuller meaning is of one who aids someone who needs assistance, and who works *beside* rather than *beneath*. It is a true partnership when each partner *helps* the *other*. And now in the new Christian church, the relationship between men and women is restored and marriage is once again a true partnership. Whether we put this into practice in our own marriages may depend on how closely we follow Jesus—how far we are along in becoming His true disciple.

 How do you feel about this definition of a true marriage partnership?

_____

_____

_____

Another new aspect of her being whole in Jesus Christ is that as a Christian, Priscilla had immediate access to God through Christ, again something Jewish women were not "allowed." Christian women do not need to go through men or any other human intermediary to commune directly with God.

Scripture does not tell us why Priscilla and Aquila settle in Corinth, but perhaps this was another of God's plans to put them in touch with Paul so that they could help him begin and sustain a Christian church there. God never limits his purposes to men only.

"**There he found a Jew named Aquila, a native of Pontus, who had recently come from Italy with his wife Priscilla, because Claudius had ordered all Jews to leave Rome.**"

Acts 18:2

PAUL MEETS HIS MATCH: A WORKING PARTNERSHIP

Verse in Which the Woman Appears: Acts 18:2
"There he [Paul] found a Jew named Aquila, a native of Pontus, who had recently come from Italy with his wife Priscilla, because Claudius had ordered all Jews to leave Rome."

Priscilla and Aquila shared Paul's trade as tentmakers, or probably more accurately, leatherworkers. The hair of goats was used to weave cloth. They were apparently prosperous artisans; since their home was large enough to become a base for Christians in Corinth after Paul began lodging with them there and also later in Ephesus. In 1 Corinthians 1:11, Paul mentions another woman named Chloe, who *could* also have been the leader of another house church in Corinth. As for their partnership in the work of the Gospel, Priscilla and Aquila were a missionary "team" who ministered and traveled with Paul. They were well known by the early church as important and well-traveled missionaries and traveling companions of Paul. He also mentions other male-female teams at the end of Romans 16, which indicates that they were common. Paul looked on everyone he worked with, including Priscilla, as *equal* partners in the spread of the gospel and for the sake of the gospel. It wasn't about him or anyone else except Christ.

Another quality of discipleship is this recognition that it isn't about us, but about God and working *together* for the gospel, rather than in competition with each other for some kind of attention for ourselves. That was a problem from the beginnings of the Christian church and is still a problem in today's church.

APPLY How do the people of your church work together for the sake of the gospel? How does any division affect the spread of the Word?

_____

_____

_____

_____

In the Corinthian letters, there are many admonitions about getting along with each other and not fighting, but rather being *"united in the same mind and the same purpose"* (1 Corinthians 1:10). In Paul's second letter to the Corinthians, he states that *"we are workers with you for your joy, because you stand firm in the faith"* (2 Corinthians 23:24). Priscilla, Aquila, and Paul were of the same mind and purpose regarding the spread of the gospel.

Priscilla and Aquila in their house church in Corinth ministered *to* and *with* Paul for eighteen months. Corinth was a major commercial port of the Hellenistic world, characterized by typical Greek culture, with an emphasis on philosophy and wisdom, and a center of rampant immorality. Up to this point, the city was probably Paul's greatest challenge, as it contained twelve temples, one of which was the temple of Aphrodite, the goddess of love, whose worshipers practiced religious prostitution. In his letters to the Corinthians, Paul mentions this wickedness many times.

📖 Read Acts 18:18-19. How does this give insight into how they ministered to the pagan culture of Corinth? What does it say about how we are to "be in Christ?"

_____

_____

_____

How do you think God gifted Priscilla for leadership in such a place?

_____

_____

_____

"After staying there (Corinth) for a considerable time, Paul said farewell to the believers and sailed for Syria, accompanied by Priscilla and Aquila. . . . When they reached Ephesus, he left them there. . . ." (Acts 18:18-19)

Priscilla and Aquila accompanied Paul to Ephesus, where they once again set up another house church. They apparently had the economic independence to acquire yet another house in Ephesus large enough to become a base for the Christian church. These house churches provided enough space for worship, the preaching of the gospel, the breaking of bread, and prayer.

Ephesus was equal to Corinth in its worship of idols and was a center of magic arts and superstition in the ancient world. The great temple of Artemis (Greek) or Diana (Latin) also possessed the right of asylum and

Paul looked on everyone he worked with, including Priscilla, as equal partners in the spread of the gospel and for the sake of the gospel.

Priscilla and Aquila in their house church in Corinth, ministered to and with Paul for eighteen months.

They apparently had the economic independence to acquire yet another house in Ephesus large enough to become a base for the Christian church.

thus had become the home to many criminals, who were "protected" by the goddess—not an easy place to proclaim a "new" way and person to worship. In Ephesus, they ministered in the shadow of the looming temple of Artemis, the great goddess of the Ephesians. The strength of her hold on the Ephesians was great. Devotion to her and the selling of silver shrines caused a run-in with Paul, known as "the revolt of the silversmiths."

While in Ephesus, Priscilla and Aquila apparently saved Paul's life and exposed themselves to danger in the process. Their unspecified intervention, which could have been connected with the silversmiths, won them Paul's endless gratitude, as reported in Romans 16:3–4, where he says: *"Greet Prisca and Aquila, who work with me in Christ Jesus, and who risked their necks for my life, to whom not only I give thanks, but also all the churches of the Gentiles."*

How do you think our ministers of today stay focused in the face of modern idols?

_____

_____

_____

In Paul's letter to the Ephesians, he tells the Christians there how to become true disciples of Christ.

"You were taught to put away your former way of life, your old self, corrupt and deluded by its lusts, and to be renewed in the spirit of your minds, and to clothe yourselves with the new self, created according to the likeness of God in true righteousness and holiness" (Ephesians 4:22–24).

How hard do you think it was for a woman like Priscilla to minister in these places? How did her faith and trust in God help her?

_____

_____

_____

Priscilla of Rome

DAY FOUR

A TEACHER OF TEACHERS: A MORE ACCURATE WITNESS

Verse in Which the Woman Appears: Acts 18:26
*"He (Apollos) began to speak boldly in the synagogue; but when **Priscilla** and Aquila heard him, they took him aside and explained the Way of God to him more accurately."*

In Ephesus, Priscilla and her husband become the teachers of the brilliant Old Testament scholar, Apollos. One of the most impressive aspects of the spiritual influence of Priscilla and Aquila was the way in which they were used to open the eyes of this great teacher. His training and teaching were based only on the baptism of John, and he, as yet, did not know Jesus as the Messiah or the baptism of the Holy Spirit. He was teaching only part of the story.

Priscilla and Aquila were present at one of his popular presentations. As they listened, they detected Apollos' lack of the full knowledge of the gospel, and they quietly took him aside to correct this deficiency. It is to their credit that they took him aside to do this privately so they did not shame him in public. It is both Priscilla and Aquila who gave him a fuller and more accurate instruction about Christ as the Messiah. They taught him about the baptism of the Holy Spirit and brought him to an understanding of conversion through Christ.

Apollos became even bolder and mightier in the preaching of the gospel as a result of the teaching he received by these two spirit-filled and enlightened believers. Paul later recruits him for help in Corinth. The *New Interpreter's Study Bible* notes say: "This is a rare instance in which Luke portrays a woman disciple as teaching—and to a prominent theologian."[5] But there is no hint in this story that Priscilla is out of bounds in teaching Apollos, or that she is entering territory reserved only for men. She is a learned woman in her own right, a capable teacher and full of the Holy Spirit. Arlandson puts it this way: "A mere female tentmaker (or leatherworker) instructs the well-studied, powerful, wealthy, male rhetorician."[6] It is God through the Holy Spirit who empowers each of us to use the gift he gives us.

How does this relate to the original twelve that Jesus called as his disciples?

_____

_____

_____

Paul refers to Apollos nine more times in his letters. If it hadn't been for Priscilla and Aquila, Apollos would not have had a complete understanding of Christ. Anyone who knows Christ and whom the Spirit has gifted for teaching should be able to use that gift in the church, as Priscilla did then. Are there those today who preach and teach who do not know Christ? Most likely there are.

APPLY If you met someone teaching the Christian message and you knew that it was only part of the story, or that the interpretation of it was flawed in some way, what would you do?

_____

_____

How has your church either discouraged or encouraged women to participate in the full spectrum of ministry? How do you reconcile this story with 2 Timothy 2:12, where it says that women should not teach a man? (This is a whole lesson in itself and is often misinterpreted).

_____

_____

_____

_____

"He began to speak boldly in the synagogue; but when Priscilla and Aquila heard him, they took him aside and explained the Way of God to him more accurately."

Acts 18:26

It was both Priscilla and Aquila who gave him a fuller and more accurate instruction about Christ. They taught him about the baptism of the Holy Spirit and brought him to an understanding of conversion through Christ.

In the remaining two New Testament references to Priscilla and Aquila, they are named by Paul. *"The churches of Asia send greetings. Aquila and Prisca, together with the church in their house, greet you warmly in the Lord"* (1 Corinthians 16:19), and *"Greet Prisca and Aquila, and the household of Onisephorus"* (2 Timothy 4:19).

After the emperor's edict was lifted in the year 54, Priscilla and her husband may have returned to Rome, where they re-established a house church and continued their *team* ministry. Some historians believe that Priscilla and Aquila were martyred in Nero's persecution of the Christians in the year 64. But Priscilla's legacy lives on. And Edith Deen offers in her book, *All of the Women of the Bible,* "One of the oldest catacombs of Rome—the Coemeterium Priscilla, was named in her honor. And a church, 'Titulus St. Prisca,' was erected on the Aventine in Rome. It bore the inscription 'Titulus Aquilla et Prisca.' Prisca's name appears often on monuments of Rome. And 'Acts of St. Prisca' was a legendary writing popular in the tenth century."[7]

She was clearly one of the most influential women in the early church. Tertullian records, *"By the holy Prisca, the gospel is preached."* Her life and ministry speak reams about the role of women that God intended for His church.

Without *partnership* and working *together* in everything related to the gospel of Jesus Christ, God's purposes can be greatly diminished. Do you know any women today who have been kept from using their gifts in the church?

_____

_____

_____

Priscilla was given the privilege of serving God in many ways—as co-leader of house churches in Corinth, Ephesus, and Rome, of supporting Paul's ministry, of teaching the proper understanding of Jesus and of spreading the gospel *with* Paul. They worked *together,* they traveled *together* and they ministered *together.*

APPLY What part of Priscilla's story do you relate to the most? Why?

_____

_____

_____

Does Priscilla's story change your attitudes toward Paul in regard to women's roles in the body of Christ? Why or why not?

_____

_____

_____

_____

_____

_____

_____

Priscilla was clearly one of the most influential women in the early church. . . . Her life and ministry speak reams about the role of women that God intended for His church.

FOR ME TO FOLLOW GOD

Life Principle for Lesson Ten: True Discipleship

Priscilla or Prisca, as Paul affectionately called her, was a giant in the early spread of Christianity. She was the epitome of what I believe God intended for women—equal partner and helper in every way—to her husband, to her coworkers and to her church. Priscilla openly and freely preached the Word, traveled with Paul as an associate equal to men like Barnabas, Silas, and Timothy, and taught one of the most brilliant scholars of the time the right way of God. She accomplished this by *believing* that she belonged to God and was freed by Jesus Christ. How does this relate to other Christian leaders or converts we have met so far?

_____

_____

_____

She went about being Christian without concerning herself with what others thought, said, or did. She got on with living out the gospel in spite of persecution, controversy, disagreement and idol worship in Rome, Corinth, and Ephesus, *sure* of who she was and whose she was. And she went to her death still holding onto herself in Christ. He was her strength, her hope, her life and her eternal life. In Him she lived, moved, and had her being.

 What inspires you most about her story? How does it help you with your own witness?

_____

_____

_____

I wish more women could be treated as equal partners in their marriages. The abuse of women in many marriages, including Christian marriages, is appalling. If there is no partnership in a marriage, there is no understanding of God's purposes for women *or* men.

I wish more women could be treated as equals in the workplace. Even in the twenty-first century, we're not there yet. Even in high professional positions, women are still harassed, put down, or not taken seriously. If there is no partnership in the workplace, there is diminished productivity and little understanding of how much ability and sensitivity women bring to "work."

And, more than any other, I wish more women could be treated as equals in the church of Jesus Christ. God's opinion of women is very high. The Holy Spirit gifts many women for leadership roles in the church, and the church desperately needs women in those roles. Women can add insights that men don't even think of. And Christian women are among the best teachers around.

> *She got on with living out the gospel in spite of persecution, controversy, disagreement and idol worship in Rome, Corinth and Ephesus, sure of who and whose she was.*

Women and men need to submit to God in all situations, not to any human authority (see Acts 5:29).

Women do not need a man's permission or approval to do anything in ministry because God is the giver of life, talent, and identity. It is God who calls women to himself and to the work in His church. Women and men need to submit to *God* in *all* situations first, not to any human "authority" (see Acts 5:29).

I wish more women could have the confidence and faith of Priscilla. Priscilla got hers from Jesus Christ, not from any other person. And because of that, she was able to function as a *full* member of the church. And to his credit, Paul loved her as a sister in Christ, respected her gifts and welcomed her help and partnership in the spread of the gospel. How would the church of Jesus Christ be different today if more women were like Priscilla?

_____

_____

_____

How would the church of Jesus Christ be different today if more men could partner with women in its work and witness?

_____

_____

_____

Our churches and our world need more women like Priscilla. And they need more partnerships with men like Paul, who are open to their gifts and help.

Our cities today are not unlike Rome, Corinth, and Ephesus. They are full of evil, rampant immorality, idol worship and unbelief. And like the first-century church, our churches are also full of controversy, disagreement, and inequality. Our churches and our world need more women like Priscilla. And they need more partnerships with men like Paul, who are open to their gifts and help.

Read Paul's letters to the Romans, to the Ephesians and to the Corinthians to get a full perspective on what ministry was like for Paul, Priscilla and Aquila.

 Lord of partnership, restore us to the lives you intended for us. Help us work together in our homes, in our marriages, in the workplace and especially in your church, that we might show the world your true intentions and purposes. Transform us into the image of your son, Jesus Christ, that we might be his true disciples in all we say and do. In Jesus' name, Amen.

Works Cited

1. Allen C. Myers, Revision Editor, *The Eerdman's Bible Dictionary* (Grand Rapids, MI: William B. Eerdman's Publishing Company, 1987), 1016.

2. Garry Wills, *What Paul Meant* (New York, NY: Viking, Published by the Penguin Group, 2006), 93.

3. *The NIV Study Bible, 10th Anniversary Edition* (Grand Rapids, MI: The Zondervan Corporation, 1995), 1684.

4. Carol Meyers, General Editor; Toni Craven and Ross S. Kraemer, Associate Editors; *Women in Scripture, A Dictionary of Named and Unnamed Women in the Hebrew Bible, The Apocryphal/Deuterocanonical Books, and the New Testament* (Grand Rapids, MI/Cambridge, U.K., William B. Eerdman's Publishing Company, 2000), 136.

5. *The New Interpreter's Study Bible, New Revised Standard Version with the Apocrypha* (Nashville, TN: Abingdon Press, 2003), 1991.

6. James Malcolm Arlandson, *Women, Class, and Society in Early Christianity* (Peabody, MA: Hendrickson Publishers, 1997), 146.

7. Edith Deen, *All of the Women of the Bible* (New York, Harper & Brothers Publishers, 1955), 229.

Notes

11

Wives, Daughters, and a Sister

Family has always been important to God. In this lesson, we see how the female members of different families help each other, the church and Paul.

Transition: Chapter 19

Paul's third missionary journey takes him to Ephesus, where he stays for two years. There, God does "extraordinary miracles" through him. He heals the sick and casts out evil spirits. As a result, many people become believers and are baptized, including many who had practiced magic. He continues to encounter resistance from the Jews, but in spite of this, God's word is heard by *"all the residents of Asia, both Jews and Greeks"* (Acts 19:10).

Paul's next encounter is with the "power" that the pagan goddess, Artemis, has over the people of Ephesus. The silversmiths have a thriving business making silver shrines of her, and when they see Paul persuading many away from worshiping her (thus drawing much business away from them) they drag two of his traveling companions into the theater and cause a near-riot. The town clerk intervenes to stop the revolt, and Paul escapes with his life.

Transition: Chapter 20

Paul sails for Macedonia. He encourages the disciples all along the way and stops in Greece for three months. A plot to kill him is discovered, and he changes his route. While in Troas, he restores the life of a young man, Eutychus, who had fallen from a window and died.

In this lesson, we see how the female members of different families help each other, the church and Paul.

As he is eager to be in Jerusalem for Pentecost, he sails past Ephesus to Miletus, where he meets the elders from Ephesus to encourage them to keep up the ministry he started with them. He tells them to keep watch over the people and warns them about false teachers who will come in and distort the message of Christ, including even some of them.

Chapter 21 has Paul continuing on his way toward Jerusalem with stops in Tyre, Ptolemais, and Caesarea. He greets the disciples in each place. Before leaving Tyre, the disciples with their **wives** and children, kneel on the beach and pray for his safe passage. In Caesarea, he stays at the house of Philip the Evangelist, who has **four unmarried daughters with the gift of prophecy**. While in Caesarea, a prophet named Agabus comes from Judea and tells Paul that he will be bound and imprisoned in Jerusalem. But Paul replies that he is ready to die for Christ.

After arriving in Jerusalem, Paul meets with the elders and tells them all the things he has done among the Gentiles. When they hear it, they praise God. They tell him how many thousands of believers there are among the Jews, but many are still zealous for the law. They suggest that Paul go through the rite of purification so the Jews can see that he also observes the law.

But the Jews from Asia see him in the Temple, stir up the crowd, seize Paul and try to kill him. Word gets to the tribune, or military officer in charge that Jerusalem is in an uproar. Soldiers are called in to save him from certain death. He is arrested, bound in chains and taken to the barracks. After determining Paul's identity, he is given permission to speak to the people. Verses that deal with the Holy Spirit include: 19:2 21; 20:22, 23, 28; 21:4, 11.

The Importance of Family

I think we all long to be part of a family, especially in these times when so many families are broken or scattered. We not only need love and support, but we need families we can depend on in times of trouble. We also need families of faith. But if we don't have a perfect human family (no one does) or if we have no family at all, we can still be sure that we are part of the family of God because He created us to be *his children*. The concept of family runs all the way through the Bible, and it is always important to God. God *planned* for us to be his children.

In the beginning, it was about God the Father and God the Son (John 1:1–4). Jesus was with the Father from the beginning of creation and nothing was made without him.

☐ Read these verses along with John 1:10–18. How do the Father and the Son relate at this point?

_____

_____

_____

God, our heavenly Father, created all of the families of the earth and promised that He would be their God. *"I will be the God of all the families of Israel, and they shall be my people"* (Jeremiah 31:1). In Acts, Peter reminds the Jews

But if we don't have perfect human families (no one does), or if we have no families at all, we can still be sure that we are part of the family of God, because He created us to be His children.

that through the descendants of Abraham, *"all the families of the earth shall be blessed"* (Acts 3:25). Throughout the Old Testament, God continually walks with His people, the Jews, and watches over them, even in their disobedience. And when disobedience and sin overwhelms them, God has a plan for their salvation *and* ours. God's Son, Jesus Christ, comes into the world.

📖 Read John 1:10–13. How does God include all of us in His plan of salvation? Write down the verse about how we become children of God.

_____

_____

_____

In the incarnation, another family is involved. God is made flesh in Jesus Christ, born as a baby into a human *family*. Read the story of the promised Messiah in Luke 2:10–12. Read also the genealogy of Jesus in Matthew 1:1–16 to see how many human families are included in the miracle of the incarnation. How many of these names are you familiar with? Research some of the family names in your own background.

_____

_____

_____

It is through Jesus Christ that we are *all* called to be God's children. God, through Christ, has *adopted us* as His own children. We have a heavenly inheritance as heirs of God and joint heirs of Christ (Romans 8:16–17). *"See what love the Father has given us, that we should be called the children of God; and that is what we are"* (1 John 3:1). . . . *"for in Christ Jesus you are all children of God through faith"* (Galatians 3:26). God calls us to be His children, and has adopted us as His own and has promised us an inheritance with Christ. And *we* must do our part and cling to Christ and walk in his ways. How do we inherit the kingdom of God? What are some of the ways we can be like Christ?

_____

_____

_____

Jesus gave us a final definition of family when He redefined it to mean that we are all brothers and sisters in Him. *"Whoever does the will of God is my brother and sister and mother"* (Matthew 12:50). In Christ, we have all become brothers and sisters in faith.

APPLY Who are your brothers and sisters (or mothers or fathers) in faith? Write how they encourage you to stay in the family of God?

_____

_____

_____

> **"But to all who received him, who believed in his name, he gave power to become children of God."**
>
> **John 1:12**

> **Jesus gave us a final definition of family when He redefined it to mean that we are all brothers and sisters in Him.**

"When our days there were ended, we left and proceeded on our journey; and all of them, with wives and children, escorted us outside the city. There we knelt down on the beach and prayed and said farewell to one another. Then we went on board the ship, and they returned home."

Acts 21:5–6

WIVES OF TYRE: A SPIRITUAL FAMILY

Verse in Which the Women Appear: Acts 21:5–6
*"When our days there were ended, we left and proceeded on our journey; and all of them, with **wives** and children, escorted us outside the city. There we knelt down on the beach and prayed and said farewell to one another. Then we went on board the ship, and they returned home."*

Here again, we see Luke making it a point to mention *both* women and men, even children, in the text. Women were among the disciples present to bid farewell to Paul on his final missionary journey to Jerusalem. At a time when women were restricted from public places, these female Christian disciples appear right alongside their husbands (and children) to see Paul off.

 Have you ever been prevented from appearing somewhere with your spouse, such as at a private club or other single-gender group? How did that make you feel?

_____

_____

_____

In reading the passage, it *appears* that the disciples are male and they are simply accompanied by their wives. However, the Greek does not use the word wives, but says: *"escorting us all with women and children."* The Greek word for woman and wife (*gynaikes*) is the same. Some scholars say that the more accurate translation is *"and all of them, with women and children."* Ross S. Kraemer in *Women in Scripture* adds: "That the women and children are presented as sending off Paul and his companions would also seem to imply that they, too, are 'Christians' (the term itself does not occur here; it occurs only once, in Acts 11:26)."[1]

Gail R. O'Day, in the *Women's Bible Commentary,* says: "Acts 21:5 actually describes the inclusiveness of the Christian community at Tyre. Men, women, and children pray with Paul and bid him farewell."[2] Christian women have gained equality in Christ that transcends their own cultures. This unity is reminiscent of that very first scene in the house in Jerusalem, when the women were praying with the men.

 How do you think these women felt that they were allowed to appear in public with their husbands *and* children?

_____

_____

_____

_____

It is impossible to define them further in terms of occupation (or leadership in the church) but they probably reflected city life, Tyre being one of the most important port cities in Phoenicia. The story of Dorcas and the widows of Joppa, south of Tyre, and also on the coast, could shed some light on possible similarities as to the activities of women in the church. What would be the similarities between Dorcas and these women?

_____

_____

_____

There is no mention here of a church at Tyre, but the fact that Luke says, *"We looked up the disciples"* indicates the presence of one. It has been suggested that one was established soon after Stephen's martyrdom, when the faithful fled Jerusalem and preached the gospel wherever they went. And Paul and Barnabas knew of the church there, since they had visited there (in Phoenicia) to report the conversion of the Gentiles (Acts 15:3).

It is also possible that the people were already familiar with the gospel even before anyone arrived, since Jesus *"went away to the district of Tyre and Sidon,"* where He healed the Syro-Phoenician woman's daughter. And people from that region were among the *"great multitude"* that came from Galilee to hear Jesus preach—*"they came to him in great numbers from Judea, Jerusalem, Idumea, beyond the Jordan, and the region around Tyre and Sidon"* (Mark 3:8; Luke 6:17–19). They had possibly already heard the good news directly from the mouth of Jesus, and that, as with the Samaritan woman at the well, may have already resulted in many conversions. How did Jesus open the door for the church in Tyre?

_____

_____

_____

Paul and his team stayed in Tyre for a week, doing what they always did when they visited the disciples—encouraging them. The disciples then, with whole families, escorted him out of the city to the beach, where they knelt down and prayed for them. *Today's English Version* (TEV) says that they *all* did this. Women and children were all part of this prayer meeting, just as they were all together just as they were all together in prayer at Pentecost.

Arlandson concludes that "this public participation [of women] accomplishes three feats: it elevates Christian women to parity with pagan women; Christian women are also allowed in public; and this in turn elevates, to some degree at least, Christian women to parity with Christian men."[3] In Christ there is no male or female—all are one in the Spirit and one in the Lord (see Galatians 3:28). There is a tremendous unity and acceptance of each other between these early Christians. The fact that they appear openly and unified in public as Christian women and men could have great impact on those who saw them. They are, in a sense, publicly "living out their faith." The impact on the women has, in one way, already happened in that they feel free to do this.

APPLY How is this unity expressed in today's church? In your church?

_____

_____

_____

_____

Christian women had gained equality in Christ that transcended their own culture.

It is interesting to note the similarity between this scene on the beach and the one described in Acts 20:36–38, when Paul leaves Miletus:

> *"When he had finished speaking, he knelt down with them all and prayed. There was much weeping among them all; they embraced Paul and kissed him, grieving especially because of what he had said, that they would not see him again. Then they brought him to the ship."*

"The next day we left and came to Caesarea; and we went into the house of Philip the evangelist, one of the seven, and stayed with him. He had four unmarried daughters who had the gift of prophecy."

Acts 21:8–9

THE DAUGHTERS OF PHILIP: TWO GENERATIONS OF WITNESSES

The Psalms are full of passages about God being faithful to all generations. An example is Psalms 89:1: *"I will sing of your steadfast love, O Lord, forever with my mouth I will proclaim your faithfulness to all generations."* And God calls families of all kinds to himself to proclaim His faithfulness. Many times he calls multiple generations of the same family to his service, as in families who have several generations of ministers, missionaries, teachers, musicians, or prophets. In the case of Philip the Evangelist, who had taken the gospel to the Samaritans, the Ethiopian eunuch, and many other people and places up the coast of the Mediterranean, he has four daughters, who minister as prophetesses.

 Does your family have two or more generations who have proclaimed the gospel in any way?

_____

_____

_____

In Acts, God is already using the second generation of those first Christians to continue in his service. And the prophecy of Joel (Acts 2:17–18), quoted by Peter at Pentecost, is also already being fulfilled in this generation. The daughters are prophesying. God is being faithful to all the generations *through* each generation.

The Verse in Which the Women Appear: Acts 21:9
"The next day we left and came to Caesarea; and we went into the house of Philip the evangelist, one of the seven, and stayed with him. "He had **four unmarried daughters who had the gift of prophecy.**"

There is one single verse about the four daughters of Philip. We are told only two things about them: they are unmarried and they have the gift of prophecy. Some have suggested that Luke's identification of Philip's daughters as unmarried is significant. The prophetic gift among women seems to be with those who are unmarried or virgins. In 1 Corinthians 7:34, Paul says: *"And the unmarried woman and the virgin are anxious about the affairs of the Lord, so that they may be holy in body and spirit."* Like Paul himself, they may have chosen to remain unmarried to devote themselves exclusively to God's work.

Only one other thing is sure—they have the gift of prophecy. Other translations say *"who proclaimed God's word,"* (TEV) and *"all of whom spoke by the Spirit of God"* (JBP). The Greek says, *"four virgins prophesying."*

Prophecy can be defined as "the communication of a divine message through a human messenger" and "one who interprets divine revelation." These four women have been given their own unique spiritual endowment, *not* because of their father's fame, but by the *Spirit's choosing and gifting of them*.

Prophecy was considered a significant gift in the early church. In Paul's first letter to the Corinthians, he defines how important this gift is to the church.

📖 Read 1 Corinthians 14:1–4 and write down the ways in which prophecy is so important. Read about the gifts of the Spirit in 1 Corinthians 12:8–10.

_____

_____

_____

 Do you know anyone who has been given the gift of prophesy? How is it manifested?

_____

_____

Rose Sallberg Kam in *Their Stories, Our Stories,* adds more insight into this important gift:

> Paul lists prophecy as second only to apostleship among ministries, and second only to love among gifts of the Spirit. In his time, prophecy was a ministry distinguished from speaking in tongues and associated rather, with proclamation and teaching. According to 1 Corinthians 14:1–6 and Acts 13:1–3, prophets and teachers presided at worship, made official decisions, and commissioned others for special missions.[4]

Here we are given some insight into the fact that prophecy in the early church was associated with other ministries. And when there was a divine revelation spoken, there were those who made sure that the message agreed with the accepted beliefs and customs of the early church, thus preventing many false prophets from invading the community. False prophets became an increasing problem in the church later on, and have invaded the church even up to the present. Referring again to 1 Corinthians 14:1–4, tell why prophecy was more important than speaking in tongues. Who are the false prophets of today?

_____

_____

_____

In this verse about Philip's daughters, we have an example of Luke's tendency to emphasize the transformed role of women in Christianity—at times. Here he limits himself to simply introducing them. He does not have them doing anything in this story, nor does he tell about any of their prophecies. He is perhaps being very careful not to upset his audience or threaten the social order of the day. In fact, he places a male prophet, Agabus, at the scene to prophesy about Paul's fate in Jerusalem. (He is also the one who

These four women have been given their own unique spiritual endowment, not because of their father's fame, but by the Spirit's choosing and gifting of them.

In this verse about them, we have an example of Luke's tendency to mention the transformed role of women in Christianity—at times.

predicted the severe famine in Acts 11:28.) There are other references in Acts to the fact that there were prophets in the various churches (Acts 15:32; 11:27; 13:1). Can we possibly deduce from this that the four daughters of Philip were the prophetesses present and working in the church at Caesarea? Unfortunately, we can't be sure.

 How do you think God might have used these women in his church?

_____

_____

_____

The church historian Eusebius says that late-second century tradition reports Philip's daughters moving to Hierapolis in Phrygia (present-day Turkey), where they served as prophets, and where they are buried. References to their burial place in documents of the second century suggest that their influence was long lasting. He viewed them as "belonging to the first stage of apostolic succession." Other traditions say that one or more of them were later married and that Philip gave his daughters in marriage.

The daughters of Philip are part of an evangelistic family and have been given gifts of the Spirit for use in proclaiming the gospel. Since none of their prophecies are told, it is hard to tell their impact, but if they practiced their gift, they must have made a major impact. Tradition tells us that they were quite successful in their witness and prophecy in Asia.

Transition: Chapter 22
Paul is addressing the Jews in Jerusalem in the Hebrew language. He tells them his own history—where he was born, that he was taught in Jerusalem by Gamaliel, and how he is as zealous about God as they are. He tells them how he persecuted the Christians and then about his conversion on the way to Damascus and his vision of Jesus telling him of his mission.

But the crowd does not want to listen to him anymore and again calls for his death. The tribune, or military officer, takes him into the barracks and attempts to learn the reason for the crowd's reaction toward him. Paul tells him he is a Roman citizen and the order to flog him is repealed. The next day he is released and brought before the chief priests and the entire council of the Jews.

Wives, Daughters, and a Sister

DAY FOUR

PAUL'S SISTER: A FAMILY'S HELP IN DANGER

Transition: Chapter 23
Paul tells the council that he is Pharisee and that he is on trial because he teaches the resurrection of the dead. This causes a violent dissention between the Pharisees and the Sadducees because of their differing beliefs regarding resurrection and the existence of angels and spirits. The tribune again intervenes and takes him back to the barracks. The Lord appears to him and tells him to keep up his courage.

The next morning forty Jews plan to ambush and kill Paul. They tell the tribune that they must bring him down to them on the pretext that they want to examine his case further. But the son of **Paul's sister** learns of the ambush and goes to the barracks to tell Paul about it. Paul calls a centurion and tells him to take his nephew to the tribune to report it. Paul's nephew tells the tribune what he knows about the plot to kill Paul. He is then dismissed by the tribune with the order, "Tell no one that you have informed me of this." (Acts 23:22).

The tribune orders the centurions to ready the horses for Paul for travel to Caesarea that night. He writes a letter to Felix the Governor, telling him that he finds nothing deserving death or imprisonment. Felix keeps Paul under guard in Herod's headquarters until his accusers arrive. The Holy Spirit is not specifically mentioned in chapters 22 and 23.

The Verse in Which the Woman Appears: Acts 23:16

"Now the son of **Paul's sister** *heard about the ambush; so he went and gained entrance to the barracks and told Paul."*

Paul's sister is a minor female figure mentioned in Acts, whose son plays a major role in keeping Paul from being killed. This is the only passage that has a specific reference to any of the apostle Paul's natural relatives, though at the end of the book of Romans, Paul greets Andronicus and Junia, *"my relatives who were in prison with me . . ."*; *"Greet my relative Herodion"*; and *"Lucius and Jason and Sosipater, my relatives"* (Romans 16:7, 11, 21). In the Greek, and in all three cases, the translation is *"the kinsmen of me."* This suggests that they *might* be blood relatives.

Paul's sister and her son evidently reside in Jerusalem, since that is where we meet them. Paul says later: *"All the Jews know my way of life from my youth, a life spent from the beginning among my own people and in Jerusalem"* (Acts 26:4). N. T. Wright, in *Acts for Everyone,* says:

> "This tells us, of course, something we didn't know and would love to know more about. Did Paul have lots of family members in Jerusalem? Were they Christians? How much contact did he have with them, and were they enthusiastic supporters of what he was doing or embarrassed by the attention he was drawing to the family? We know none of this. All we know is that the same night that Paul received a vision of the Lord telling him that he would make it safely to Rome, a little boy happened to be at the right place at the right time, pricked up his ears and knew what to do. It wouldn't be too unlikely, in a crowded city like Jerusalem."[5]

Paul's natural family is loyal and protective of him. The nephew's eagerness to save his uncle from imminent danger suggests that there are deep family ties.

APPLY Have you ever kept a family member from danger? Has another family member of yours ever protected you from danger?

_____

_____

_____

_____

_____

"Now the son of Paul's sister heard about the ambush; so he went and gained entrance to the barracks and told Paul."
Acts 23:16

Paul's sister and her son evidently reside in Jerusalem, since that is where we meet them.

Paul's natural family is loyal and protective of him. The nephew's eagerness to save his uncle from imminent danger suggests that there are deep family ties.

This story tells of a conspiracy planned by some of the Jews in Jerusalem to ambush and kill Paul while he is in Roman custody. This is the second of three attempts on Paul's life by his opponents in Jerusalem, the first described in Acts 21:31 and the third in Acts 25:3. But Paul sees a vision of the Lord telling him, *"Keep up your courage! For just as you have testified for me in Jerusalem, so you must bear witness also in Rome"* (Acts 23:11).

APPLY Have there been any times in your life when you felt the protection and assurance of God in difficult circumstances?

_____

_____

_____

Paul's unnamed nephew, son of his unnamed sister, learns about it and reports the plot to Paul. Some scholars suggest that he is just a boy, others say about twenty or in his twenties, but we cannot be certain of his age. Being part of Paul's family, do you think he or his mother were also in danger?

_____

_____

_____

He is able to gain entrance to the barracks where Paul is being held and tell him. Paul sends him to the tribune via one of the centurions to tell him of the plot. As a result, the tribune tells his nephew not to inform anyone about what he has told him.

APPLY Would you speak out about a dangerous plot against someone or keep quiet?

_____

_____

_____

Paul's unnamed sister's son, his unnamed nephew, protected Paul from being killed by an angry mob in Jerusalem.

The tribune orders the centurion to take Paul safely by night to Felix the Governor in Caesaera. They stop first in Antipatris, a town that is approximately thirty miles north of Jerusalem, but its exact location is uncertain. Caesarea is another twenty-eight miles from Antipatris. It is interesting to note that God used the Roman government to transport Paul safely to Caesarea. The Romans were very concerned with justice, and God's purpose is always achieved. He will use whomever he needs to in order to accomplish it.

Our earthly families protect us from many things, including danger. In this brief and only mention of Paul's earthly family, they are seen in the role of protectors. When we protect anyone from danger, especially our families, we are walking in the ways of God. Protection is something that God gives all of His children because He loves them so much. Psalms 12:7 says, *"You, O Lord, will protect us."* In turn, we protect our own families because we love them so much and are concerned with their safety and welfare.

Paul's unnamed sister's son, his unnamed nephew, protected Paul from being killed by a Jewish mob in Jerusalem. How? Because God's ways are not our ways. Just as he used a mere female tent worker to teach a renowned

Bible scholar, he used two unnamed relatives of Paul to save his life for the sake of the gospel. God can use anyone who is willing to be used by him. A fancy title, job, education (the twelve disciples were uneducated men), or any other *worldly* "qualification," is not necessary—just a willing heart and faith in a God who can do more than we can even think or imagine for the sake of His kingdom.

FOR ME TO FOLLOW GOD

Life Principle for Lesson Eleven: The Importance of Family

These three sections on seemingly minor figures in the early church and how God used them in major ways remind me a little of my performing days. As we say in the theater, "There are no small parts, just small actors." And yet, everyone still clamors for the starring role or a part that is more important than just a walk-on or cameo appearance. Through all the many plays and musicals I have appeared in, I have had many different parts, from the leading role to usher and everything in between. And each part was equally important to the play's performance.

I used to do an exercise with women's groups comparing the parts of a play to our gifts and place in the family of God (Body of Christ).

First, I made signs out of poster board, punched holes, and threaded some string so they could be put around the necks of the participants. On one side of the sign, I wrote every part of a production I could think of, from the playwright, to the producer, to the understudy, to the sound engineer, to the prop man, all the performing roles, and finally, the audience. There were thirty-eight different parts in all. On the other side of the sign, I pasted a large star.

I passed out the signs and instructed the women to put them around their necks, with the part they were playing facing out. I then arranged them as to where they would stand during the production, either on the stage or backstage, in the lighting booth or in the house (theater seating area). Then I asked everyone how they felt about the parts they had been assigned. There were grumbles from the ones with the minor roles and smiles from the ones in the spotlight. I explained that the production could not take place without *all* of the parts involved. If the lighting crew didn't turn on the lights, you couldn't see the star or any of the other performers. Something would be missing if even one of the parts weren't there. Then, the drama critic would be involved! I then had the women turn their signs around so that everyone could see that they were all "stars." I told them that this was a model for the body of Christ, with all the different parts being equally important to the whole. I told them there were no small parts or people in God's family, which includes all of us.

Just as everyone is important to the smooth running of the play, everyone is important to the smooth running of God's church. There are different gifts and different roles and different purposes in the body of Christ. I had them each write down on the star sides what they considered to be their role or gift from God. Then, we set up God's production. We joined hands and formed a circle so we could see each other, be connected to each other, and learn what roles *each* were playing.

The women in this lesson may seem unimportant, insignificant, or not even worth mentioning to some, but they are not that way to God.

 What role has God given to you? How do you feel about it? Is it "important" enough?

_____

_____

_____

The women in this lesson may seem unimportant, insignificant, or not even worth mentioning to some, but they are not that way to God. He used them for the purpose for which He needed them , and they complied. Just as we have studied more visible women in the early church, we have also seen God using unnamed women and groups of women in roles that *appear* to be invisible, but are in fact, equally important to His purposes.

God lifted the Tyrian women to a place they had not had in their cultures before, and they responded with joy. These women were a part of the spiritual family who loved and supported not only Paul, but each other. It is clear that they are united in sending him off on his next journey. They are equal as families, with the men, women and children all appearing together on the beach to pray for him.

God made it possible, through his Holy Spirit, to gift women, the four daughters of Philip, for prophecy. There were major female prophetesses in the Old Testament whom God used (see Exodus 15:20; Judges 4:4; 2 Kings 22:14; Nehemiah 6:14) and other New Testament prophetesses, such as Anna. He is carrying out his plan for women to prophesy in his new church.

And finally, the sister of Paul, whom many may not even have heard of, God used to save Paul's life. This is not either a minor role or an invisible role to God.

God is continuously acting not only to bring the whole of creation to Himself, but He is assigning us the roles that He needs us to play for His purpose. Do we still complain when we are not elected to the Board of the church? Do we sneer at those who clean the church toilets because they don't *appear* to play a very important role?

William Shakespeare said: *"All the world's a stage, and all the men and women merely players."* The great Danish theologian Søren Kierkegaard said: "We are all actors and God is our audience as we play out the roles in our lives."

God said, you are my child, part of my family, and I have an important role for you to play.

God says, "You are my child, part of my family, and I have an important role for you to play."

 Lord, help us eagerly take on the roles You have for us in Your body, the church, so that it can accomplish all of Your purposes in the world. Help us look to You first for our eternal protection, then to our earthly families for love and support, and finally, to our church families for spiritual fellowship. And help us keep in mind that You are God and we are Your children whom You love more than we can even fathom. Keep us close to Your will and your ways through the precious name of Your son, Jesus Christ, our Savior and our brother.

Works Cited

1. Carol Meyers, General Editor; Toni Craven and Ross A. Kraemer, Associate Editors; *Women in Scripture, A Dictionary of Named and Unnamed Women in the Hebrew Bible, The Apocryphal/Deuterocanonical Books, and the New Testament* (Grand Rapids, MI/Cambridge, U.K: William B. Eerdman's Publishing Company, 2000), 467.

2. Carol A. Newsom and Sharon H. Ringe, eds., *Women's Bible Commentary, Expanded Edition* (Louisville, KY, Westminster John Knox Press, 1992), 396.

3. James Malcolm Arlandson, *Women, Class, and Society in Early Christianity, Models From Luke-Acts* (Peabody, MS, Hendrickson Publishers, Inc., 1997), 147.

4. Rose Sallberg Kam, *Their Stories, Our Stories, Women of the Bible* (New York, Continuum, 1995), 254–255. Used by Permission of the Author.

5. N. T. Wright, *Acts For Everyone, Part One* (Louisville, KY, Westminster John Knox Press, 2008), 172.

Notes

12

Drusilla, Bernice, and Others

Two female members of the Herodian family, the Jewish sisters, Drusilla and Bernice, (spelled "Berenice" by Josephus), make brief appearances in the Book of Acts. Other members of this infamous family of Herod the Great are also mentioned in Acts and play various major and minor roles in connection with Paul and his witness.

Chapter 24 begins with the high priest Ananias, some elders, and an attorney named Tertullus, reporting their case against Paul to his Excellency, Felix the governor. Paul is accused of being *"a pestilent fellow, an agitator among all the Jews throughout the world, and a ringleader of the sect of the Nazarenes"* (Acts 24:5–6).

Paul responds to the charges of the Jews by denying that he stirred up the crowd or profaned the Temple. He does admit to being part of the Way, which the Jews call the sect of the Nazarenes. He says that the crime against him is about the resurrection of the dead. Felix adjourns the hearing by stating that he will decide the case at a later date.

Several days later, Felix comes with his wife **Drusilla**, who is Jewish, to hear Paul again. Paul speaks this time about his faith in Jesus Christ and discusses justice, self-control, and the coming judgment. Felix becomes frightened and tells Paul he will see him later. Over the next two years, in an attempt to obtain bribe money from him, Felix meets with Paul, but leaves him in prison to appease the Jews. Felix is succeeded by Porcius Festus. The Holy Spirit is not specifically mentioned in chapter 24.

> Two female members of the Herodian family, the Jewish sisters, Drusilla, and Bernice (spelled Berenice by Josephus), make brief appearances in the Book of Acts.

"**Some days later when Felix came with his wife Drusilla, who was Jewish, he sent for Paul and heard him speak concerning faith in Christ Jesus.**"

Acts 24:24

DRUSILLA: A BEAUTIFUL APPEARANCE, AN EMPTY SPIRIT

The Bible does not give much information about either of these sisters (Drusilla and Bernice). The main record of their lives is found in the writings of the historian Josephus, whose information helps us understand the role they play in Acts.

The Herodian family was infamous, both in its success and its brutality. This family has been present since before the birth of Jesus and various members of it appear in Acts. A short introduction to them will help you understand the background of the two Herodian women who appear in the latter half of Acts.

The sisters were great granddaughters of Herod the Great, who succeeded in overthrowing the king of Judea in 37 BC, beginning his own ruthless reign of thirty-three years as King of Judea. Herod was an Edomite and also a Jew, but he was also considered an outsider, a half-Jew by most Jews. He rebuilt the Temple in an attempt to gain their approval. Herod married ten wives and had children by all of them. He executed one of them and three of his own sons, and ordered the massacre of all male children in Bethlehem under the age of two because he viewed Jesus as a threat to his own power.

Drusilla and Bernice were nieces of Herod Antipas, the most prominent of the Herods during the time of Jesus, who had John the Baptist beheaded at the request of Salome, his wife Herodias' daughter, and returned Jesus to Pilate for condemnation.

These two sisters were daughters of Herod Agrippa the First, who has gone down in history as the first royal persecutor of the church, who *"laid violent hands upon some who belonged to the church"* (Acts 12:1), who ordered the execution of James the son of Zebedee and had Peter imprisoned. The Herod dynasty, which ended with the death of Agrippa II, their brother, was known for its cruelty, immorality, and pompous self-interest. Drusilla and Bernice, unfortunately followed in their footsteps.

History further tells us that they had great hate for each other. Drusilla, the younger, was beautiful and was persecuted by Bernice, who was much plainer in appearance.

Verse in Which the Woman Appears: Acts 24:24
*"Some days later when Felix came with his wife **Drusilla**, who was Jewish, he sent for Paul and heard him speak concerning faith in Christ Jesus."*

Drusilla: feminine diminutive form of Drusus, one of the elite Roman families of the gens, or clan, Livius; a notable Roman; name meaning "watered by the dew."

All that Scripture tells us about Drusilla is that she was Jewish and married to Felix, the governor of Judea. But from history, we learn that she was born in AD 38, one of the daughters of Herod Agrippa I and his wife and first cousin, Cypros. Her father first promised her in marriage to Epiphanes, son of Antiochus IV of Commagene (on the Euphrates River), but he refused to convert to Judaism. At fourteen, her brother Agrippa II arranged that she marry Syrian king Azizus of Emesa, who did agree to be circumcised.

But in AD 53, less than a year into this marriage, a Jewish magician persuaded Drusilla to leave Azizus and marry Antonius Felix, Roman procurator of Judea. It is said that Felix had employed this magician to seduce her from her husband because he was attracted to her great beauty. In defiance of Jewish law, Drusilla, a Jewess, left her husband to marry Felix, a Gentile, and had come to Caesarea to live with him. It is said that she never bothered divorcing her previous husband before marrying Felix. Drusilla was Felix's third wife and accompanied him at least once when Paul appeared before him.

In the meantime, Paul had arrived at Caesarea under heavy guard. The letter written by the tribune in Jerusalem was presented to Felix, and he told Paul that he would give him a hearing when his accusers arrived. The high priest Ananias and an attorney named Tertullus, arrived from Jerusalem five days later and presented their case against him. Write down the accusations against Paul presented by Tertullus in Acts 24:2–9.

_____

_____

_____

📖 Now read Paul's defense in Acts 24:10–21. How does he answer his accusers? How would you answer someone who accused you of being a Christian?

_____

_____

_____

Felix does not decide the case at this point, but indicates he will wait for Claudius Lysias, the tribune who wrote the letter to him, to arrive. In the meantime, Felix sends for Paul to hear him speak again about his faith. On this occasion, Drusilla is present.

Drusilla hears Paul speak about Jesus Christ first, before her sister. The *Eerdman's Bible Dictionary* states that, "According to the Western text, it was she who prompted her husband to summon Paul."[1]

If she did summon him, why do you think Drusilla would be interested in what Paul had to say?

_____

_____

After Paul had spoken of his faith, he turned to reason with them on justice, self-control and the judgment to come (Acts 24:25). But he was talking about these things to a man who had a corrupt administration and an unlawful marriage to Drusilla—and a woman who was spoiled and loved the trappings of the world. What might Drusilla have thought of what Paul said to Felix? Do you think she took any of it seriously?

_____

_____

In defiance of Jewish law, Drusilla, a Jewess, left her husband to marry Felix, a Gentile, and had come to Caesarea to live with him. She was his third wife.

Did You Know?
WESTERN TEXT

The Western Text is an early form of the Greek text of the New Testament. One of its features is that it has a tendency to paraphrase, thus making the Book of Acts ten percent longer than that which is commonly regarded as the earliest text of Acts. It also contains errors that minimize the historically important roles of some early Christian women. The reasons behind these additions and errors often lie with the freedom used by some of the scribes in copying ancient manuscripts.

Felix trembled at Paul's words, dismissed him and said he would call him back later. Luke tells us in the next verse (Acts 24:26), that Felix hoped Paul would bribe him with money so that he would be released. Over the next two years, Felix would send for him often and talk with him. (Acts 24:26). But he never seemed convinced of Paul's guilt. We don't know if Drusilla was also present at these other meetings or what she thought of Paul. She may also have feared and hated him for making her more conscious of her own sins that she had no intention of doing anything about.

She was a Herod, after all, and a lover of pomp, power, and position, who was willing to enter into an illegitimate relationship with Felix.

Although never charged with any crime, Paul remained imprisoned. Felix was recalled to Rome to answer for his less than stellar performance as Governor. The time of power for Felix and Drusilla was only two years and they barely escaped with their lives. Drusilla met an untimely end. At the age of forty-two, it is said that she and her son by Felix, also named Agrippa, perished in the eruption of Mt. Vesuvius in AD 79.

 How do you think Drusilla could have impacted the church had she believed what Paul said?

_____

_____

_____

> ### *Drusilla, Bernice, and Others*
>
> DAY TWO

> "So the next day Agrippa and Bernice came with great pomp, and they entered the audience hall with the military tribunes and the prominent men of the city."
>
> Acts 24:24

BERNICE: POMP AND CEREMONY

Verses in Which the Woman Appears: Acts 25:13, 23
*"After several days had passed, King Agrippa and **Bernice** arrived at Caesarea to welcome Festus. . . . So the next day Agrippa and Bernice came with great pomp, and they entered the audience hall with the military tribunes and the prominent men of the city."*

"Bernice," from the Greek *pherenike,* **meaning "victory" or "victorious"**

Bernice was born around 28 CE, and was another great-granddaughter of Herod the Great and daughter, along with Drusilla, of Agrippa I. She, too, married young the first time. At fifteen, she married Marcus Julius Alexander from a prominent Alexandrian Jewish family. He was a nephew of philosopher Philo and son of Alexander, Alabarch (a Roman official) of Egypt. After he died, Agrippa married her off to his own brother, Herod of Chalcis, who was her uncle. When she was twenty-two and once again a widow with two small sons, she began to go about publicly with her own brother, Agrippa II, and ruled as his queen. In Rome, Bernice was known largely for her incestuous conduct with him. To hush up the scandal caused by the relationship with her brother, she arranged to marry again—this time to a non-Jew named Polema, king of Cilicia, who agreed to be circumcised. But Josephus claims that she tired of him and soon went back to her brother.[2]

Other scandals filled Bernice's life. She became the mistress of Titus Vespasian, but when he became emperor, he cast her aside. The Roman historian Dio Cassius says that she acted as if she were his wife.

History further tells us that Bernice was in Jerusalem in the spring of AD 66 during the Jewish war and she performed the one redeeming act in her infamous life. She and other leading Jews went before Cestius to complain of the iniquities of the brutal Florus. She had been depicted as going before him barefooted and with her hair disheveled. But Florus paid no attention to the once proud Bernice, and even in her presence, he scourged and murdered Jews.

Chapter 25 has the new procurator, Porcius Festus, going to Jerusalem, where he hears a report against Paul. The chief priests and the leaders of the Jews ask him to have Paul transferred back to Jerusalem, so they can ambush and kill him on the way. But Festus tells them Paul will remain in Caesarea and that, if they have anything against him, they should go there. The Jews go to Caesarea, and Festus orders Paul to appear before them. They make many accusations against him but can prove none of them. Paul rejects all of the charges.

Wanting to do the Jews a favor, Festus asks Paul if he wants to go back to Jerusalem to be tried. But Paul appeals to the Emperor. Festus, after conferring with his council, agrees to let him go to Rome. Festus tells the king about Paul's case, the charges of the Jews against him, his offer to let Paul go to Jerusalem for trial, and his appeal to the Emperor. Agrippa asks Festus if he can hear Paul himself.

As the official consort of her brother, Bernice sat down with Agrippa and Festus to hear Paul recount the story of Jesus. As she entered the hall, she presented herself with *"great pomp"* and probably looking all the while that she was the most important one there. Other translations say *"in full state;"* (NEB); *"pomp and ceremony"* (JBP); and *"made a big show"* (CEV). The Greek says, *"much display."*

The New English Bible translation says that they entered with the "prominent citizens" rather than just "men of the city," suggesting possible women in the audience. In addition, Bernice may have had female attendants.

Chapter 26 opens with the king giving Paul permission to speak for himself. He appeals to the king by saying that he spoke nothing against them, but quoted Moses and the prophets in regard to the Messiah.

📖 Read Acts 26:2–23 and compare this defense with the previous one before Felix. Write down the similarities.

_____

_____

_____

_____

Festus interrupts Paul, calling him out of his mind. But Paul tells him that he is speaking the truth and that the king is familiar with the customs of the Jews. Paul counters by addressing the king directly: *"King Agrippa, do you believe the prophets? I know that you believe"* (Acts 26:27). The king replies: *"Are you so quickly persuading me to become a Christian?"* (Acts 26:28).

> *The New English Bible translation says that Agrippa and Bernice entered with the "prominent citizens" rather than just "the men of the city," suggesting possible women in the audience. In addition, Bernice may have had female attendants.*

Do you think some others had the same reaction as the king?

_____

_____

_____

Paul replies: "Whether quickly or not, I pray to God that not only you but also all who are listening to me today might become such as I am—except for these chains." (Acts 26:29). How do you think Bernice felt when her husband, Agrippa, seemed almost persuaded by Paul? What if she were almost persuaded herself?

_____

_____

_____

The witness is thus complete. The hearers all have an opportunity to respond positively or negatively to the gospel message.

Verse in Which the Woman Appears: Acts 26:30-31
"Then the king got up, and with him the governor and Bernice, and those who had been seated with them, and as they were leaving, they said to one another, 'This man is doing nothing to deserve death or imprisonment.'"

For one golden moment, Bernice had heard the witness of Paul about Jesus Christ and had the opportunity to embrace it. What do you think Bernice might have contributed to the discussion among the group after they left the audience hall?

_____

_____

_____

Bernice and Drusilla never experienced anything but worldly pleasures and scandalous lives, for which they paid a heavy price. They come into Bible history for one reason alone, because they were present and occupied influential positions at the trials of the apostle Paul. Even though they were both introduced to life in Jesus Christ, they quickly retreated into the darkness of their own sensual and selfish lives.

They disappeared into the obscure pages of history as two of the most shameless women of their time.

> **"Then the king got up, and with him the governor and Bernice, and those who had been seated with them; and as they were leaving, they said to one another, 'This man is doing nothing to deserve death or punishment.'"**
>
> **Acts 26:30-31**

Drusilla, Bernice, and Others

OTHER WOMEN WITH PAUL: SAILING FOR ROME (ACTS 27:1–28:16)

I believe there are women in these chapters, even though Luke does not specifically point them out. As we travel with Paul on his final journey to Rome, let us see who and where they might be.

After appearing before King Agrippa at Caesarea, Paul and other prisoners are transferred to a ship from the ancient city of Adramyttium, a seaport in Mysia on the west coast of Asia Minor. This ship carried goods and passengers up and down the coast along established trade routes. And because sailing was so much a part of the lives of people in the ancient world (for business and pleasure), there might have been women among its passengers.

From Caesarea Paul, along with some other prisoners, sets sail for Rome. When his ship reaches Sidon, Paul is allowed to visit the believers there. Sidon was a Mediterranean seaport and the first Phoenician city to sail ships on the open sea. We know there was a church in Sidon with female and male disciples that had been founded much earlier, possibly by the Christians who were scattered from Jerusalem. We also know that Jesus visited the areas of Tyre and Sidon and that people from both places came to Galilee to listen to Jesus (See Lesson Eleven on the Tyrian disciples). In addition, Paul and Barnabas visited the churches in Samaria and Phoenicia to report the conversion of the Gentiles (Acts 15:3).

The people were dependent on the sea for their livelihood. Perhaps there were women like Dorcas who provided for the widows and children of the fisherman who were killed at sea. Or, perhaps there were women like Lydia who were sellers of purple cloth. The *Eerdman's Bible Dictionary* reports: "Mounds of murex shells at Sidon attest to the city's participation in Phoenicia's profitable dye production industry."[4] These are the same shells described in the story of Lydia.

They continue their journey, passing the island of Cyprus, and arriving at Myra in Lycia, where they are transferred to a large Alexandrian ship bound for Italy. It was most likely one that carried grain and passengers from Egypt to Rome. There were 276 persons on the ship (Acts 27:37). Some ships in the ancient world could actually hold up to six hundred passengers. There could have been women, even children, on Paul's ship. As stated before, sailing was done in the ancient world not only for trade, but also for pleasure, and a large ship bound for Italy could very easily have had female passengers. Nowhere are we told that all of the passengers were prisoners *or* men. Various translations hint at this with words like *souls, persons, a total of, altogether, and all told.* The Greek says *souls,* again not identifying them all as men. Perhaps there were women like Priscilla, who sailed with Paul and her husband Aquila, because there were other missionary teams in the early church.

As they continue the journey, the sailing becomes difficult because of the stormy season on the Mediterranean, but they finally reach Fair Havens on the island of Crete. They decide, since much time has been lost, to continue. Paul warns them that it will be dangerous, but they do not listen to him and set sail in an attempt to reach the port of Phoenix to spend the winter.

On the way, a violent storm, called a northeaster, engulfs them and they are forced to throw the cargo and tackle overboard. After many days, they lose all hope of being saved.

📖 Read the account of the storm in Acts 27:9–20. How has God brought you through a "storm" in your life?

_____

_____

_____

I believe there are women in these chapters, even though Luke does not specifically point them out.

We know there was a church in Sidon, with male and female disciples that had been founded much earlier, possibly by the Christians who were scattered from Jerusalem.

We have seen from the time of the first persecution of the Christians in Jerusalem that women have been among those experiencing all of the hardships and joys that come with following Christ.

In the midst of it all, an angel appears to Paul and tells him that God will save all of them and that they will be shipwrecked on an island. Paul tells them to keep up their courage and urges them to eat some food to keep up their strength. They finally discover land, but when they hit a reef the ship is broken up by the waves. There is a plan to kill all the prisoners, quite likely because the soldiers were afraid of the consequences if they allowed even one of the prisoners to escape. But the centurion prevents the soldiers from doing so in order to save Paul. Everyone escapes the sinking ship and safely reaches land.

Read the rest of the story of the shipwreck (Acts 27:21–44). While reading the lengthy account of this harrowing voyage, think about *all* the passengers experiencing everything together. We have seen from the time of the first persecution of the Christians in Jerusalem that women have been among those experiencing all of the hardships and joys that come with following Christ.

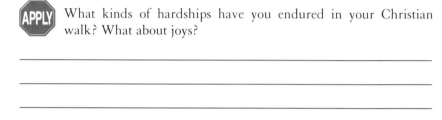

What kinds of hardships have you endured in your Christian walk? What about joys?

_____

_____

_____

_____

After drifting for two weeks amidst the great storm and being shipwrecked on the island of Malta, they are greeted by friendly natives, undoubtedly both women and men (Acts 28:2). They show them unusual kindness and are entertained "hospitably" by Publius, whose household surely included women. Perhaps there were women like Rhoda—servants—who participated in that hospitality. After Paul heals Publius' father of a fever, the rest of those with diseases came to him to also be healed.

Perhaps there were among them women like the Philippian slave girl or women like those healed by Jesus. Perhaps there were women like the Jerusalem disciples, both women and men, who brought their sick to Peter, that only his shadow might heal them (Acts 5:15). Perhaps there were women like the Samaritans, who were healed by Philip (Acts 8:7).

Paul and all the other passengers who were on the doomed ship stay for three months and then set sail on a ship that had wintered on the island, making several stops along the way. Acts 28:14–15 tells us that there were believers found in Puteoli, where Paul is invited to stay for a week. As they approach Rome, other believers come several miles from there to the towns of the Forum of Appius and Three Taverns to meet them. These places were along the Appian Way, the major road into Rome. Three Taverns was about thirty miles from Rome, and the Forum of Appius was another ten miles out. They are willing to come a considerable distance to greet him, for he had written to them over two years before that he was coming. The fact that there were established churches in both Puteoli and Rome tells us that Paul did not start those churches. Again, all of these areas, including Rome, had been evangelized by Jewish Christians of the Diaspora, scattered after their expulsion from Jerusalem. Finally, Paul arrives in Rome.

WOMEN IN THE CHURCH AT ROME: THE CONTINUING WITNESS (ACTS 28:17-30)

Paul is allowed to live by himself in Rome with only one soldier guarding him. And he, as is his way, does not waste any time in his continuing witness. Paul does the same thing he has done everywhere—he preaches the gospel to the Jews, trying to convince them about Jesus.

He calls together the leaders of the Jews and tells them why he was brought there. Read this in Acts 28:17–20. They tell him that no one has reported or spoken anything evil about him, and they invite him to speak to them in regard to the sect that everyone speaks against.

They set a day to meet and people come in great numbers, most likely both women and men, to listen to him speak about Jesus. As in every case with the Jews, some are convinced, and others refuse to believe. Perhaps there were women like those in Thessalonica and Berea who eagerly accepted the gospel, or ones like Damaris who gave up the worship of idols to follow Christ. On the other hand, perhaps there were women like those in Antioch of Pisidia who were unconvinced, or women like Drusilla and Bernice, who were so caught up in their own power and wealth that they could not be convinced to give it all up.

Finally, Paul quotes the prophet Isaiah about their refusal to understand. The Holy Spirit speaks through the prophet Isaiah (6:9–10) concerning the Jews' rejection of the Messiah, and Paul uses his prophecy to focus the meaning of it on those who have rejected his own presentation of the gospel. It is interesting to note that Jesus used this same prophecy to explain why some of the Jews rejected His teaching (Matthew 13:14–15; Mark 4:12; Luke 8:10; John 12:39–40). This is another example of the parallelism between the Gospels and Acts.

📖 Read this prophecy from Isaiah 6:9–10. How does it still speak to us today?

_____

_____

_____

He again tells them that salvation has gone to the Gentiles because "they will listen" as they have done many times before. Perhaps there were many women among all those who came to Paul who received the message of Jesus, as they have done throughout the entire story of Acts, from Jerusalem to Rome.

Acts ends with the following verses (Acts 28:30–31):

"He lived there two whole years at his own expense and welcomed all who came to him, proclaiming the kingdom of God and teaching about the Lord Jesus Christ with all boldness and without hindrance."

Paul and all those who traveled with him, women and men alike, ministered to and with him, and never stopped proclaiming the gospel with faith,

Paul and all those who traveled with him, women and men alike, ministered to and with him and never stopped proclaiming the gospel with faith, enthusiasm, commitment, and love in the face of every hardship or setback.

enthusiasm, commitment, and love in the face of every hardship or setback. As he wrote in his letter to the Romans:

"For I am convinced that neither death, nor life, nor angels, nor rulers, nor things present, nor things to come, nor powers, nor height, nor depth, nor anything else in all creation, will be able to separate us from the love of God in Christ Jesus our Lord." (Romans 8:38–39)

 With these verses in mind, write your own version of them, thinking of things that you may have endured for the gospel.

_____

_____

_____

_____

The Women in the Church at Rome
From the greetings at the end of the letter to the Romans, we know that there were several prominent women in the church there. Paul lists ten women at the end of chapter sixteen, as well as other brothers and sisters:

- He asks them to welcome Phoebe, a deacon of the church at Cenchreae, who is thought to have carried his letter to Rome. The Greek word, *diakonos,* is the same title that Paul applies to himself and includes preaching and teaching.
- Priscilla and Aquila have returned to Rome and, as we learned in Lesson Ten, she was a prominent teacher and traveling missionary with Paul.
- There are four women, Mary, Tryphaena, Tryphosa, and Persis whom Paul singles out as having "worked hard" in the church. In the case of Mary, Tryphaena, and Tryphosa, he uses the same Greek word to refer to his own missionary work. In the case of Persis, Paul describes her in words that he uses for his own and other leaders' work in the churches.
- There is Junia, a relative of Paul, who is "prominent among the apostles" and who was imprisoned with him. This was the woman whose name was translated as a male name, Junais, and interpreted that way for centuries because some male scholars did not think a woman could be an apostle. But, Paul calls her an apostle, suggesting that she *may* have been among the women to see the risen Christ.
- He greets the mother of Rufus, who was "a mother to me also," perhaps by showing him hospitality or serving as a patron.
- Julia and the sister of Nereus, along with those mentioned with them, could have been part of the same congregation in Rome.

 All of these women were crucial to the church and its witness and were faithful disciples of Jesus and important coworkers of Paul. Think of and describe some of the women in your church who nurture the body of Christ by "acting" both behind and in front of the scenes to proclaim the gospel.

For Me To Follow God

Life Principle for Lesson Twelve: The Choice Is Yours

Two sisters who had never known material need had the chance to hear Paul witness his faith in Jesus Christ. Yet, neither of them, according to history, made a choice to accept the Christian gospel.

Ruth Emily, whom I knew, was also a woman who inherited great wealth. She had the opportunity to have everything in life that she wanted—everything that Drusilla and Bernice had, and more.

But in spite of it all, she did accept the gospel and that made all the difference in the way she lived. She lived very simply and quietly, stayed in the background, never flaunted her wealth, was endowed with great humility, and gave much of her fortune away. A great deal of it went to the church of Jesus Christ. She, unlike the two Herodian sisters mentioned in the Bible, knew her Savior and lived like she did.

I often wonder, when I read the stories of the lives of these two women, how different their lives might have been had they responded positively to Paul's message. I wonder what kind of impact they *could* have made on the early church. They had the opportunity. Maybe they heard it more than once. But they were too taken with themselves, with their wealth and power, and with the riches of this world to take a chance on the riches of the kingdom of God.

APPLY Do you know God's riches for you? How do you balance your life in terms of the worldly and the spiritual?

_____

_____

_____

_____

I cannot read the book of Acts and not be moved by the faith and perseverance of the women and men who first brought the gospel to the world. Most of them, with just a few exceptions like Drusilla and Bernice, responded positively to the message of Christ.

All along the way, there are the followers of Jesus Christ—women like those with the apostles in Jerusalem and those who believed and followed him first. There are prophetesses, like Philip's daughters, because of a fulfilled prophecy on Pentecost. There are the widows whom the church cares for and who give so much of themselves back to the church. And we can remember the daughter of Pharaoh because Paul continuously reminds the Jews of their history. In his letter to the Romans, he mentions his relatives and we remember what his sister's son did for him.

Most of the women we have met throughout Acts have been eager to believe in something that frees them to be themselves, frees them to use their Spirit-given gifts and frees them from bondage to a culture, a man, an institution, or anything else that tells them they are less than God made them to be.

I cannot read the Book of Acts and not be moved by the faith and perseverance of the women and men who first brought the gospel to the world.

Most of the women we have met throughout Acts have been eager to believe in something that frees them to be themselves, frees them to use their Spirit-given gifts, and frees them from bondage to a culture, a man, an institution or anything else that tells them they are less than God made them to be.

Any woman who believes that God frees her in every way has an impact on whatever she touches, be it her own family, her church, or her society. That is because God can use her to help bring those she touches to Himself, that all may have dignity, hope, salvation, and love in the best definition of those words.

Ruth Sallberg Kam, in her book, *"Their Stories, Our Stories,* ends with a piece called "We Remember" which includes this verse: "When our church denies us a voice, we remember the Samaritan woman, Magdalene, Prisca, and Junia and know that God nevertheless calls us."[5]

God indeed calls *all* women and men to *all* kinds of positions in his church. Just because you are a woman doesn't mean you don't have a gift for leadership. And, just because you are a man doesn't mean that you do. The Spirit blows as it wills and gives us each unique and important gifts to use for the glory of God and for the upbuilding of his church—and none is more important than any other. Any woman who believes that God frees her in every way has an impact on whatever she touches, be it her own family, her church, or her society. That is because God can use her to help bring those she touches to Himself, that all may have dignity, hope, salvation and love in the best definition of those words.

Acts is the story of how our Christian church began—first, with the disciples of Jesus, then with the thousands of faithful women and men who believed and spread the message, and finally, with Paul and his missionary associates, which included many women. They did their part. And millions of faithful women and men have continued to spread its message throughout history.

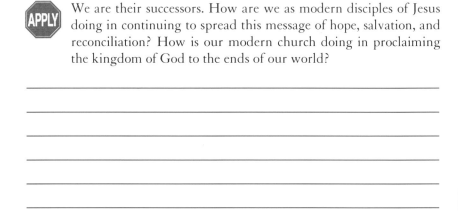 We are their successors. How are we as modern disciples of Jesus doing in continuing to spread this message of hope, salvation, and reconciliation? How is our modern church doing in proclaiming the kingdom of God to the ends of our world?

_____

_____

_____

_____

_____

_____

My prayer for the church today is that we can live our lives so anchored in Christ that we can be like these brave women in Acts—free to be our best selves and to treat each other with a love that can transform our world. God grant us the same faith and perseverance so that our "acts" will continue to grow and build up the Christian church.

 Lord, of journeys, as You were with Paul and all the women and men who went with him, be with us as we travel our own journeys of faith. Keep us from trusting in worldly things for the abundant and eternal life You promise. Rather than gain the whole world and lose ourselves, help us get lost in Your love that we might gain life. Keep us safe through the storms, sure of Your presence, and strong in the faith that You will always be with us wherever we go. Teach us Your word, that it may be a lamp to our feet and a light on all the paths of our lives (prayer from Psalm 119:105). In the name of Jesus Christ we pray, Amen.

Works Cited

1. Allen C. Myers, Revision Editor, *The Eerdman's Bible Dictionary* (Grand Rapids, MI: William B. Eerdmans Publishing Company, 1987), 948.

2. Carol Meyers, General Editor; Toni Craven and Ross A. Kraemer, Associate Editors; *Women in Scripture, A Dictionary of Named and Unnamed Women in the Hebrew Bible, The Apocryphal/Deuterocanonical Books, and the New Testament* (Grand Rapids, MI/Cambridge, U.K., William B. Eerdman's Publishing Company, 2000), 60.

3. Edith Deen, *All of the Women of the Bible* (New York, NY: HarperOne, 1988), 237.

4. Meyers, *The Eerdman's Bible Dictionary,* 948.

5. Rose Sallberg Kam, *Their Stories, Our Stories, Women of the Bible* (New York, NY: Continuum, 1995), 274. Used by permission of the author.

Bibliography

Arlandson, James Malcolm. *Women, Class, and Society in Early Christianity: Models From Luke-Acts.* Peabody, MA: Hendrickson Publishers, Inc., 1997.

Bagster, Samuel and Sons LTD, Editors. *The Zondervan Parallel New Testament in Greek and English, The Interlinear Greek-English New Testament, The New International Version, The King James Version.* New York: Iverson-Norman Associates, 1975, Copyright transferred to The Zondervan Corporation, 1980.

Barclay, William. *The New Daily Study Bible: The Acts of the Apostles.* Louisville, London: Westminster John Knox Press, The William Barclay Estate, 1975, 2003.

Barker, Kenneth, General Editor. *The NIV Study Bible, 10th Anniversary Edition.* Grand Rapids: Zondervan Publishing House, 1995.

Brown, Raymond E., Donfried, Karl P., Fitzmeyer, Joseph A., Reumann, John, Editors. *Mary in the New Testament.* Philadelphia: Fortress Press, New York,/Ramsey/Toronto, Paulist Press 1978.

Carroll, James. "Who Was Mary Magdalene?". *Smithsonian Magazine.* June 2006, 108–119.

Carroll, James. *Practicing Catholic.* New York: Houghton Mifflin Harcourt Publishing Company, 2009 .

Chicago Manual of Style: The Essential Guide for Writers, Editors and Publishers 15th Edition. Chicago: The University of Chicago Press, 1982, 1993, 2003.

Deen, Edith. *All of the Women of the Bible.* New York: Harper & Brothers, 1955.

Eiselen, Frederick Carl, Lewis, Edwin, and Downey, David G., Editors. *The Abingdon Bible Commentary.* New York, Nashville: Abingdon Press, 1929.

Erdman, Charles R. *An Exposition, The Acts.* Philadelphia: The Westminster Press, 1919.

Gardner, Joseph L., Editorial Director. *Reader's Digest Who's Who in the Bible: An Illustrated Biographical Dictionary.* Pleasantville, New York, Montreal: The Reader's Digest Association, Inc., 1994.

Goss, Leonard G. and Carolyn Stanford. *The Little Style Guide to Great Christian Writing and Publishing.* Nashville: Holman Reference, 2004.

Grady, J. Lee. *10 Lies the Church Tells Women: How the Bible Has Been Misused to Keep Women in Spiritual Bondange.* Lake Mary, FL: Charisma House, a part of Strang Communications Company, 2000.

Hall, Stuart G. *Doctrine and Practice in the Early Church.* Grand Rapids: William B. Eerdman's Publishing Company, 1991.

Harrelson, Walter J., General Editor. *The New Interpreter's Study Bible: New Revised Standard Version with the Apocrypha.* Nashville: Abingdon Press, 2003.

Hollyday, Joyce. *Clothed with the Sun: Biblical Women, Social Justice & Us.* Louisville: Westminster John Knox Press, 1994.

Kam, Rose Sallberg. *Their Stories, Our Stories: Women of the Bible*. New York: Continuum, 1995. Used by permission of the author.

Keck, Leander E., Convener. *The New Interpreter's Bible: a Commentary in Twelve Volumes* (Volume X: The Acts of the Apostles, Introduction to Epistolary Literature, The Letter to the Romans, The First Letter to the Corinthians). Nashville: Abingdon Press, 2002.

Lockyer, Herbert, *All the Kings and Queens of the Bible: The Life and Times of Biblical Royalty*. Grand Rapids: Zondervan Publishing House, 1961.

Lockyer, Herbert. *All the Women of the Bible*. Grand Rapids: Zondervan, 1967.

MacHaffie, Barbara J. *Her Story*. (Second Edition: Women in Christian Tradition). Minneapolis: Fortress Press, 2006.

Maier, Paul, Eusebius. *The Church History, A New Translation with Commentary*. Grand Rapids: Kregel Publications, 1999.

Maier, Paul L. *First Christians: Pentecost and the Spread of Christianity*. New York: Harper & Row Publishers, 1976.

Meeks, Wayne A., General Editor. *The Harper-Collins Study Bible: New Revised Standard Version*. London: Harper-Collins Publishers, 1989.

Meyers, Carol, General Editor, Craven, Toni and Kraemer, Ross S., Associate Editors. *Women in Scripture, a Dictionary of Named and Unnamed Women in the Hebrew Bible, The Apocryphal/Deuterocanonical Books, and the New Testament*. Grand Rapids, Cambridge, UK: Willam B. Eerdman's Publishing Company, 2000.

Metzger, Bruce M., Coogan, Michael D., Editors. *The Oxford Companion to the Bible*. New York, Oxford: Oxford University Press, 1993.

Metzger, Bruce M., Editorial Consultant. *NRSV Exhaustive Concordance: Includes the Apocryphal and Deuterocanonical Books*. Nashville: Thomas Nelson Publishers.

Myers, Allen C., Revision Editor. *The Eerdman's Bible Dictionary*. Grand Rapids: William B. Eerdman's Publishing Company, 1987.

Newsom, Carol A., and Sharon H. Ringe, Editors. *Women's Bible Commentary: Expanded Edition*. Louisville: Westminster John Knox Press, 1992.

Richards, Sue Poorman and Lawrence O. *Women of the Bible: The Life and Times of Every Woman in the Bible*. Nashville: Nelson Reference and Electronic, a Division of Thomas Nelson Publishers, 2003.

Webster's New World Dictionary of the American Language. Nashville: The Southwestern Company, 1965.

Wills, Garry. *What Paul Meant*. New York: Viking: Penguin Group, 2006.

Willmington, Harold L. *The Outline Bible: The Most Comprehensive Outline of the Bible Available*. Wheaton, IL: Tyndale House Publishers, Inc., 1999.

Wright, N.T. *Acts for Everyone: Part One and Part Two*. Louisville: Westminster John Knox Press, 2008.

Notes

Notes

Made in the USA
Columbia, SC
23 February 2021